Handbook to British Standard BS 8110:1985

Structural Use of Concrete

HANDBOOK TO BRITISH STANDARD BS8110:1985 STRUCTURAL USE OF CONCRETE

R. E. Rowe, CBE, MA, ScD, DEng, FEng, FICE, FIStructE, FIHT, FACI
Cement and Concrete Association

G. Somerville, BSc, PhD, FEng, FICE, FIStructE, FIHT, FACI
Cement and Concrete Association

A. W. Beeby, BSc, PhD, CEng, MICE, MIStructE
Cement and Concrete Association

J. B. Menzies, BSc, PhD, CEng, FIStructE
Building Research Establishment

J. C. M. Forrest, TD, BSc, CEng, MICE, FIStructE, MConsE
Kenchington Little and Partners

T. A. Harrison, BSc, PhD, CEng, MICE, MICT
Cement and Concrete Association

J. F. A. Moore, MA, PhD, MIStructE
Building Research Establishment

K. Newman, BSc, CEng, MICE
Quality Scheme for Ready Mixed Concrete

H. P. J. Taylor, BSc, PhD, CEng, FICE, FIStructE
Dow-Mac Concrete Ltd

A. J. Threlfall, BEng, DIC
Cement and Concrete Association

R. Whittle, MA, MICE
Arup Research and Development

PALLADIAN PUBLICATIONS LTD

Viewpoint Publications

Books published in the VIEWPOINT PUBLICATIONS series deal with all practical aspects of concrete, concrete technology and allied subjects in relation to civil and structural engineering, building and architecture.

First published 1987

Publication no. 14.015

ISBN 0 86310 025 2

VIEWPOINT PUBLICATIONS are designed and published by:

PALLADIAN PUBLICATIONS LIMITED
11 Grosvenor Crescent
London SW1X 7EE
England

Printed by Gwynne Printers Limited, Hurstpierpoint, Sussex

© Palladian Publications Limited

FOREWORD

D. D. Matthews, MA, DEng, FEng, FICE, FIStructE, FAmSocCE
Chairman of the Code Committee

It may be recalled that for over half a century there has been a Handbook to the current British Concrete Code. First there was Scott and Glanville on the DSIR Code, later Scott, Glanville and Thomas on CP114 and Walley and Bate on CP115. This practice was continued for CP110:1972 by the Handbook produced by the Cement and Concrete Association under the general authorship of Drs Bate and Rowe. The Drafting Committee CSB/39 in its preparation of BS 8110:1985 welcomed the proposal of the current Handbook under the general editorship of Dr Rowe, Director-General of the Cement and Concrete Association and currently Chairman of the Structural Codes Advisory Committee of the Institution of Structural Engineers, Dr Menzies of the Building Research Establishment, and Drs Somerville and Beeby of the Cement and Concrete Association. The drafting of a British Code of Practice for the Structural Use of Concrete is necessarily dependent on the contributions provided by the serving panels of the Structural Codes Advisory Committee of the Institution of Structural Engineers, by the Building Research Establishment and the Cement and Concrete Association.

The explanations of the changes between CP110:1972 and BS 8110:1985 should be invaluable to readers interested in the up-to-date art and science of practical structural concrete.

It is a pleasure to recommend the Handbook to the reader because it supplements the Code with the highest possible authority and is written in a manner which reflects the successful interaction between the authors and the other members of the Drafting Committee.

PREFACE

It has been a tradition since the first DSIR Code for reinforced concrete, published in 1934, for an explanatory handbook to be prepared. This work was undertaken by the team of Scott, Glanville and Thomas, and the version of the Handbook to CP114:1965, published in 1965, is still relevant. Similarly, for prestressed concrete, a guide to CP115:1959 was prepared by Walley and Bate and published in 1961.

With the combination of the various codes into the Unified *Code of practice for the structural use of concrete* and the incorporation of limit state design procedures, the Code drafting committee expressed the desire and need for the tradition to be continued. However, the scope and content of CP110 necessitated a somewhat different approach from that in the past in that, firstly, there was a need to involve more authors who had been intimately concerned in preparing the draft clauses for the Code committee and, secondly, the sheer volume of material precluded the inclusion of the actual code clauses. The Cement and Concrete Association, having already taken over responsibility for publishing the existing Handbook and Guide, agreed to publish the Handbook to CP110, and an appropriate team of authors agreed to undertake the task of producing the material. An editorial group, consisting of Drs Bate, Cranston, Rowe and Somerville, integrated and correlated the material.

Now that the revised version of CP110 has been published as BS 8110, a new edition of the Handbook was required and Palladian Publications Ltd has assumed the responsibility for publishing it. As before, a group of authors was assembled and an editorial team appointed – this consisted of Dr Rowe, Dr Somerville and Dr Beeby of the Cement and Concrete Association together with Dr Menzies of the Building Research Establishment.

Note on numbering of Tables and Figures

Tables and Figures in this Handbook are prefaced by 'H' (e.g. Figure H3.19) to distinguish them from Tables and Figures in the Code itself, which are referred to by the number alone (e.g. Table 3.1). Tables and Figures in Part 2 of the Handbook are also prefaced by (2) (e.g. Figure H(2)3.1).

CONTENTS

PART 1 – CODE OF PRACTICE FOR DESIGN AND CONSTRUCTION

Section one. General

Section two. Design objectives and general recommendations

Section three. Design and detailing: reinforced concrete

Section four. Design and detailing: prestressed concrete

Section five. Design and detailing: precast and composite construction

Section six. Concrete: materials, specification and construction

Section seven. Specification and workmanship: reinforcement

Section eight. Specification and workmanship: prestressing tendons

PART 2 – CODE OF PRACTICE FOR SPECIAL CIRCUMSTANCES

Section one. General

PART 1. CODE OF PRACTICE FOR DESIGN AND CONSTRUCTION

SECTION ONE. GENERAL

1.1 Scope

1.2 Definitions

See relevant sections.

1.3 Symbols

The huge number of variables with slightly different definitions which have to be used in Codes of Practice, make notation a difficult problem. To list a different symbol for every possible marginally different parameter would result in a totally unwieldy system. The BS 8110 and CP110 Committees took an alternative approach, using a concept employed in computer programming of 'local' and 'global' variables. On this basis it was decided that where a symbol was used only in a particular clause or equation, it could be defined within that clause without it implying any meaning to the symbol in a more general sense. This was developed further by adopting the American system of providing a list of symbols at the beginning of each section defining the symbols used in that section rather than a general list at the start of the Code. An attempt has been made here to give a general list of symbols. In a number of cases the list appears to contain ambiguities. However, as the Handbook is designed to be used in conjunction with the Code, the reader will find that no ambiguities actually occur in use.

A	area of tensile reinforcement or prestressing tendons
A_c	area of concrete
A_{cc}	area of concrete in compression
A_h	area of steel required to resist horizontal shear
A_{ps}	area of prestressing tendons in the tension zone
A_s	area of tension reinforcement
A_{sb}	area of bent-up bars
A_{sc}	area of compression reinforcement, or in columns, the area of reinforcement
A_s'	area of compression reinforcement
$A_{s,prov}$	area of tension reinforcement provided at mid-span (at support for a cantilever)
$A_s'_{,prov}$	area of compression reinforcement provided
$A_{s,req}$	area of tension reinforcement required at mid-span to resist the moment due to design ultimate loads (at support for a cantilever)
A_{st}	area of transverse steel in a flange
A_{sv}	area of shear reinforcement, or area of two legs of a link
a	deflection
a'	distance from the compression face to the point at which the crack width is being calculated
a_b	centre-to-centre distance between bars (or groups of bars) perpendicular to the plane of bend
a_{cr}	distance from the crack considered to the surface of the nearest longitudinal bar
a_f	angle of internal friction between the faces of the joint
a_u	deflection of column at ultimate limit state
$a_{u\,av}$	average deflection of all columns at a given level at ultimate limit state
a_v	length of that part of a member traversed by shear failure plane
b	width (breadth) or effective width of section
b'	effective section dimension of a column perpendicular to the y axis
b_c	breadth of the compression face of a beam measured mid-way between restraints (or the breadth of the compression face of a cantilever)
b_e	breadth of effective moment transfer strip (of flat slab)
b_t	width of section at the centroid of tension steel

b_v	width (breadth) of section used to calculate the shear stress
b_w	breadth or effective breadth of the rib of a beam
C	torsional constant, or cover to main reinforcement
C_{ave}	effective cover
C_x, C_y	plan dimensions of column
c	width of column
c_{min}	minimum cover to the tension steel
c_x, c_y	plan dimensions of column, parallel to longer and shorter side of base respectively
d	effective depth of section or, for sections entirely in compression, distance from most highly stressed face of section to the centroid of the layer of reinforcement furthest from that face
d'	depth to the compression reinforcement
d_h	depth of the head (of a column)
d_n	depth to the centroid of the compression zone
d_t	depth from the extreme compression fibre either to the longitudinal bars or to the centroid of the tendons, whichever is the greater
E_c	static modulus of elasticity of concrete
E_{cq}	dynamic modulus of elasticity of concrete
$E_{c,t}$	static modulus of elasticity of concrete at age t
E_{eff}	effective (static) modulus of elasticity of concrete
E_n	nominal earth load
E_s	modulus of elasticity of reinforcement
E_t	modulus of elasticity of concrete at the age of loading t
E_u	modulus of elasticity of concrete at age of unloading
E_0	initial modulus of elasticity at zero stress
e	eccentricity, or the base of Napierian logarithms
e_a	additional eccentricity due to deflections
e_x	resultant eccentricity of load at right angles to the plane of the wall
$e_{x,1}$	resultant eccentricity calculated at the top of a wall
$e_{x,2}$	resultant eccentricity calculated at the bottom of a wall
F	total design ultimate load on a beam or strip of slab
F_b	design force in a bar used in the calculation of anchorage bond stresses
F_{bst}	design bursting tensile force in an anchorage zone
F_{bt}	tensile force due to ultimate loads in a bar or group of bars in contact at the start of a bend
F_s	force in a bar or group of bars
F_t	basic force used in defining tie forces
f	stress
f_{bs}	bond stress
f_{bu}	design ultimate anchorage bond stress
f_c	maximum compressive stress in the concrete under service loads
f_{ci}	concrete strength at transfer
f_{cp}	design compressive stress due to prestress
f_{cpx}	design stress at distance x from the end of member
f_{cu}	characteristic strength of concrete
f_{pb}	design tensile stress in the tendons
f_{pe}	design effective prestress in the tendons after all losses
f_{pu}	characteristic strength of a prestressing tendon
f_s	estimated design service stress in the tension reinforcement
f_t	maximum design principal tensile stress
f_y	characteristic strength of reinforcement
f_{yv}	characteristic strength of shear or link reinforcement
G	shear modulus
G_k	characteristic dead load
H	storey height
h	overall depth of the cross-section measured in the plane under consideration
h'	effective section dimension in a direction perpendicular to the x axis
h_{agg}	maximum size of the coarse aggregate
h_c	effective diameter of a column or column head
h_f	depth (thickness) of flange

h_{max}	larger dimension of a rectangular section
h_{min}	smaller dimension of a rectangular section
I	second moment of area of the section
K	coefficient, as appropriate
L	span of member or, in the case of a cantilever, length
l	span or effective span of member, or anchorage length
l_a	clear horizontal distance between supporting members
$l_{b,1}$	breadth of supporting member at one end or 1.8m, whichever is the smaller
$l_{b,2}$	breadth of supporting member at the other end or 1.8m, whichever is the smaller
l_c	dimension related to columns (variously defined)
l_e	effective height of a column or wall
l_{ex}, l_{ey}	effective height in respect of the major or minor axis respectively
l_h	effective dimension of a head (of column)
l_o	clear height of column or wall between end restraints
l_p	length of prestress development
l_r	distance between centres of columns, frames or walls supporting any two adjacent floor spans
l_s	floor to ceiling height
l_t	transmission length
l_x, l_y	length of sides of a slab panel or base
l_z	distance between point of zero moment
l_1	panel length parallel to span, measured from centres of columns
l_2	panel width, measured from centres of columns
M	design ultimate resistance moment
M_{add}	additional design ultimate moment induced by deflection of beam
M_i	initial design ultimate moment in a column before allowance for additional design moments
M_o	moment necessary to produce zero stress in the concrete at the extreme tension fibre
M_t	design moment transferred between slab and column
$M_{t,max}$	maximum design moment transferred between slab and column
M_u	design moment of resistance of the section
M_x, M_y	design ultimate moments about the x and y axis respectively
$M_{x'}, M_{y'}$	effective uniaxial design ultimate moments about the x and y axis respectively
M_1	smaller initial end moment due to design ultimate loads
M_2	larger initial end moment due to design ultimate loads
m_{sx}, m_{sy}	maximum design ultimate moments either over supports or at mid-span on strips of unit width and span l_x or l_y respectively
N	design axial force
N_{bal}	design axial load capacity of a balanced section
N_d	number of discontinuous edges ($0 \leqslant N \leqslant 4$)
N_{uz}	design ultimate capacity of a section when subjected to axial load only
n	design ultimate load per unit area, or number of columns resisting sidesway at a given level or storey (in 3.8.1.1)
n_o	number of storeys in a structure
n_w	design ultimate axial load
P_o	prestressing force in tendon at the jacking end (or the tangent point near the jacking end)
P_x	prestressing force in tendon at distance x along the curve from the tangent point
Q_k	characteristic imposed load
R	restraint factor (against early thermal contraction cracking)
r	internal radius of bend
r_{ps}	radius of curvature
$\dfrac{1}{r_b}$	curvature at mid-span or, for cantilevers, at the support section
$\dfrac{1}{r_{cs}}$	shrinkage curvature
$\dfrac{1}{r_x}$	curvature at x

S_s first moment of area of reinforcement about the centroid of the cracked or gross section

s_b spacing of bent-up bars

s_v spacing of links along member

T torsional moment due to ultimate loads

t_e effective thickness of a slab for fire resistance assessment

t_f thickness of non-combustible finish (for fire resistance)

u length (or effective length) of the outer perimeter of the zone considered

u_o effective length of the perimeter which touches a loaded area

V shear force due to design ultimate loads, or design ultimate value of a concentrated load

V_b design shear resistance of bent-up bars

V_c design ultimate shear resistance of the concrete

V_{co} design ultimate shear resistance of a section uncracked in flexure

V_{cr} design ultimate shear resistance of a section cracked in flexure

V_{eff} design effective shear force in a flat slab

V_t design shear force transferred to column

v design shear stress

v_c design shear stress in the concrete

$v_{c'}$ design concrete shear stress corrected to allow for axial forces

v_{max} maximum design shear stress

v_{sx}, v_{sy} design end shear on strips of unit width and span l_x or l_y respectively and considered to act over the middle three-quarters of the edge

v_t torsional shear stress

$v_{t,min}$ minimum torsional shear stress, above which reinforcement is required

v_{tu} maximum combined shear stress (shear plus torsion)

W_k characteristic wind load

x neutral axis depth, or dimension of a shear perimeter parallel to the axis of bending

x_1 smaller centre-to-centre dimension of a rectangular link

y_o half the side of the end block

y_{po} half the side of the loaded area

y_1 larger centre-to-centre dimension of a rectangular link

z lever arm

α coefficient of expansion, or angle between shear reinforcement and the plane of beam or slab

$\alpha_{c,1}, \alpha_{c,2}$ ratio of the sum of the column stiffness to the sum of the beam stiffness at the lower or upper end of a column respectively

$\alpha_{c,min}$ lesser of $\alpha_{c,1}$ and $\alpha_{c,2}$

α_e modular ratio (E_s/E_{eff})

α_{sx}, α_{sy} bending moment coefficients for slabs spanning in two directions at right angles, simply supported on four sides

β coefficient, variously defined, as appropriate

γ_f partial safety factor for load

γ_m partial safety factor for strength of materials

Δt difference in temperature

ε strain

ε_{cc} final (30 year) creep strain in concrete

ε_{cs} free shrinkage strain

$\varepsilon_{c,1}$ strain in concrete at maximum stress

ε_m average strain at the level where the cracking is being considered

ε_r thermal strain assumed to be accommodated by cracks

ε_{sh} shrinkage of plain concrete

ε_1 strain at the level considered, calculated ignoring the stiffening effect of the concrete in the tension zone

μ coefficient of friction

ξ proportion of solid material per unit width of slab

ρ area of steel relative to area of concrete

ϕ creep coefficient, or diameter

ϕ_e effective bar size

SECTION TWO. DESIGN OBJECTIVES AND GENERAL RECOMMENDATIONS

2.1 Basis of design

2.1.1 Aim of design

The aim or purpose of design is explicitly stated and hence should ensure that all the criteria relevant to safety, serviceability and durability are considered in the design process. These criteria are related to the performance of the structure or, equally, its unfitness for use and each is associated with a limit state. Thus the aim of design is to provide an acceptable probability that the structure, or part of it, will not attain any specific limit state during its expected life.

The intended life of the structure must, obviously, be considered at the outset together with the defined, or likely, maintenance. Further, changes in use, in environment and in ownership are almost inevitable during the normal life of buildings and structures and thus imply that the designer treats each aspect of the performance with both judgement and an awareness of the imponderable aspects.

As with other structural materials, knowledge is not yet adequate to allow concrete structures to be designed for a specific durability and life. Structures designed and built according to the recommendations in the Code may normally be expected to be sufficiently resistant to the aggressive effects of the environment that maintenance and repair of the concrete will not be required for several decades, i.e. a life before significant maintenance generally in the region of say 50-100 years.

It is for the client, designer, specifier, manufacturer or contractor, as appropriate, to make the choices necessary for the construction of a specific structure. These choices should be made following consideration of the uncertainties which are likely to be present in particular aspects of the design and construction phases and also of the subsequent use and environment of the structure in service. Where a greater uncertainty than usual is judged to be present in a particular aspect it should be offset by adopting a more cautious, or stringent, approach or by introducing alternative safeguards.

Where a higher than usual degree of assurance of durability is required, choices should be made which ensure that the structure and its maintenance will be of higher than usual quality.

2.1.2 Design method

The limit state concept has gained international acceptance[2.1,2.2,2.3] but, in particular, has been adopted within the European Economic Community as the basis for the draft Eurocodes. The acceptable probabilities for the various limit states have not been defined or quantified by the Code Committee but care has been taken throughout the Code to ensure that structures designed in accordance with the Code have sensibly the same level of safety as those designed in accordance with the previous Codes. Furthermore, much more attention has been devoted to the serviceability requirements of structures, which form an integral part of the limit state design process.

The durability of structures has come to the fore in recent years and it should be recognised that durability has to be designed into a structure at the concept and detailing stages, the designer's intents must be clearly expressed and then implemented effectively in practice.

2.1.3 Durability, workmanship and materials

2.1.4 Design process

2.2 Structural design

2.2.1 General

The limit states to be considered fall into two categories, namely ultimate and serviceability limit states. The criteria given in Part 2 for the serviceability limit states are those which are generally applicable but obviously, in certain circumstances, more or less stringent criteria may be specified by a controlling authority or client, or be deemed necessary by the engineer. In Part 1, all the criteria are dealt with by deemed-to-satisfy clauses.

2.2.2 Ultimate limit state (ULS)

This limit state is concerned with the strength of the structure being adequate in the sense of giving an acceptable probability of its not collapsing under the action of defined design loads; as such it is treated by appropriate formal calculations which take account of both primary and secondary effects in the members and the structure as a whole.

The possibility of collapse being initiated by foreseeable, though indefinable and perhaps exceedingly remote, effects which are not treated formally in design e.g. explosive pressure, vehicle impact, should be considered in design either

(a) by adopting a structural concept (including layout) or form of construction which can accept a decrease in, or complete loss of, the structural effectiveness of certain members albeit with a reduced level of safety for the structure as a whole; or

(b) by the provision of appropriate devices to limit the effects of these accidental occurrences to acceptable levels, e.g. the use of controlled venting, crash barriers.

For special-purpose structures, there may well be particular hazards which, in effect, require a special limit state to be considered. In these cases, unless the hazard can be specified in sensible and effective loading terms, the assessment of what will be acceptable is left to the engineer.

2.2.3 Serviceability limit states (SLS)

2.2.3.1 *General*

2.2.3.2 *Deflection due to vertical loading*

2.2.3.3 *Response to wind loads*

2.2.3.4 *Cracking*

2.2.3.4.1 *Reinforced concrete.* The evidence on the significance of crack width on the corrosion of reinforcing steel is conflicting but it is generally accepted that, for the environmental conditions obtaining for most structures in the United Kingdom, a surface crack up to 0.3mm wide may exist from both aesthetic and performance viewpoints provided that the quality of the concrete and the cover to the reinforcement are controlled (**3.3**). More information on acceptable crack widths can be found in CEB Bulletin 166[2.4]. It must be emphasized that cracking is influenced by many factors and is a variable phenomenon; hence, absolute limits to the widths of cracks cannot be given or complied with and the requirements given in the Code merely provide an acceptable probability of the limiting widths not being exceeded.

2.2.3.4.2 *Prestressed concrete.* The criteria given for Class 1 and 2 structures are essentially the same as those in the previous codes. For Class 3 structures, which correspond to what have been termed partially prestressed structures, the limiting width of crack is 0.1mm for "very severe" and "extreme" category environments, and for all other conditions is 0.2mm. Thus, there is a progression from Class 1, 2 and 3 to reinforced concrete structures.

2.2.3.5 *Vibration*

In the majority of structures, the stiffness provided to comply with the requirements of the deflection limit state will be such that no further consideration of vibration is necessary. Where specific consideration of vibration is required by virtue of known repeated loading, the following should be included:

(a) the damping characteristics of the material
(b) the dynamic magnification effects on the structural members
(c) the sensitivity of human beings to vibration.

Steffens[2.5] reviews the problem and gives a detailed bibliography. BRE Digest No 278, 1983, *Vibrations: building and human response*, is also relevant. BS 6472:1984 *Guide to evaluation of human exposure to vibration and shock in buildings* (1 Hz to 80 Hz) gives further guidance.

2.2.4 Durability

This is a function of the conditions of exposure, the quality of the concrete as placed, the cover to the steel and the crack width if significantly greater than 0.3mm. The first three of these are controlled by the requirements of **3.3** and Table **3.4**. The quality of the concrete in turn is controlled by the requirements of **6.2** to ensure adequate durability in the various exposure conditions.

In design, both strength and durability requirements have to be satisfied and so the quality of concrete chosen will depend on which of these two criteria governs. In conditions of severe exposure, a high minimum cement content may be specified and it may well therefore be appropriate to utilize the strength associated with this in design.

Where exceptionally severe environments are encountered which are outside the categories indicated in Table **3.2**, reference should be made to Lea[2.6].

2.2.5 Fatigue

Fatigue loading is extremely unlikely on most structures, particularly fatigue loading which is appreciable in relation to the characteristic imposed load. Even in very special cases where the primary loading is of a fatigue type, the behaviour of both reinforced and prestressed concrete (Class 1, 2 and 3), designed in accordance with **3**, **4** and **5**, is such that the endurance limit is of the order of millions of cycles. The only significant effects are on the widths of cracks and the deflections, these increasing by between 20 and 25% compared with equivalent static loading. More detailed information may be found in references 2.7, 2.8 and 2.9.

2.2.6 Fire resistance

See **3.3.6**.

2.2.7 Lightning

2.3 Inspection of construction

See reference 2.10.

2.4 Loads and material properties

2.4.1 Loads

2.4.1.1 *Characteristic values of loads*

2.4.1.2 *Nominal earth loads, E_n*

2.4.1.3 *Partial safety factors for load, γ_f*

Strictly speaking, γ_f is the partial safety factor for loads and load effects as indicated by the effects it embraces. The design load for each limit state is the product of the characteristic load and the relevant partial safety factor γ_f; hence, γ_f may be considered as covering the following:

(a) (i) Possible unusual increases in the actual load not covered in deriving the characteristic load,

(ii) reduced probability that exist for combinations of loads all at characteristic value

(b) Assumptions made in design which affect the distribution of stresses, or load effects, in the structure. It is implied that the assumptions normally made and given in **3**, **4** and **5** give an acceptable accuracy in the assessment of the effects of loading.

(c) The dimensional accuracy achieved in construction. It is implied that the tolerances defined in the relevant clauses of **3**, **4** and **5** are complied with.

(d) The nature of the limit state and its significance as assessed from the economic consequences of attaining it and the safety aspect with regard to human life associated with it. In strict limit state terminology[2.1, 2.2], this particular aspect is covered by a special partial safety factor γ_c. For simplicity, and because the economic and social consequences cannot as yet readily be quantified, the Code implicitly assumes γ_c is unity.

2.4.1.4 *Loads during construction*

2.4.2 Material properties

2.4.2.1 *Characteristic strengths of materials*
The characteristic strength of materials is defined on the basis of test results, from appropriate standard test specimens, as that value below which not more than 5% of all possible results fall, i.e. the 5% fractile. For a normal, or Gaussian, distribution of test results in which the mean value is f_m and the standard deviation is s, then the characteristic value f_k is given by

$$f_k = f_m - 1.64s$$

2.4.2.2 *Partial safety factors for strengths of materials, γ_m*
The partial safety factor for materials, γ_m, is necessary to relate the strength of the material in the actual structure and its members, which is a function of the construction or production process, to the characteristic strength derived as above. γ_m also takes account of model uncertainties i.e. in the calculation models for the strength of sections. Its definition implies a certain standard of construction covered in the case of concrete by **6** and for steel by **7** and **8**. Thus, the design strength is obtained by dividing the characteristic strength by the relevant value of γ_m.

2.4.2.3 *Stress–strain relationships*
In analysis, the response of the structure is governed by the average properties of the materials throughout the structure; for convenience, however, it is assumed that the characteristic strength, and the properties associated with it, will obtain since these have to be specified by the designer. This assumption will be conservative but it does imply that a single analysis will suffice for all limit states thus simplifying the design process. The design strengths of the materials are relevant only when considering the behaviour of cross-sections within the structure and it is then that the relevant values of γ_m obtain.

The stress-strain curves given in Figures 2.1–2.3 have been derived from the available data to be representative for design purposes. For concrete (Figure 2.1), the curve differs from that given in reference 2.1 by having a variable strain at the intersection of the parabola and straight line, which is a function of the strength of the concrete, and a defined tangent at the origin. This is more consistent with the available data, particularly for the higher concrete strengths, although slightly more complicated; it is also more useful in the non-linear analysis which may become more important in the future.

The elastic modulus for concrete as a function of the significant parameters affecting it is discussed in Section **7** of Part 2 (particularly Table 7.2). The moduli given for the various types of steel are typical and are accurate enough for all design calculations. For reinforcement, the modulus of elasticity ranges between 200 and 205kN/mm^2.

For prestressing tendons, it is advisable to use the actual secant modulus of elasticity in determining the expected extension during stressing.

2.4.2.4 *Poisson's ratio for concrete*

2.4.3 Values of loads for ultimate limit state (ULS)

2.4.3.1 *Design loads*

2.4.3.1.1 *General.* The selection of the γ_f factors for the various combinations of load has been governed largely by the consideration that structures designed in accordance with the Code should have sensibly the same degree of safety and serviceability as structures designed in accordance with previous codes and will have the same general standards of workmanship and quality control. Therefore the global factors of safety, the product $\gamma_m \times \gamma_f$, ranges from $1.15 \times 1.4 = 1.61$ to $1.15 \times 1.6 = 1.84$ for structures sustaining wholly dead load to wholly live load.

Although the three load combinations 1, 2 and 3 should be considered for all the structural members, of the three, load combination 1 will govern design in most building structures, particularly since for this load combination the minimum design dead load $1.0\ G_k$ has to be considered[2.11]; combination 2 will govern in those structures where the wind loading is the primary imposed load, e.g. chimneys, cooling towers, etc., and for this case the minimum and maximum values of γ_f are 1.0 and 1.4 respectively.

The ultimate strength of sections and the ultimate load of structures are not significantly affected by the effects of temperature, creep or shrinkage because the deformations produced by these causes are much less than those associated with the collapse conditions. These effects are therefore considered only for the serviceability limit states.

2.4.3.1.2 *Partial factors for earth pressure.* See Section **2** of Part 2.

2.4.3.2 *Effects of exceptional loads or localized damage*

2.4.3.3 *Creep, shrinkage and temperature effects*

2.4.4 Strengths of materials for the ultimate limit state

2.4.4.1 *Design strengths*
The values of γ_m are relevant to the control and workmanship requirements given elsewhere in the Code. Obviously, where data exist, e.g. in the manufacture of precast units, these may be used to justify lower values for γ_m for concrete[2.1]. When considering misuse or accident, the reduced probability of occurrence is reflected in the lower values of 1.3 and 1.0 for γ_m.

2.4.4.2 *Effects of exceptional loads or localized damage*

2.4.5 Design loads for serviceability limit states
See **3.3** of Part 2.

2.4.6 Material properties for serviceability limit states

2.4.6.1 *General*
Since for these limit states it is deformation in general which is the criterion, and this depends on the behaviour of the structure as a whole, the properties of the materials are taken as those related to the characteristic strength although, strictly speaking, the mean strength should be used, but it is the former that is known and specified; hence γ_m is 1.0 in general. For the treatment of individual sections such as in cracking, the local properties of the concrete assume a greater importance and so γ_m is taken as 1.3 to ensure an acceptable probability. See **3.2** of Part 2.

2.4.6.2 *Tensile stress criteria for prestressed concrete*

2.4.7 Material properties for durability

To achieve appropriate durability for the expected life of the structure requires an integrated approach to design, specifications and construction as mentioned earlier (**2.1.2**). The specific material related aspects are itemized here with forward references to sections and clauses covering their treatment; then the clause provides a check list. Summarizing the subject is possible succinctly by the 4 C's, namely:

constituents
compaction
curing
cover

to which could be added control, checking and care.

2.5 Analysis

2.5.1 General

The more fundamental approaches are those which are based upon the moment-curvature and moment-rotation relations for reinforced and prestressed concrete sections; descriptions of these are given in references 2.12 and 2.13.

2.5.2 Analysis of structure

Of the assumptions permitted for the stiffness of members in elastic analysis, that associated with the gross concrete section (a) will for obvious reasons, generally be used; (b) and (c) may be relevant when checking existing structures for new loadings associated with change of use.

Some useful sources on yield-line theory and the strip method for slabs are references 2.14–17.

2.5.3 Analysis of sections for the ultimate limit state

2.5.4 Analysis of sections for serviceability limit states

2.6 Designs based on tests

2.6.1 Model tests

See reference 2.18.

2.6.2 Prototype tests

See reference 2.19.

It should be emphasized that, appropriate testing having been carried out to establish a design procedure for a structure or structural members, this is equivalent to design by calculation in accordance with **3**, **4** and **5**. There is, therefore, no further need for testing the production units other than for quality control, or assurance, purposes.

REFERENCES

2.1 COMITE EURO-INTERNATIONAL DU BETON – FEDERATION INTERNATIONALE DE LA PRECONTRAINTE. Model Code for concrete structures, 1978.

2.2 INTERNATIONAL STANDARDS ORGANIZATION. General principles for the verification of the safety of structures. Geneva. 12 pp. International Standard 2394:1973.

2.3 ROWE, R.E. CRANSTON W.B. and BEST, B.C. New concepts in the design of structural concrete. The Structural Engineer. Vol.43, No.12. December 1965. pp.399-403. Discussion. Vol.44, No.4. April 1966. pp.127-133. Further Discussion. Vol.44, No.11. November 1966. pp.411-421.

2.4 COMITE EURO-INTERNATIONAL DU BETON. Draft CEB guide to durable concrete structures. May 1985. 264 pp. CEB Bulletin 166.

2.5 STEFFENS, R.J. Structural vibration and damage. London, HMSO, 1974. 56 pp.

2.6 LEA, F.M. The chemistry of cement and concrete. Third edition. London, Edward Arnold, 1970. pp.659-676.

2.7 SNOWDON, L.C. The static and fatigue performance of concrete beams with high-strength deformed bars. London, Construction Industry Research and Information Association, August 1970. 31 pp. CIRIA Report 24.

2.8 BATE, S.C.C. A comparison between prestressed-concrete and reinforced-concrete beams under repeated loading. Proceedings of the Institution of Civil Engineers. Vol.24. March 1963. pp.331-358.

2.9 STEVENS, R.F. Tests on prestressed concrete beams. Concrete. Vol.3, No.11. November 1969. pp.452-457.

2.10 INSTITUTION OF STRUCTURAL ENGINEERS. Inspection of building structures during construction. London, 1983. 22 pp.

2.11 BEEBY, A.W. and CRANSTON, W.B. Influence of load systems on safety. Civil Engineering and Public Works Review. Vol.67, No.797. December 1972. pp.1251-1253, 1255, 1257-1258.

2.12 BAKER, A.L.L. Limit-state design of reinforced concrete. London, Cement and Concrete Association, 1970. 360 pp. Publication 12.037. (Now out of print.)

2.13 COMITE EUROPEEN DU BETON. Appendix to International Recommendations (1970) – Hyperstatic Structures, Paris, 1972.

2.14 JONES, L.L. and WOOD, R.H. Yield-line analysis of slabs. London, Thames & Hudson, Chatto & Windus, 1967. 405 pp.

2.15 JOHANSEN, K.W. Yield-line formulae for slabs. Translated from Danish. London, Viewpoint Publications, 1972. 106 pp. Publication 12.044.

2.16 WOOD, R.H. and ARMER, G.S.T. The theory of the strip method for design of slabs. Proceedings of the Institution of Civil Engineers. Vol.41. October 1968. pp.285-311.

2.17 ARMER, G.S.T. The strip method: a new approach to the design of slabs. Concrete. Vol.2, No.9. September 1968. pp.358-363.

2.18 ROWE, R.E. and BASE, G.D. Model analysis and testing as a design tool. Proceedings of the Institution of Civil Engineers. Vol.33. February 1966. pp.183-199.

2.19 SOMERVILLE, G. Development testing for structural concrete. Engineering. Vol.205, No.5321. 12 April 1968. pp.558-559.

SECTION THREE. DESIGN AND DETAILING: REINFORCED CONCRETE

3.1 Design basis and strength of materials

3.1.1 General

The methods of analysis and design have been chosen primarily for their simplicity in use and the wide range of conditions over which they produce acceptable results. Other methods are permitted but it is suggested that they should not be more complicated in use than those recommended.

The limitations of the methods should be fully recognized; in many cases, limitations are stated, but often it will be necessary to rely on the experience and judgement of the engineer carrying out the design. It is for this reason that all design should be supervised by suitably qualified and experienced engineers.

3.1.2 Basis of design for reinforced concrete

In general, the initial analysis and design of a reinforced concrete structure will be for the ultimate limit state and the final stages will involve checking for the serviceability limit states. It will be prudent, however, when assessing preliminary proportions for the structure to perform a rough check on the ratios of the span to effective depth in accordance with **3.4.6.3**.

3.1.3 Alternative methods (serviceability limit state)

These are discussed under Part 2, Section 3.

3.1.4 Robustness – general requirements

Since the partial collapse of the Ronan Point block of flats and of a precast structure at Aldershot, it has become accepted that designing a structure to withstand the specified design loads is not sufficient in itself to guarantee a structure with the required level of safety. An additional property is required of the structure which can be described as *robustness*. This can possibly best be defined as an ability to withstand all the minor unforeseen occurrences and accidents to which the structure may be subjected during its life without major consequences. In particular, it is essential to avoid structural solutions where damage to one member can lead to a major collapse (progressive collapse or a 'house of cards' type of failure). The general requirement for robustness was expressed in CP110 as follows:

"No structure can be expected to be resistant to the excessive loads and forces that could arise due to an extreme cause, but it should not be damaged to an extent disproportionate to the original cause".

Clause **2.2.2.2** in BS 8110 attempts to express the same idea in a slightly different form:

"Structures should be . . . not unreasonably susceptible to the effects of accidents. In particular, situations should be avoided where damage to small areas of a structure or failure of single elements may lead to collapse of major parts of the structure."

While it is generally understood what is meant by a robust building, the development of design rules which will ensure this has been less easy since robustness, unlike strength, is not a concept that can be expressed mathematically.

Attempts have been made to define what constitutes 'major parts of the structure', though not in BS 8110. Building Regulation A3 states that, if one member is considered removed by an accident then:

(a) structural failure consequent on that removal would not occur within any storey other than the storey of which the member forms part, the storey next above (if any) and the storey next below (if any); and

(b) any structural failure would be located within each such storey.

It is further stated that (b) may be "deemed to be satisfied if the area within which structural failure might occur would not exceed 70m^2 or 15% of the area of the storey (measured in the horizontal plane), whichever is the less". It is understood that, under the revised Building Regulations, similar limits will be given in an 'Approved document'.

The Code specifies three basic measures to ensure that a design is robust:

1. ensure that there is no inherent weakness in the structural layout (see **3.1.4.1** below);
2. for buildings where the wind loads are low, ensure that the structure can withstand at least a nominal horizontal load equal to 1.5% of the dead weight (**3.1.4.2**); and
3. ensure that the loss of one member will not result in the collapse of a major part of the structure.

This last provision may be met in one of two ways: either each member may be considered to be removed in turn and the remaining structure checked to ensure that it will remain standing when subjected to the accidental combination of loads or a 'deemed to satisfy' solution may be adopted using ties.

Methods for designing for element removal are set out in Part 2, Section **2.6** and will be discussed more fully later.

It is recognized that it may occasionally be impossible to avoid having single members which support what might be considered to be a 'major part of the structure' and whose failure would thus automatically cause the collapse of a 'major part of the structure'. Such elements are classed as 'key elements'. If possible, they should be avoided. However, where they are unavoidable, special rules for their design are given in Part 2, Section **2.6**. The Code does not explicitly define a key element but it would seem reasonable to assume that such an element was one which supported more than 70m² or 15% of the area of a storey.

The 'deemed to satisfy' provisions for ties are set out in **3.12.3** but, for completeness of this general discussion, the principles of the method will be outlined here.

The basic element of the tie system is a peripheral tie or continuously reinforced strip around the entire perimeter of each floor. Internal ties, continuous over the whole length or breadth of the building and anchored to the peripheral tie at both ends, are provided to maintain the integrity of the whole floor should some part of it suffer severe damage. Similarly, vertical ties are provided over the whole height of vertical load bearing members. Where such members are located outside the peripheral tie, they are tied back into it. Figure H3.1 illustrates these principles.

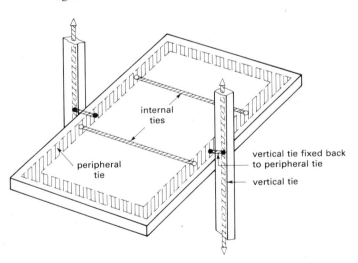

Figure H3.1: Schematic illustration of tying system.

3.1.4.1 *General check of structural integrity*

This and other codes ask for a robust and stable planform without specifying what constitutes such a structural layout. It is not possible to give an exact definition of what the Code requires but some general guidelines can be given. There seem to be two basic principles which can be stated here:

1. the overall form of the structure should be chosen so that it is not excessively flexible to any mode of deformation;

2. the form of the structure should be such that the centre of resistance of the structure to a particular loading should be close to the line of action of the loading.

These concepts can be explained more fully by examples. Consider the building layout sketched in Figure H3.2(a). This layout is reasonably stiff relative to uniform lateral loading but would have a very low torsional stiffness. We would not, of course, design this structure for torsion but torsions will inevitably occur (possibly due to gusting, eddying of wind around a structure etc) and this planform could hardly be considered to be robust.

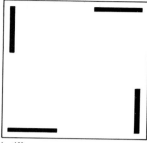

(a) lack of torsional stiffness

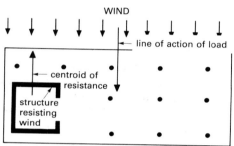

(b) lines of action of load and resistance not coincident

Figure H3.2: Poor structural layouts
(a) lack of torsional stiffness
(b) lines of action of load and resistance not coincident

Figure H3.2(b) shows a situation where the centroid of the structure resisting lateral load is well away from the line of action of the load. It will be seen that the lateral load can only be transferred to the structure designed to carry it by inducing substantial torsional distortion in the structure. Again, this could not be considered to be a robust structural layout.

3.1.4.2 *Notional horizontal load*

3.1.4.3 *Provision of ties*
See **3.12.3**.

3.1.4.4 *Key elements and bridging structures*
See **2.6** in Part 2.

3.1.4.5 *Safeguarding against vehicular impact*

3.1.4.6 *Flow chart of design procedure*

3.1.5 Durability and fire resistance of reinforced concrete
As far as design is concerned, durability is dealt with largely in terms of the choice of

a suitable concrete quality and nominal cover. This is covered in Section **3.3** with more general information in **6.2**. The Handbook will deal with the background to these clauses under **6.2**. Fire resistance is covered at two levels. Section **3.3** gives simple, safe rules for cover and member size while Part 2, Section **4** gives a much more thorough treatment.

The fire resistance of a reinforced concrete structure is treated on an elemental basis i.e. column, beam, slab, wall etc. The tables in this Code refer to widths or thicknesses of sections and the amount of cover necessary to main and secondary reinforcement.

Part 1 of the Code contains simplified tabular data for general use in ordinary reinforced concrete construction. Where the requirement of the design is not encompassed by the range of values given in the tables then the designer should refer to Part 2, Section **4** for a more detailed treatment.

3.1.6 Loads

3.1.7 Strength of materials

3.1.7.1 *General*

3.1.7.2 *Selection of compressive strength grade of concrete*
The BS 5328 Table of preferred grades is reproduced as Table H6.5. Note that C25 can only be used under rather special circumstances and that probably C35 is a likely common minimum.

3.1.7.3 *Age allowance for concrete*
Data from water cured cubes should not be taken as evidence of the potential development of strength. Concrete which is allowed to dry below a relative humidity of 85% will cease to gain in strength. Concretes which are exposed to the UK weather, exposed but protected from rain or effectively sealed from the time of casting e.g. the centre of a large pour, will all continue to gain in strength. The rate of gain in strength will depend on the exposure, the quality of concrete and the type of cement.

3.1.7.4 *Characteristic strengths of reinforcement*

3.2 Structures and structural frames

3.2.1 Analysis of structures

3.2.1.1 *Complete structures and complete structural frames*
It will rarely be necessary, or advantageous, to attempt an analysis of the complete structure where vertical load only is considered. It may more frequently be necessary to consider the complete structure of an unbraced frame, except in the case of basically simple structures (e.g. portal frames), or certain special structures (an example might be one of the more complex forms of grandstand).

3.2.1.2 *Monolithic frames not providing lateral stability*

3.2.1.2.1 *Simplification into sub-frames.* The frame can be considered by breaking it down into sub-frames; the sub-frames permitted are illustrated in Figure H3.3. Analyses of these sub-frames under the prescribed loadings give results which do not differ significantly from those obtained from analyses of the complete frame. The simpler sub-frames (Figure H3.3(c)) have the advantage that an explicit solution can be written down in terms of the rotations of the joints at the ends of the beam considered. The equations for these two rotations are:

$$\theta_1 = k_1 \sigma . M_{F1} + k_2 \sigma . M_{F2}$$

$$\theta_2 = k_3 \sigma . M_{F1} + k_4 \sigma . M_{F2}$$

$\sigma.M_{F1}$ and $\sigma.M_{F2}$ are respectively the algebraic sums of the fixed-end beam moments on either side of the joints at ends 1 and 2 of the beam under the loading considered. θ_1 and θ_2 are the rotations of joints 1 and 2 and k_1, k_2, k_3 and k_4 are constants which depend on the relative stiffnesses of the members connected to each joint. They are given by:

$k_1 = K_2/B$

$k_4 = K_1/B$

$k_2 = k_3 = -K_b/2B$

where $B = K_1K_2 - K_b^2/4$

$K_1 =$ the sum of the stiffnesses of all members connecting to joint 1

$K_2 =$ the sum of the stiffness of all the members connecting to joint 2

$K_b =$ the stiffness of the beam ($4EI/1$)

The moments at ends 1 and 2 of the beam are given by:

$M_1 = M_{F1} - K_b(\theta_1 + 0.5\theta_2)$

$M_2 = M_{F2} - K_b(\theta_2 + 0.5\theta_1)$

M_{F1} and M_{F2} are respectively the fixed-end moments at ends 1 and 2 of the beam.

In the interests of simplicity, the concrete section should be used for assessing relative stiffnesses. Of course, the gross or transformed sections can be used only if a prior estimate of reinforcement area is available or where a reassessment of an existing structure is being carried out.

In most structural frames, the beams are integral with the floor slabs and designed as T beams. In such cases, the beam stiffness can be assessed by taking the effective width, as described in **3.4.1.5** to apply over the entire span.

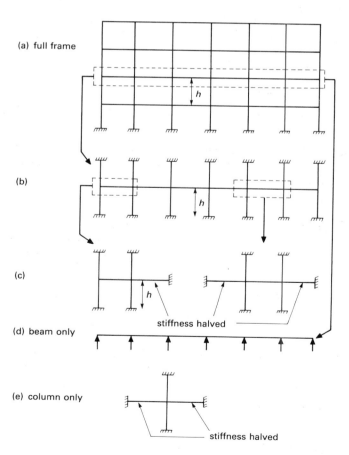

Figure H3.3: Permissible simplification of a frame for analysis.

3.2.1.2.2 *Choice of critical loading arrangements*. The load patterns are a simplification of previous practice. The old 'alternate spans loaded' and 'adjacent spans loaded' load patterns could require n + 1 cases to be considered, where n is the number of spans of a continuous beam. The provisions of this clause require a maximum of 3. The actual difference made to the design moments is fairly small: maximum sagging moments are unchanged but maximum support moments are reduced by a few percent. Assuming some degree of ductility, it can be shown[3.1] that overall safety is not significantly affected by this change since the 'alternate spans loaded' pattern defines the critical failure mechanisms. The only real effect is a slight increase in stress near the supports under service conditions. This is not of practical significance.

3.2.1.2.3 *Alternative simplification for individual beams*. This has been dealt with under **3.2.1.2.1**.

3.2.1.2.4 *'Continuous beam' simplification*. While the simplest analysis to carry out, it should be noted that it can be very conservative, especially when there are fairly stiff columns in the frame. The possible degree of conservatism may be seen from Figure H3.4.

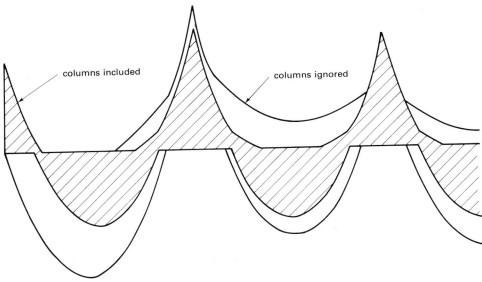

Figure H3.4: Comparison of analyses including and ignoring the columns.

3.2.1.2.5 *Asymmetrically-loaded columns where a beam has been analysed in accordance with 3.2.1.2.4*. The moments in columns may be assessed using the formulae given in Table H3.1.

Table H3.1 Moments in columns

	Moments for frames of one bay	Moments for frames of two or more bays
External (and similarly loaded) columns		
Moment at foot of upper column	$M_o \dfrac{K_u}{K_1+K_u+0.5K_b}$	$M_o \dfrac{K_u}{K_1+K_u+K_b}$
Moment at head of lower column	$M_o \dfrac{K_1}{K_1+K_u+0.5K_b}$	$M_o \dfrac{K_1}{K_1+K_u+K_b}$
Internal columns		
Moment at foot of upper column		$M_{es} \dfrac{K_u}{K_1+K_u+K_{b1}+K_{b2}}$
Moment at head of lower column		$M_{es} \dfrac{K_2}{K_1+K_u+K_{b1}+K_{b2}}$

where M_o is the bending moment at the end of the beam framing into the column, assuming fixity at both ends of the beam;

M_{es} is the maximum difference between the moments at the ends of the two beams framing into opposite sides of the column, each calculated on the assumption that the ends of the beams are fixed and assuming one of the beams unloaded;

K_b is the stiffness of the beam;

K_{b1} is the stiffness of the beam on one side of the column;

K_{b2} is the stiffness of the beam on the other side of the column;

K_1 is the stiffness of the lower column;

K_u is the stiffness of the upper column.

For the purposes of this Table, the stiffness of a member may be obtained by dividing the moment of inertia of a cross-section by the length of the member, provided that the member is of constant cross-section throughout its length.

The equations for the moment at the head of the lower column may be used for columns in a topmost storey by taking K_u as zero.

Where the bending moment is calculated in the internal columns it is permissible to take into account the reduction in load resulting from the beam on one side of the column being fully loaded and the beam on the other side being loaded with dead load only.

3.2.1.3 *Frames providing lateral stability*

3.2.1.3.1 *General*. The division between frames providing lateral stability (sometimes called unbraced frames) and frames not carrying horizontal loads (braced frames) is, of course, somewhat artificial in many cases. Any monolithic frame will redistribute the horizontal forces between the vertical members as a function of their relative stiffnesses. It so happens that elements of structure such as lift shafts, stair wells and walls are commonly so stiff relative to columns that it is a legitimate simplification to assume that all the horizontal loads are carried by the stiff vertical elements and ignore any contribution from the columns. This Section is concerned with frames in structures which do not contain such very stiff vertical elements of structure so that the influence of the horizontal forces on the frame cannot be ignored. Occasionally, the designer may nevertheless arbitrarily decide that certain members in such structures will be designed to carry the lateral loads and the remainder be considered as elements of braced frames. This approach should be viewed with considerable caution if the stiffnesses of the elements chosen as bracing elements do not greatly exceed the total stiffness of the remainder. The lateral loads will be shared in proportion to the stiffnesses and will only be shed to

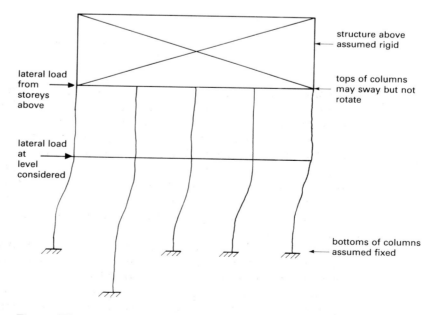

Figure H3.5: Alternative treatment of laterally-loaded unbraced frame.

the members designed to carry them after excessive cracking or failure of the 'braced' elements has greatly reduced their stiffness.

3.2.1.3.2 *Sway-frame of three or more approximately equal bays.* Studies have shown that the methods suggested in this clause are often inadequate when applied to one- or two-bay frames. For these, or for frames with very unequal bay sizes, a more complete analysis should be employed. An approximate method which seems to give reasonable results is to adopt a modified version of the sub-frame described in **3.2.1.2.1**. This is sketched in Figure H3.5.

3.2.2 Redistribution of moments

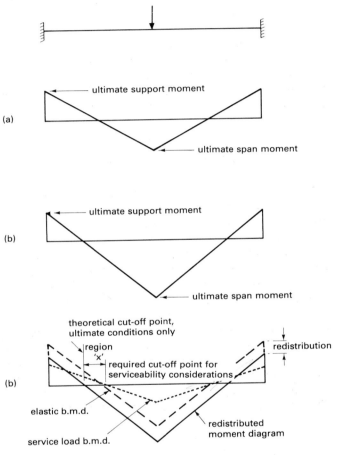

Figure H3.6: Development of bending moments in an encastré beam.

3.2.2.1 *General*
Reinforced concrete behaves in a manner intermediate between the elastic-plastic behaviour of the reinforcement and the behaviour of the concrete which, in normal circumstances, is capable of very little plastic deformation. The exact behaviour depends on the relative quantities of the two materials and their properties; however, it may be considered to be roughly elastic until the steel yields and then roughly plastic until the concrete fails in compression. The concrete failure limits the amount of this plastic behaviour or, more specifically, it limits the amount of rotation which a plastic hinge can undergo. Thus a system of analysis is required for indeterminate structures which will allow for plastic hinges forming as the collapse load is approached while controlling their rotation.

Figure H3.6 shows how the bending moments develop in an elastic-plastic member. As the load is increased, the beam behaves elastically until the plastic moment of one or more critical sections is reached (in Figure H3.6(a) the support moments). Further loading causes these hinges to rotate while the moments do not change. The extra moment required to balance the load is carried by other parts of the member. This continues until the mid-span section reaches its plastic moment, when the structure becomes a mechanism and collapses. Figure H3.6(b) shows the final bending moment diagram when all the critical sections are carrying their plastic moments. From the design point of view, this same bending moment diagram can be obtained by calculating the elastic bending moment diagram under the collapse loading, and then reducing the support moments while increasing the mid-span moment by a corresponding amount to maintain equilibrium (Figure H3.6(c)). This operation is known as redistribution of moments. The percentage by which a moment is reduced from the elastic value is a measure of the rotation of the hinge. Design can therefore conveniently be done by carrying out an elastic analysis and then applying a limited amount of redistribution. The design of the critical sections must then be such that they can carry the rotations implied by the redistribution.

The effect of condition 2 is to limit the neutral axis depth at ultimate to 0.3 of the effective depth if the full 30% reduction in moment has been made; as the neutral axis depth is increased, the amount of redistribution is reduced. Where the neutral axis depth exceeds 0.6 of the effective depth, no reductions in moment are permitted.

Condition 3 is required to deal with serviceability conditions, where an elastic response will be appropriate. From Figure H3.6(c), it will be seen that service loading in this case will produce hogging moment in region 'x'. Ultimate load conditions require no reinforcement here and plainly very wide cracking would develop in this region. Supplying reinforcement to carry at least 70% of the maximum moment means that the structural response will remain roughly elastic at loads equal to or less than 70% of total ultimate load. The loading corresponding to the serviceability limit state is always less than this, and thus the possibility of wide cracking is ruled out.

The limitation of 30% in reducing moments is to restrict the rotation which will develop at critical sections. It should be noted that no limit is placed on the amount by which moments can be increased.

Redistribution will also affect the shears. Depending on how the redistribution is done, these may be either decreased or increased. It is considered that it is prudent to take the worst of the redistributed and unredistributed shears as the design values. A reason for this is that, if the redistribution reduces the shears and, possibly because the strength of the reinforcement was above its design value, the redistribution did not take place then design for the reduced shears could lead to the structure having a reduced safety factor (note that an increase in steel strength would increase the flexural strength of a section but not its shear strength).

The question of appropriate strategies for redistribution from the point of view of economy of design and ease of construction is not simple. It is considered in some detail in reference 3.2.

3.2.2.2 *Restriction to redistribution of moments in structures over four storeys where structural frame provides lateral stability*

The limitation of 10% for tall unbraced frames is because the formation of plastic hinges at the onset of redistribution may induce a premature failure due to frame instability[3.3].

3.3 Concrete cover to reinforcement

Concrete cover has to perform the following functions:

1. provide adequate bond between steel and concrete for load transference
2. protect the steel from corrosion and the effect of aggressive agencies
3. protect the steel from fire.

It must also meet other practical requirements e.g. in relation to placing concrete. All such requirements are given in this clause (together with **4.12.3** for prestressed concrete) because cover influences the position of reinforcement within the overall cross-section and hence the design resistance of the section.

3.3.1 Nominal cover

3.3.1.1 *General*

BS 8110 uses the term 'nominal cover' in an attempt to clarify what, in the past, has caused some confusion. The vital factor is that 'nominal cover' is the specified cover to **all reinforcement including links**. It is envisaged that, in line with the recommendations of the joint Institution of Structural Engineers/Concrete Society report on detailing[3.4], spacers should be fixed on the links and not on the main bars in a beam or column. In the past, where it was the normal procedure to fix the spacers to the main bars, the cover to the links could be very much less than intended. This has resulted in numerous cases where links have corroded and have caused local spalling of the concrete. All limits to cover given in Part 1 of BS 8110 are quoted as nominal covers. It should be noted, however, that this is not the case in Section **4** of Part 2 (Fire resistance) where a definition more appropriate to fire resistance considerations has been adopted.

The reference to surface treatments which reduce the effective depth of protective concrete is a further example of the wide range of considerations in a properly integrated design. In **7.1** attention is drawn to the possibility of using coated or stainless steel reinforcement in special circumstances such as may occur when protection of reinforcement against corrosion cannot be achieved in the usual way, i.e. by provision of an appropriate depth and quality of concrete cover, or when an exceptional assurance against cracking of the concrete arising from reinforcement corrosion is required.

3.3.1.2 *Bar size*

There are two reasons for ensuring that the cover to the main bars is not less than the bar diameter. The first is that smaller covers may make the proper placing and compaction of the concrete around the bars difficult. The second is related to structural performance. Bond strength is very dependent on the ratio of cover to bar size, though this variable does not appear in the bond provisions in this Code, and the safety factor against bond failure could well be reduced to an unacceptably low value if the cover was significantly less than the bar size. Furthermore, local bond stresses could lead to cracks forming along the line of the bars which might pose a corrosion risk.

3.3.1.3 *Nominal maximum size of aggregate*

The requirement that the cover should not be less than the nominal maximum aggregate size has been introduced to help ensure the proper flow around the bars of the concrete and hence proper compaction.

3.3.1.4 *Concrete cast against uneven surfaces*

Clearly a much larger uncertainty exists about obtaining the necessary cover in the circumstances and so a substantially greater tolerance needs to be provided for. The provisions of this clause repeat those given in CP2004.

3.3.2 Ends of straight bars

This clause covers a distinction not made in CP110 but suggested in Section 3.11.2 of the Handbook to CP110. It is in effect a relaxation for a specific limited application which should not be extended. The possibility of rust staining during construction will, of course, have to be considered. Experience suggests that some corrosion of the ends of bars will occur but that this is not progressive or harmful.

3.3.3 Cover against corrosion

The essence of this clause is contained in Table 3.4. The advance from CP110 which it represents is the direct linking of mix design parameters to cover and conditions of exposure, in effect a merger of the previous Tables 19 and 48, together with a general strengthening of the recommendations.

The stimulus to this integration was increasing evidence that concrete has not always been specified and placed to the necessary thickness and quality to provide reasonable assurance of adequate long-term protection to reinforcement, in the absence of other deleterious or particularly extreme effects.

In particular, sufficient cement content and limited water content are essential, along with proper compaction and curing, to ensure a concrete sufficiently impermeable to the ingress of carbon dioxide which leads to carbonation and loss of the alkaline characteristics which inhibit corrosion (see also **6.2**).

3.3.4 and **3.3.5** deal with various aspects of Table 3.4 (which is based on 20mm nominal maximum size of aggregate) and the technical basis for the Table is discussed under **6.2**.

3.3.4 Exposure conditions

3.3.4.1 *General*
The first point of entry to Table 3.4 is assessment of the exposure conditions. These are described in Table 3.2 and should be considered as design parameters. It has not been possible yet to quantify the conditions assigned to the five environments – mild, moderate, severe, very severe and extreme – so the definitions comprise descriptions of the exposure conditions.

This Table is reproduced below, modified to include examples of most of these conditions. These examples were not included in the Code because it is the designer's responsibility to assess the environment in the light of all relevant factors, which may indicate sometimes a more severe environment than the examples indicate. Nevertheless, they are likely to cover most common situations.

The four more severe environments are now aligned with those in BS 5400 for bridges and incorporate that involving chlorides from external sources.

Table 3.2 Exposure conditions

Environment	Exposure conditions	Example
MILD	Concrete surfaces protected against weather or aggressive conditions but conditions may be aggressive for a brief period during construction	Internal concrete e.g. shops, offices
MODERATE	Concrete surfaces sheltered from severe rain or freezing whilst wet	Underside of suspended ground floors
	Concrete subject to condensation	
	Concrete surfaces continuously under water	Reservoirs
	Concrete in contact with non-aggressive soil (see class 1 of Table 6.1)	All foundations except those described in **6.2.4.1**
SEVERE	Concrete surfaces exposed to: severe rain, alternate wetting and drying or occasional freezing or severe condensation	Most external concrete above ground, washing and cooking areas (pipes and ducts: see BS 5911)
VERY SEVERE	Concrete surfaces exposed to: Sea water spray, de-icing salts (directly or indirectly)	Concrete adjacent to the sea, car parks, structures adjacent to carriageways
	Corrosive fumes or severe freezing conditions whilst wet	Swimming pools and halls
EXTREME	Concrete surfaces exposed to abrasive action e.g. sea water carrying solids or flowing water with pH $\leqslant$4.5 or machinery or vehicles	All parts of marine structures including piers or harbour works, moorland water, with abrasion

3.3.4.2 *Freezing and thawing and de-icing salts*
See Section **6** (**6.1.5** and **6.2.3.2**).

3.3.5 Concrete materials and mixes
These clauses (**3.3.5.1-6**) provide qualifications to the use of Table 3.4 to take account of practical difficulties in demonstrating compliance with requirements for cement content and free water/cement ratio, of benefits of specially well controlled conditions of manufacture, of different sized aggregates, of the use of pulverized-fuel ash or ground granulated blastfurnace slag and of sulphate resisting cement. The rationale for the adjustments or restrictions is given in Section **6.2** of the handbook.

3.3.6 Cover as fire protection

Section 10 of CP110: 1972 gave values of cover to main reinforcement against minimum widths or thicknesses of sections without any opportunity to vary cover with increase or decrease in section dimensions.

Since 1972 international fire testing of concrete elements has demonstrated that moderate increases in beam and rib widths can lead to small but significant reductions in concrete cover to maintain the required fire resistance. Also the Building Research Establishment has relaxed its view on the depth of cover at which it is necessary to include measures to control spalling. CP110: 1972 required supplementary reinforcement to be inserted in beams and ribs whenever the cover to the main reinforcement, irrespective of the aggregate used, exceeded 40mm. This Code now requires additional measures to reduce the risk of spalling when the nominal cover exceeds 40mm in dense concrete elements and 50mm in lightweight concrete elements.

These two developments (i.e. variation of cover with section size and the cover depth requiring anti-spalling measures) are the principal changes in this new Code.

Variation of cover with section size

The sketches and dimensions in Figure H3.7 indicate the differing approaches to beam cover requirements in the 1972 and 1985 codes, for two hour fire resistance.

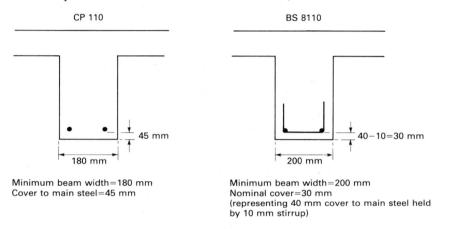

Figure H3.7: Comparison of CP 110 and BS 8110 for two hours fire resistance.

A comparison between the section sizes/covers given in Figure 3.2 and the tabular data for elements in Part 2, Section **4** reveals differences in the minimum widths for beams and ribs.

Figure 3.2 brings the minimum width of a beam or rib up to a dimension which suits practical considerations on site such as blockwork infilling between floor and beam soffits and the setting out dimensions for trough and waffle floors. By increasing the width of a beam or rib a corresponding small reduction in the cover to the main reinforcement can be made in accordance with Table 4.1 in Clause **4.3.5** in Part 2 of the Code.

Referring to the example in Figure H3.7, for two hour fire resistance, continuous construction and dense concrete, Tables 4.1 and 4.2 in Part 2 can be used as follows:

Minimum increase in width 50mm (from 150 to 200)
Decrease in cover 10mm (from 50 to 40)
After allowance for 10mm stirrup nominal cover is 30mm

The nominal cover of 30mm is the figure to be found in Table 3.5 for a two hour fire resistant continuous reinforced concrete beam.

Additional measures necessary to reduce the risk of spalling

Table 3.5 sets out the nominal covers to all reinforcement (including links) to meet specified periods of fire resistance for dense concrete. The sketch in Figure H3.8 illustrates the differing approaches to cover in CP110: 1972 and nominal cover in BS 8110: 1985.

The use of fine mesh as supplementary reinforcement to control spalling indicated in CP110 has met with almost universal condemnation as detrimental to the placing of good

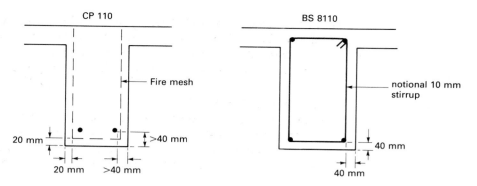

Figure H3.8: Comparison of CP 110 and BS 8110 fire provisions.

homogeneous concrete around the reinforcement. Consequently the new Code does not advocate this method as a means to control spalling.

To maintain the concept of nominal cover in the new Code whilst still relating basic cover to main tensile steel, it has been necessary to make allowance for the thickness of a stirrup in beam and column constructions. Consequently a stirrup thickness of 10mm has been used as an average of the range 8 to 12mm used in practice in the majority of constructions.

The values of nominal cover in Table 3.5 therefore reflect the stirrup allowance of 10mm in comparison with the tabular data in Section **4** of Part 2. Other constructions, such as ribs, floors and walls which do not incorporate stirrups, generally have nominal covers equal to the covers to be found in Section **4** of Part 2.

The horizontal lines drawn through Table 3.5 separate constructions that do not require anti-spalling measures where above the line and do require additional measures to reduce the risk of spalling where below the line. Such measures are outlined in Section **4** of Part 2.

3.3.7 Control of cover
The importance of workmanship to realise the design intentions is re-emphasised.

3.4 Beams

3.4.1 General
For considering the design of elements, the Code considers different classes of element in turn (i.e. beams, slabs, columns, etc). It is generally clear how a particular element should be classified but not always so and it should be understood that, in the limit, the boundaries between the different types of element are entirely arbitrary. For example, the element sketched in Figure H3.9 could possibly be classified as either a beam or a

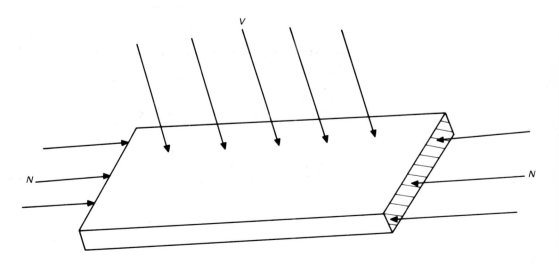

Figure H3.9: Is it a wall, beam, column or slab?

column or a slab or a wall. Frequently, the Code does not provide specific definitions which will allow a direct answer to be obtained in particular circumstances. The designer in these circumstances should use his common sense in judging the most appropriate design rules to use rather than looking for quasi-legal interpretations of the wording.

3.4.1.1 *Design limitations*
The basic assumptions about beam behaviour only hold where the span is reasonably large compared with the depth. Their validity certainly does not hold where the clear span is less than twice the depth. For the design of such members, reference could be made to CIRIA Guide 2: *The design of deep beams in reinforced concrete*[3.5].

3.4.1.2 *Effective span of simply-supported beams*
The objective of this provision is to make allowance for the influence of wide supports.

3.4.1.3 *Effective span of a continuous member*
Wide supports will also influence the behaviour of continuous beams and the same provision could be applied as for simply-supported members. This would, however, make practical difficulties in the analysis of continuous beams as the spans used would differ from those shown on drawings. It was felt that the resulting confusion was not justified.

3.4.1.4 *Effective length of a cantilever*
The clause is drafted to give consistency with the provisions of **3.4.1.2** and **3.4.1.3**.

3.4.1.5 *Effective width of flanged beam*
The concept of an effective width to a flanged beam is a device which will permit an

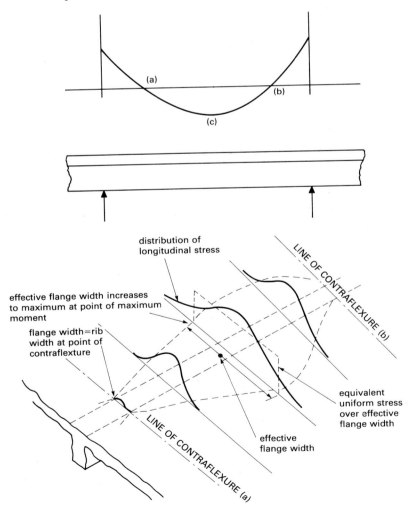

Figure H3.10: Effective flange width concepts.

essentially three-dimensional problem to be considered as a two-dimensional one. The behaviour of a beam with a wide flange is illustrated in Figure H3.10. At a point of contraflexure, the compressive stress is clearly zero. With increasing distance into the sagging region, the compressive force increases as the moment increases. However, stress can only get into the flanges by the action of shear. This increases the breadth of slab subject to significant compression with increasing distance from a point of zero moment. The effective flange width is the width of flange which, if assumed to have the same stress condition at all points across its width, will be equivalent to the actual behaviour (see Figure). It will be seen that the effective flange width is not constant and will be at its maximum at the point of maximum moment. The Code approach gives a conservative estimate of this maximum width.

3.4.1.6 *Slenderness limits for beams, for lateral stability*
These rules preclude failure by sideways bending and buckling. Lateral restraint should normally be provided by construction attached to the compression zone of the beam. In the case of parapet beams, lateral restraint may be assumed to be provided by slabs attached to the tension zone, provided that the slab thickness is at least one-tenth of the effective depth of the parapet beam and the parapet beams themselves do not project above the slab more than ten times their width. The limit to the value which need be taken was introduced so that lightly stressed members should not be penalised.

The limits are derived from work by Marshall[3.6].

3.4.2 Continuous beams

3.4.3 Uniformly-loaded continuous beams with approximately equal spans: moments and shears
The factors given in Table 3.6 are close to those which would be obtained from accurate analysis of a number of equal spans on point supports. In a practical case, with the permitted variation in span, calculated moments in excess of those given can arise. In addition, where load is transferred to the beam from a slab, no allowance is made for the type of distribution of loading specified in **3.5.3.7**; some allowance for redistribution has therefore already been included in Table 3.6 and this is why no further redistribution is permitted. Hence it will be prudent to limit the neutral axis depth at critical sections to $0.5d$(**3.4.4.4**).

3.4.4 Design resistance moment of beams

3.4.4.1 *Analysis of sections*
These assumptions are now well established and need little comment. The simplified stress block in Figure 3.3 gives answers which are generally very close to those which would be obtained using the parabolic-rectangular diagram. It will, therefore, be adequate for all practical purposes. The limit to the lever arm may be considered to serve two possible purposes: it provides a limit to the maximum tensile strain in reinforcement of 0.028 and it avoids reliance on what might be poor quality concrete at the top of a beam or slab section.

The presence of a small axial thrust of up to $0.1f_{cu}$ times the cross-sectional area actually increases the calculated ultimate moment, if taken into account, but at the expense of considerable added complexity in calculation.

3.4.4.2 *Design charts*
Full details on the design charts are given in Part 3 of the Code. They have been prepared for a range of concrete grades and are based on the stress-strain curve for concrete given in Figure 2.1.

Where redistribution has been done in the analysis for beams or slabs, the charts may be used to design sections which comply with the neutral axis limitations given in **3.2.2.1**. Lines are marked on the charts for neutral axis depths at ultimate load of 0.3, 0.4 and 0.5 of the effective depth. Any point on the chart to the left of one of these lines corresponds to a section which will have a neutral axis depth at failure less than the value appropriate to the line.

3.4.4.3 *Symbols*

3.4.4.4 *Design formulae for rectangular beams*

The derivation of these formulae assume that the tension steel will be yielding at the ultimate limit state. The limit to the value of K' ensures that the neutral axis depth at failure does not exceed half the effective depth. This will ensure that the tension steel will have yielded for all currently available grades of reinforcing steel. The derivation of the formulae is given below. Figure H3.11 illustrates the assumptions used.

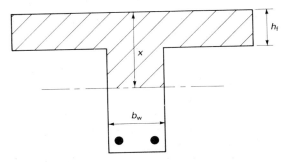

Figure H3.11: Flanged beam.

Consider first a singly reinforced section:

by equilibrium forces:

$$0.87f_y A_s = 0.45 \times 0.9bxf_{cu}$$

by equilibrium moments:

$$M = 0.87f_y A_s z$$

where $z = (d - 0.45x)$

From these two equations,

$$x = (0.87f_y A_s)/(0.45 \times 0.9bf_{cu})$$

$$A_s = M/0.87f_y z$$

Hence

$$x = M/(0.45 \times 0.9 \times b \times z \times f_{cu})$$

and hence,

$$z = d - (M/0.9\ bzf_{cu})$$

Substituting $K = M/bd^2 f_{cu}$ gives

$$z = d\ (1 - Kd/0.9z)$$

The solution to this quadratic in z is:

$$z = d[0.5 + \sqrt{(0.25 - Kd/0.9)}]$$

Turning now to the limitations applied by the redistribution, Clause **3.2.2.1** condition 2 states that:

$$x < (\beta_b - 0.4)d$$

Writing the moment equilibrium equation as:

$$M = (d - 0.45x)\ \underline{0.402bxf_{cu}} \quad {\scriptstyle 0.405\ bx\ fcu}$$

and substituting for 'x' gives:

$$M = 0.402bf_{cu}(\beta_b - 0.4)d\ [d - 0.45\ (\beta_b - 0.4)d]$$

writing $K' = M/bd^2 f_{cu}$ corresponding to the limiting value of z_c gives:

$$K' = 0.402\ (\beta_b - 0.4) - 0.18\ (\beta_b - 0.4)^2$$

(Note: $0.67f_{cu}/1.5 = 0.4467f_{cu}$ but the figures in the above derivation have only been written to two decimal places as $0.45f_{cu}$. The more accurate figure has, however, been used in the arithmetic.)

Substituting into this equation gives the values in Table H3.3 for K' for various amounts of redistribution.

Table H3.3 Values of K' corresponding to various amounts of redistribution

% redistribution	β_b	K'
< 10	0.9	0.156
15	0.85	0.145
20	0.8	0.132
25	0.75	0.119
30	0.7	0.104

When K exceeds K', the simplified equations provide for the addition of sufficient compressive steel to ensure that the neutral axis remains at the level corresponding to K'. The compression steel is assumed to be at yield and this will be so provided:

$$0.0035(x-d')/x > 0.87f_y/200\,000$$

or

$$d'/x < 1 - f_y/805$$

assuming $f_y = 400$, this gives $d'/x < 0.43$

The extra moment above that which would correspond to a singly reinforced section with the required neutral axis depth is $(K-K')f_{cu}bd^2$. By moments about the tension steel,

$$(K-K')f_{cu}bd^2 = 0.87(d-d')A'_s f_y$$

hence,

$$A'_s = (K-K')f_{cu}bd^2/0.87(d-d')f_y$$

The area of tension steel is that required for the moment $K'f_{cu}bd^2$ plus A'_s. This can be seen to be given by:

$$A_s = (K'f_{cu}bd^2/0.87f_y z) + A'_s$$

The equations in **3.4.4.4** thus follow directly from the basic assumptions and the neutral axis limitations of **3.2.2.1**.

Table H3.4 may be used for the calculation of steel areas for reinforcing rectangular sections as T-sections where the neutral axis lies within the flange.

Table H3.4 Design parameters for rectangular sections

K		<0.047	0.05	0.075	0.10	0.125	0.15	0.156
x/d		0.11	0.13	0.20	0.28	0.37	0.47	0.50
z/d		0.95	0.94	0.91	0.87	0.83	0.79	0.78
$0.87f_y z/d$	$f_y=250$	206.6	204.7	197.5	189.8	181.2	171.5	169.0
	$f_y=460$	380.2	376.6	363.5	349.3	333.5	315.6	311.0

$A_s = M/0.87f_y z$ $K = M/bd^2 f_{cu}$

3.4.4.5 *Design ultimate moments of resistance (of flanged beams where neutral axis falls below the flange)*

The equations given in this clause are not exact but are slightly conservative approximations. Equation 1 is derived as follows:

Moments about the centre of the flange gives:

$$M = 0.87f_y(d-h_f/2)A_s - (0.45-h_f/2)\,0.45 \times 0.9xb_w f_{cu}$$

Rearranging gives:

$$A_s = (M+(0.45x-h_f/2)\,0.402b_w x f_{cu})/(0.87A_s f_y(d-h_f/2))$$

x will not exceed $0.5d$ so substituting this value will give a generally conservative estimate of A_s. This gives:

$$A_s = (M + 0.1f_{cu}b_w d\ (0.45d - h_f))/(0.87\ A_s f_y (d - h_f/2))$$

Equation 2 can be derived directly by taking moments about the centroid of the tension steel.

3.4.5 Design shear resistance of beams

Calculations for the strength of reinforced concrete beams are based on comparing the average shear stress on a section calculated from equation 3 with a nominal value of ultimate shear stress v_c given in Table 3.9. The shear stresses given in Table 3.9 are based on an extensive study of test data (Figure H3.12). When the average shear stress is greater than the nominal stress from the Table, shear reinforcement is provided in proportions calculated on the assumption that the reinforcement forms the tension members of one or more series of pin-jointed trusses. This approach, commonly called the truss analogy, has been shown in tests to be conservative and the contribution to the shear strength from the concrete, $v_c bd$, is therefore assumed not to be lost if $v > v_c$. If v is only just greater than v_c, it will be necessary to increase the amount of shear reinforcement required from the truss analogy to the Code minimum permitted amount. When v is less than v_c, minimum reinforcement is still required in many cases; see Table 3.8.

[handwritten margin notes: up to here for general section, table 3.9 3.4.5.4, table 3.8 3.4.5.3]

[handwritten: although it is stated that in some instances reinforcement is not required it is general practice that it is.]

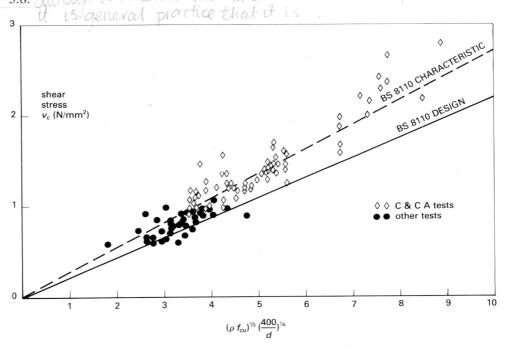

Figure H3.12: Shear strength of beams without shear reinforcement.

Where large shears are carried, it is possible for the diagonal compressive stresses to cause crushing of the web concrete. For this reason, the maximum shear carried by the beam must be limited; in the Code this limitation is given as $0.8\sqrt{f_{cu}}$ or 5 N/mm^2, whichever is lesser.

3.4.5.1 *Symbols*

3.4.5.2 *Shear stress in beams*

The actual way in which shear is carried by a section is highly complex and the value given by equation 3 should not be viewed as a stress which actually exists within a section: it is merely a mathematical device used for the interpretation of test results in the derivation of an empirical design method.

3.4.5.3 *Shear reinforcement: form, area and stress*

The intentions of Table 3.8 may be summarised diagramatically in Figure H3.13.

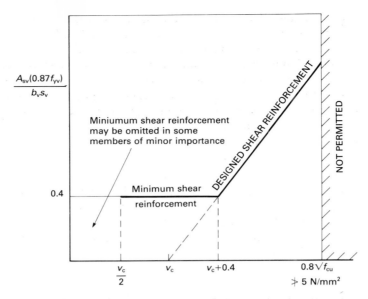

Figure H3.13: Provision of shear reinforcement in beams.

3.4.5.4 *Concrete shear stress*

Since the shear stress is a function of the amount of tension reinforcement at the section considered, it is clearly important to establish just what reinforcement can be included. This caused some confusion in CP110 and an attempt has been made to give clearer rules. In general, any bar which extends more than an effective depth on either side of the section being considered can be included. This definition will not be satisfactory at a single support but there is ample evidence to show that the full area of bottom steel at the support may be used in this case provided it is anchored according to the normal rules. The final paragraph of **3.4.5.4** aims to clarify which reinforcement should be used when nominal top steel is provided at a notional simple support. It is believed that there is a misprint in the final sentence which should read "This steel should extend into the *span* for a distance of at least three times the effective depth." Clearly, it should also be fully anchored into the support.

3.4.5.5 *Spacing of links*

The truss analogy would suggest a maximum spacing equal to the lever arm: $0.75d$ is a lower bound value for this. The logic behind the limit on lateral spacing of the legs of stirrups is less clear but experimental evidence suggests a reason why such a limit is valuable. One of the major functions of stirrups is to inhibit 'dowel' failure of the tension steel. This is a tearing out of the bars in the way sketched in Figure H3.14.

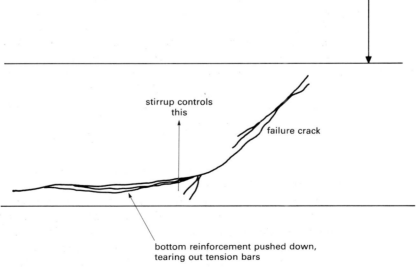

Figure H3.14: Normal mode of shear failure.

Clearly the effectiveness of the stirrup in achieving this will reduce with increasing distance of the vertical leg from the bar considered. Clearly, if a bar is placed further than 150mm from a stirrup leg, it can still be used to provide flexural strength but should be ignored in assessing v_c. The situation in slabs can be used to extend the interpretation of this clause further. In slabs, stirrups are not required until v exceeds v_c. It seems logical to argue from this that the requirement relating to the spacing of stirrup legs is to ensure that v_c can be maintained in circumstances where v exceeds v_c. It therefore seems reasonable to conclude that the limitations on lateral spacing may be ignored where v is less than v_c both in beams and slabs.

3.4.5.6 *Shear resistance of bent-up bars*
The truss analogy assumes that the tensions in the truss are carried by longitudinal and stirrup reinforcement and the concrete carries the thrust in the compression zone and the diagonal thrust across the web.

Equation 4 is derived directly from consideration of the equilibrium of this system (Figure H3.15).

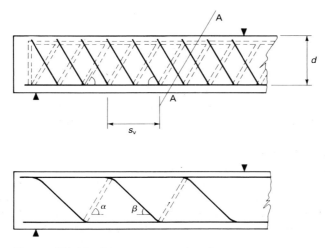

Figure H3.15: Truss systems for shear.

3.4.5.7 *Anchorage and bearing of bent-up bars*

3.4.5.8 *Enhanced shear strength of sections close to supports*
When the ratio of shear span to effective depth of a beam is reduced below 2, the shear capacity is considerably increased.

Figure H3.16 shows a plot of test results reported in references 3.7, 3.8 and 3.9 illustrating the relationship between a/d and v, for beams without stirrups. The line shown on the graph is straight for all values of a_v/d greater than 2 when v/v_c is 1. This clause defines the parabolic line shown in the Figure.

The strength of short beams depends to a large extent upon the detailing of the reinforcement. Adequate anchorage must be provided to the main tensile reinforcement. Vertical stirrups are not very effective in beams in which a_v/d is less than 0.6, in which case horizontal stirrups parallel to the main tension reinforcement are recommended.

The results shown in Figure H3.16 derive from tests on short-span, point-loaded beams but the results will hold for any failure where the failure plane is constrained to form at an angle greater than $\tan^{-1}(1/2)$ to the horizontal. The enhancement in strength can therefore be applied for any section closer to a support than $2d$.

3.4.5.9 *Shear reinforcement for sections close to supports*
Equation 5 derives from the assumption that the effect of the enhancement is only on v_c and does not affect the efficiency of shear reinforcement. Application of truss analogy might be seen to suggest that the increased truss angle implied by a failure close to a support would increase the efficiency of shear reinforcement. This may be so, in which case, equation 5 is conservative, but, while the experimental evidence for the enhancement of v_c is clear (Figure H3.16), it is doubtful if sufficient exists to show the effect of a_v/d on shear reinforcement unequivocally.

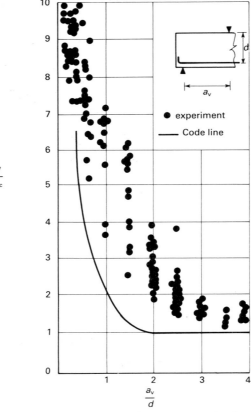

Figure H3.16: Ultimate shear stresses for beams loaded close to supports: v_c taken from Code

3.4.5.10 *Enhanced shear strength near supports (simplified approach)*

At a distance d from the support, Figure H3.16 will show that the capacity of the section is increasing very rapidly. So much so that it is most unlikely that the shear force will be increasing more rapidly. The rule given in this clause will thus normally give a safe way of gaining the advantage of the strength enhancement for minimal effort.

3.4.5.11 *Bottom loaded beams*

A load applied near the bottom of a beam could break the bottom out as sketched in Figure H3.17. The load, effectively, has to be transferred to the top by links before the design method is valid.

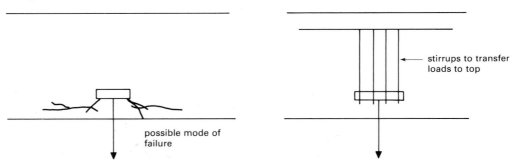

Figure H3.17: Loads on the bottom of beams.

3.4.5.12 *Shear and axial compression*

In dealing with the comments on the draft of BS 8110 circulated for public comment it became apparent that there was a considerable demand for guidance on the treatment of shear and compression, particularly in columns. Equation 6 in this clause is an entirely empirical attempt to make allowance for the increased shear capacity given by compressive axial load. Truly applicable test data are not easy to find but Figure H3.18 compares test results from several series of tests with the proposed formula. In the comparison, γ_m has been taken as 1.0 when calculating v_{co}.

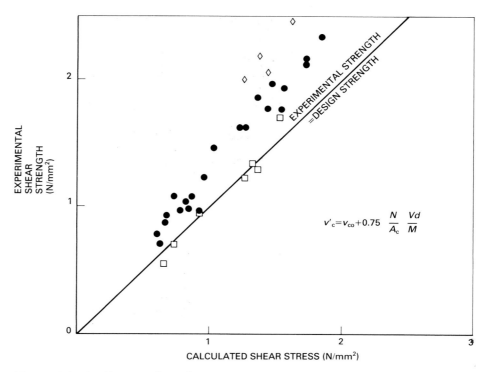

$$v'_c = v_{co} + 0.75 \frac{N}{A_c} \frac{Vd}{M}$$

Figure H3.18: Shear and axial compression.

3.4.5.13 *Torsion*

When the system is statically determinate, ultimate torsional moments must be calculated and provided for. In indeterminate structures, it will in most cases not be necessary to consider torsion at the ultimate limit state, but it may be necessary to consider it at the limit state of cracking. Figure H3.19 shows an example with edge beams in which torsion is statically indeterminate, i.e. it arises because of an imposed deformation and its magnitude will depend on the relative torsional and flexural stiffnesses in the structure. Lack of torsional strength in such cases will not cause collapse since the members will crack and deform without developing the ultimate torsional condition.

However, in some cases the twist imposed on a member may cause excessive cracking. This can happen, for example, in an edge beam where the span of the slab at right-angles to the beam is large, or as in Figure H3.19 in the short length of edge beam between the trimming beam and column where the imposed rotation from the secondary beam

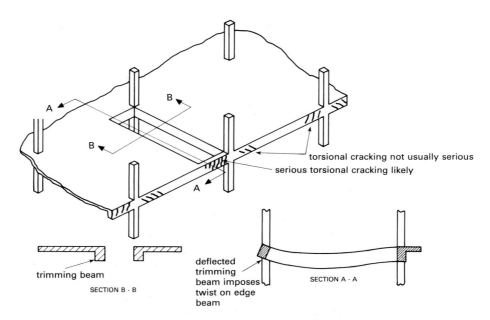

Figure H3.19: Examples of torsion due to imposed rotation.

has to be accommodated in quite a short length. For the purpose of designing the reinforcement and determining the forces exerted on adjoining members the method for calculating the imposed torque is based on tests on cracked reinforced beams[3.10] and is generally conservative.

Torsional stiffnesses are generally small with respect to flexural stiffnesses and can, therefore, be ignored in assessing the imposed twist. This will give an upper limit and one which will not be too conservative.

Explicit design for torsion is dealt with in Part 2 of the Code and will be discussed in the related section of the Handbook.

3.4.6 Deflection of beams

3.4.6.1 *General*
Where the conditions of service of a beam are known with precision, its deflection can be calculated reasonably accurately by using any of a number of semi-empirical equations. However, the calculations are tedious and time-consuming. It is not practicable to check the sufficiency of all normal members with respect to deflection by direct calculation. Furthermore, as is discussed in the commentary to Part 2 Section **3**, the calculation of a deflection requires consideration of many factors, a number of which may well not be definable at the design stage.

For this reason, the Tables of ratios of span to effective depth have been devised and it will be satisfactory to use them for all normal members. Consideration should, however, be given to the possibility of calculation where the conditions are in any way unusual.

3.4.6.2 *Symbols*

3.4.6.3 *Span/effective depth ratio for a rectangular or flanged beam*
Use of the Tables should be largely self-explanatory. The category 'continuous' in Table 3.10 may be taken to apply to any situation where at least one end of the beam is continuous. Thus, the end span of a series of continuous beams may be considered as continuous.

The derivation of the clause is discussed fully in references 3.11–3.13; however, a brief discussion of the principles involved will be given here.

To see how the setting of limits on the ratio of span to depth can be expected to control deflections, consider the case of a fully elastic rectangular beam supporting a uniformly distributed load (g_k+q_k).

If the maximum permissible stress in the material is f, the moment which the section can withstand is given by:

$$M = fbh^2/6 = (g_k+q_k)l^2/8 \qquad \qquad 3.1$$

The deflection of the beam is given by:

$$a = 5(g_k+q_k)l^4/384EI \qquad \qquad 3.2$$

Forming an expression for (g_k+q_k) from equation 3.1 and substituting this into 3.2 gives:

$$(5f/24E)\,(l/h) = (a/l)$$

Thus for a given elastic material, if the ratio l/h is kept constant, the ratio of deflection to span will remain constant. By setting a limit to the ratio of span to depth, the deflection will be limited to a given fraction of the span. This is what is required by the Code since, in general, the deflection limits are given as fractions of the span. It should be clear that, if an absolute limit is set on deflection, the ratio of span to depth must decrease with increasing span. This is the case where a limit of 20mm is specified. **3.4.6.4** is necessary to cope with this condition.

If the engineer considers that limits other than those for which the Tables have been produced are more appropriate, the Tables of basic ratios can be modified to suit the chosen limits. This may be done by multiplying the basic ratio by the ratio of the required deflection to the deflection for which the Table was derived. Thus, if the total deflection is to be limited to span/B instead of span/250, the figures in Table 3.10 should be multiplied by 250/B. Similarly, if the deflection occurring after the construction of the partitions is to be limited to some absolute value a', rather than to 20mm, the factor in **3.4.6.4** can be adjusted by multiplying it by $a'/20$.

additional information to 3.4.6.3

Span/depth ratios provide a rigorous method for controlling deflections as long as the material from which the beam is made is elastic. Unfortunately, reinforced concrete is not; the stiffness of a beam depends to a large extent upon the steel percentage and upon the state of cracking. Thus, if span/depth ratios are to be used for reinforced concrete, some way of correcting for its actual behaviour has to be found. The first step in this process is to use ratios of span to effective depth rather than span to overall depth, and the second is to introduce modifying factors.

The basic ratios given in Table 3.10 derive from experience. They can be seen to be similar to those in previous Codes which experience has shown to be of the right order. They may be considered to apply to 'average' beams. The factors in **3.4.6.5** and **3.4.6.6** modify this average figure up or down as a function of the level of steel stress and the state of loading of the section.

The logic behind the factors in Table 3.11 can be seen from considering the four cases sketched in Figure H3.20. This figure shows the strain distributions in four sections, two reinforced with 250 grade and two with 460 grade steel; of each pair, one has a high and the other a low steel percentage. All sections are loaded to their full design service load. For this example, the effects of the concrete in tension on the stiffness are ignored and the analysis is based on a cracked section. The deflection of a beam is directly proportional to the curvature at the critical section and this is given as:

$$\text{curvature} = 1/r = \varepsilon_s/(d-x)$$

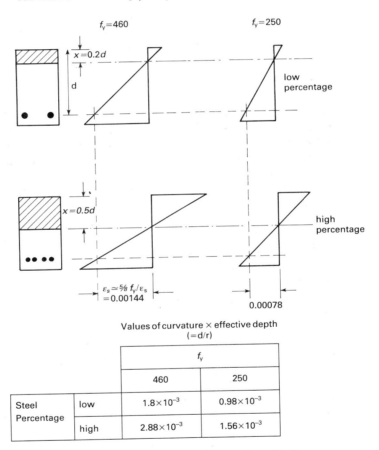

Values of curvature × effective depth
(=d/r)

		f_y	
		460	250
Steel Percentage	low	1.8×10^{-3}	0.98×10^{-3}
	high	2.88×10^{-3}	1.56×10^{-3}

Figure H3.20: Logic behind tension steel multipliers.

The figure illustrates clearly how steel percentage, which defines the neutral axis depth, and steel strength, which defines the strain, influence the deflection. From the point of view of span/depth ratios, the higher the curvature, the lower must the permissible span/depth ratio be in order to limit deflections to a constant proportion of the span. In CP110, a table of factors was included which was a function of steel percentage and steel stress. The effect of steel percentage over the full practical range is illustrated in Figure H3.21(a). In practice this was found inconvenient to use since deflections could not be checked until after the reinforcement had been detailed. Since there is a direct relationship between steel percentage, steel strength and K (M/bd^2), the table in CP110 is reformulated

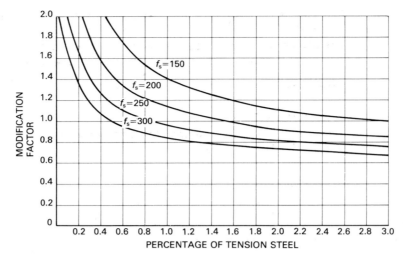

Figure H3.21 (a): Modification factors as a function of steel percentage.

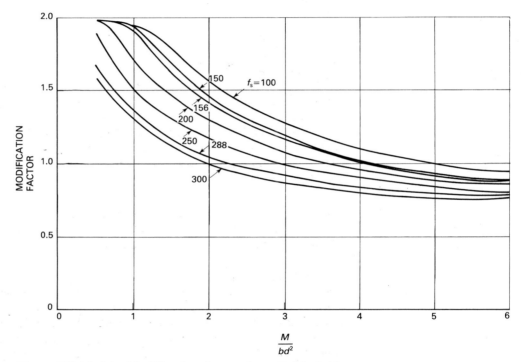

Figure H3.21 (b): Modification factors from Table 3.11.

to give factors as a function of *K* and steel stress. Thus it is now possible to check deflections as soon as an estimate of the design ultimate moments can be made. For convenience, Table 3.11 is presented graphically in Figure H3.21(b).

The analysis illustrated in Figure H3.20 ignores any influence of the concrete in the tension zone. In fact, this concrete adds considerably to the stiffness (see Part 2, Section 3) and this is allowed for in the factors given in the Code. Clearly, however, in the case of flanged beams, this stiffening will be reduced. The basic ratios given in Table 3.10 for flanged beams reflect this fact.

3.4.6.4 *Long spans*
See discussion of **3.4.6.3** above.

3.4.6.5 *Modification of span/depth ratios for tension reinforcement*
See discussion of **3.4.6.3** above.

3.4.6.6 *Modification of span/depth ratios for compression reinforcement*
The effects of compression reinforcement on deflections are twofold:

(a) compression steel reduces the neutral axis depth and hence the curvatures (Figure H3.20)

(b) compression steel significantly reduces the effects of creep and shrinkage and thus has a substantial effect on the long-term deflections.

These two factors are taken into account in the values given in Table 3.12

3.4.6.7 *Deflection due to creep and shrinkage*
This clause is self-explanatory. More information on the effects of creep and shrinkage is given in Part 2 Section **7**.

3.4.7 Crack control in beams
See Section **3.12.11.2** for discussion.

3.5 Solid slabs supported by beams or walls

3.5.1 Design

3.5.2 Moments and forces

3.5.2.1 *General*
Single-way slabs may be analysed as beams taking account of the simplified load arrangement. Most two-way solid slabs in practice are rectangular, are cast monolithically with supports and are covered by **3.5.3**. As the provisions here are based on Johansen's yield line method it is suggested that **3.5.3** be applied in all such cases. It follows that determination of moments and forces will be necessary only for non-rectangular slabs. Elastic theory for such cases is rather complex and so the Johansen or Hillerborg methods are recommended[3.14,3.15].

3.5.2.2 *Distribution of concentrated loads on slabs*
The empirical rules given for the effective widths of slab that resist bending moments due to such loads are based on loading tests to failure.

3.5.2.3 *Simplification of load arrangements*
The justification for a single-load case of maximum design load on all spans or panels is given by Beeby[3.16]. The major part of the report is taken up with justifying this simplification in terms of current knowledge of slab behaviour and imposed loadings on floors. It is reasonable for normal occupancy but cannot be rigorously proved to be so. It is not considered valid for structures designed for storage or where the live to dead load ratio is large. In such circumstances pattern loading should be considered.

The effect of redistributing the moments by 20% is shown in Figure H3.22.

Redistribution of moments affects the shear forces and these should be calculated to satisfy static equilibrium.

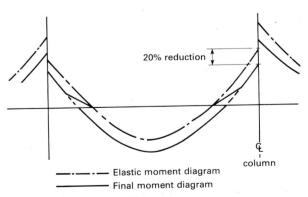

20% reduction

℄ column

— · — · — Elastic moment diagram
————— Final moment diagram

Figure H3.22: Development of bending moment envelope for slab.

It should be noted that the effect of redistributing moments by 20% affects the neutral axis depth limit and hence the value of K'. The value of K' in **3.4.4.4** is reduced to 0.132. This is not generally a limitation for solid slabs.

The moment reduction does not, of course, apply to cantilevers.

Where a cantilever extends from the last support of a continuous slab it is essential to consider the load case of cantilever loaded and adjacent slab panel or span unloaded to ensure sufficient anchorage of the cantilever top steel into the adjacent slab.

3.5.2.4 *One-way spanning slabs of approximately equal span*

3.5.3 Solid slabs spanning in two directions at right angles: uniformly distributed loads

3.5.3.1 *General*

3.5.3.2 *Symbols*

3.5.3.3 *Simply-supported slabs*
The coefficients in Table 3.14 are derived from the Grashof–Rankine formulae.

3.5.3.4 *Restrained slabs*

3.5.3.5 *Restrained slabs where the corners are prevented from lifting and adequate provision is made for torsion: conditions and rules for the use of equations 14 and 15*
The coefficients in Table 3.15 have been derived from yield-line analysis[3.17]. The particular values of β_{sx} and β_{sy} depend on the choice of yield lines, the relationship for which is given in equations 16 to 18. The values of β_{sy} were chosen to an accuracy of two decimal places. This has led to small differences occurring between the values for β_{sx} and β_{sy} for square panels.

3.5.3.6 *Restrained slab with unequal conditions at adjacent panels*

3.5.3.7 *Loads on supporting beams*
The estimation of loads on supporting beams has been changed significantly from previous codes. The new Table of coefficients (Table 3.16) provides an estimate of the load on the supporting beams which makes allowance for the support conditions. If a panel has one edge continuous and the opposite edge discontinuous, then more load will be attracted to the continuous support (in the same way as the shear coefficient in Table 3.13 for the first interior support is greater than that for an end support). The new Table (Table 3.16) takes account of this effect in developing coefficients for the shear forces in the slab along the line of the support. Those shear forces constitute the loading on the supporting beams.

When analysing the supporting beams, the loading shown in Figure 3.10 gives a maximum free bending moment of $0.117 v_s l^2$ and a fixed end moment of $0.076 v_s l^2$.

3.5.4 Resistance moment of solid slabs
Where the single load case has been used with 20% redistribution of support moments (**3.5.2.3**) the value of K' in **3.4.4.4** is reduced to 0.132.

3.5.5 Shear resistance of solid slabs
The problem of defining what is a slab for the purpose of shear design is not easy to resolve. The simple definition that any member with a ratio of width to depth greater than 4 is a slab and any member with a smaller ratio is a beam – is a first rough way of separating the types of member. In some circumstances, the way in which a slab, so defined, is designed or loaded may require it to be treated as a beam. One example is that of treating areas of slabs, which may or may not be locally thickened, as beam strips between columns; such strips should be treated as beams. This discussion does not apply to the ribs of waffle type floors; these do not have to be considered generally as beams (**3.6**).

3.5.5.1 *Symbols*

3.5.5.2 *Shear stresses*

3.5.5.3 *Shear reinforcement*

3.5.6 Shear in solid slabs under concentrated loads (3.7.7)

3.5.7 Deflection

Note that, with the exception of cantilever slabs, it is always the mid-span moment which is used in assessing the factor from Table 3.11. It is worth bearing in mind that the ratios of span to effective depth have been arranged to ensure that the deflections of flexural members do not exceed the specified limits relative to their supports. If the support for a slab consists of beams which will themselves deflect under load, the total deflection of the whole system might not be satisfactory even though each member considered individually was satisfactory relative to its own supports. It might be unwise, therefore, to design both the beams and slabs in such a system to be on the limit of the ratios of span to effective depth.

Where compression reinforcement is used in slabs Table 3.12 may be used to modify the span/effective depth ratio.

3.5.8 Crack control

See **3.12.11**. Specific crack control measures are unlikely to be required provided the spacing of bars conforms with the rules given in **3.12.11.2.7**.

When reinforcement is needed purely to distribute cracking arising from shrinkage and temperature effects the recommendation given in **3.9.4.19** and **3.9.4.20** for plain walls should be followed. Further information is given in Part 2 Section **3.8.4**.

3.6 Ribbed slabs (with solid or hollow blocks or voids)

3.6.1 General

3.6.1.1 *Introduction*

3.6.1.2 *Hollow or solid blocks and formers*

3.6.1.3 *Spacing and size of ribs*

When calculating the section resistance the maximum flange width assumed should not exceed that specified for T-beams (**3.4.15**).

Where the slab is arranged to span in one direction, it is suggested that, in addition to the condition specified in the clause, a minimum of five ribs may be provided.

The last paragraph applies to trough slabs where there may be practical difficulties in ensuring the positioning of main reinforcement or where the rib spacing is such that each will behave as a separate beam. This is likely if the spacing exceeds 1.5m.

It is not considered necessary to provide links in waffle slabs unless they are required for shear or fire resistance purposes. Fixing of the bars in one direction can be achieved by tying them to the bars in the other direction.

3.6.1.4 *Non-structural side support*

This clause neglects to point out that cracking in the adjacent flange is likely and consideration should be given to introducing ribs at right angles to the support.

3.6.1.5 *Thickness of topping used to contribute to structural strength*

Although a nominal reinforcement of 0.12% is suggested in the topping (**3.6.6.2**), it is not insisted upon, and the topping is therefore expected to transfer load to the adjacent ribs without the assistance of reinforcement. The mode of transfer involves arching action and this is the reason for the insistence that the depth be at least one-tenth of the clear distance between ribs.

3.6.1.6 *Hollow block slabs where topping not used to contribute to structural strength*

3.6.2 Analysis of structure

When considering the effects of concentrated loads in one-way slabs, the width assumed to contribute to the support of the load should not exceed the width of the loaded area plus four times the rib spacing; in addition, it should not be taken greater than 0.251 on either side of the loaded area.

For waffle flat slabs the section properties should be based on the stiffness of the waffle section. If the breadth of the solid area at the column is at least one third of the smaller dimension of the surrounding panels, it should be taken into account in the section properties.

Similarly for a flat slab with drops, the drop should be taken into account in the section properties if it is at least one-third of the smaller dimension of the surrounding panels.

Hence when analysing by equivalent frame the section properties should be based on the hatched areas as shown in Figure H3.23.

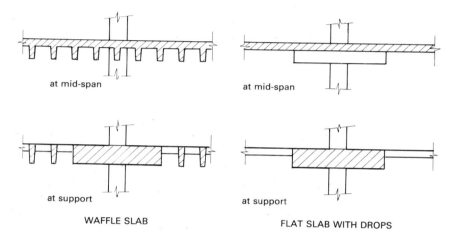

at mid-span at mid-span

at support at support

WAFFLE SLAB FLAT SLAB WITH DROPS

Figure H.3.23: Areas to be considered for section properties in equivalent frame analysis.

The lateral distribution of moments in waffle flat slabs is similar to solid flat slabs except that the solid area around a column may be considered as a drop (**3.7.1.5**, **3.7.3** and **3.7.2.10**). The presence of the solid area causes stress concentration at the outer corners. For this reason the concentration of reinforcement required generally by **3.7.3.1** does not apply. The reinforcement should be placed evenly across the column strip.

The torsional stiffness of waffle slabs is small and when analysing by grillage or finite element methods it is reasonable to neglect its effects except in solid areas.

A more detailed method of grillage analysis covering waffle flat slabs is given by Whittle[3.18].

The alternative suggestions given in **3.6.2** for situations where it is impracticable to provide sufficient reinforcement to develop the full design support moment apply to single and two-way ribbed slabs. For flat slabs **3.7.2**, **3.7.3** and **3.7.4** apply.

3.6.3 Design resistance moments

3.6.4 Shear

It is suggested that where the rib spacing exceeds 1m, nominal stirrups should be provided in the ribs in accordance with **3.4.5.3**.

3.6.4.1 *Flat slab construction*

Where shear links are required in the ribs they should be extended into the solid section to allow the concentrated stresses to disperse into the solid section (an effective depth say). The tension reinforcement should extend a further tension anchorage length.

3.6.4.2 *One or two-way spanning slabs*

3.6.4.3 *Shear contribution by hollow blocks*

3.6.4.4 *Shear contribution from solid blocks*

3.6.4.5 *Shear contribution by joints between narrow precast units*

3.6.4.6 *Maximum design shear stress*

3.6.4.7 *Area of shear reinforcement in ribbed, hollow block or voided slabs*
Advantage may be taken of enhanced shear strength of sections close to supports as given in **3.4.5.8–3.4.5.10**.

3.6.5 Deflection in ribbed, hollow block or voided construction generally
Note that if a slab is designed as simply supported it must be considered as simply supported when checking deflections.

3.6.5.1 *General*
If a slab is designed as simply supported according to the rules given in **3.6.2** then it should be treated as simply supported for the purposes of checking the ratio of span to effective depth.

3.6.5.2 *Rib width of voided slabs or slabs of box or I-section units*

3.6.6 Arrangement of reinforcement
3.6.2 allows that a continuous ribbed slab may be designed as simply supported with so-called anti-crack steel provided over the supports. The system of treating continuous slabs as simply supported has arisen in practice because of the difficulty, or even sometimes impossibility, of fixing enough top steel in the ribs over supports to resist the moments which would arise from treating the slabs as continuous. From the point of view of safety, this is likely to be satisfactory. However, from the point of view of serviceability, its sufficiency is more doubtful. Effectively, designing in this way is asking for a very large redistribution in the support section. This means that, even under dead load, the support steel will yield if the concrete cracks, and it cannot therefore act effectively as anti-crack reinforcement. It may well be that cracks in the top surface of slabs over the supports are often not serious, the cracks being covered by floor finishes or partitions. The engineer should nevertheless be aware that this method of design does have risks of serious cracking associated with it.

The necessity of providing internal ties in accordance with **3.12.3** may on occasions influence the application of these detailing rules.

Where waffle slabs have been designed as flat slabs, situations will arise where particular spacings of ribs will lead to those of the middle strip requiring more reinforcement than those in the column strip for positive moments in the span (Table 3.21). In such circumstances the reinforcement required for the total moment should be spread evenly across the middle and column strips.

3.6.6.1 *Curtailment of bars*

3.6.6.2 *Reinforcement in topping for ribbed or hollow block slabs*

3.6.6.3 *Links in ribs*
See comment on **3.6.1.3**.

The ribs along the external edges of waffle slabs should be provided with nominal links to help control torsional cracking.

3.7 Flat slabs

3.7.1 General
The design of flat slabs by the empirical method given in CP110 was generally less conservative than that of more rigorous elastic methods. Research in recent years has

shown that pattern loading for the rigorous methods is overconservative. For this reason the simplified single load case (**3.5.2.3**) has been introduced. In general, designs now carried out in accordance with the simplified rules will be more conservative than those made using equivalent frame or grillage methods.

New shear clauses have been introduced as a result of research by Regan[3.19] and Long et al[3.20]. These clauses are considered internationally to provide the closest relationship with the test results of all the existing concrete codes.

3.7.1.1 Symbols

3.7.1.2 Design

In order to satisfy the serviceability criteria, elastic methods of analysis are likely to control the design of flat slabs. The use of computers enables equivalent frame and grillage methods to become increasingly popular for modelling flat slabs. Grillage methods can provide reasonable estimates of deflection provided care is taken in selecting section properties and due account is taken of the effects of cracking and creep. Detailed methods are given by Whittle[3.18].

The distribution of moments across the width of slab for negative moment alters with respect to the aspect ratio of the panel. Figure H3.24, taken from Regan[3.19] shows the relationship.

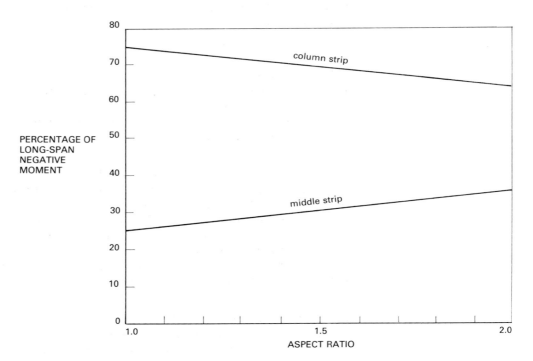

Figure H3.24: Distribution of long-span negative moment in internal panel of flat slab.

3.7.1.3 Column head

3.7.1.4 Effective diameter of a column or column head

3.7.1.5 Drops

When checking the shear resistance, two critical perimeters should be considered. One $1.5d_d$ from the face of the column and the other $1.5d_s$ from the outer edge of the drop (d_d=effective depth of drop and d_s=effective depth of slab).

3.7.1.6 Thickness of panels

3.7.2 Analysis of flat slab structures

Analysis of flat slabs is normally carried out by using one of three methods: yield line, equivalent frame, or grillage analogy. Yield line methods whilst providing the most economic solution do not provide information concerning the most suitable arrangement of reinforcement for working load conditions with consequent implications for cracking and deflection.

Elastic methods are more likely to predict the behaviour under working load conditions and they can be extended to an analysis at the ultimate limit state. The equivalent frame approach provides a reasonable representation of the behaviour of the floor by a system of columns and beams analysed separately in each span direction.

One misconception held by some engineers is to consider a reduced load when analysing the slab in one direction. A flat slab supported on columns, other than perimeter beams, can fail as a one-way mechanism just as a single-way slab, and it should be reinforced to resist the moment from the full load in each orthogonal direction.

The use of computers for the analysis of flat slabs is becoming more common and grillage programs are now often used to solve routine design problems. These can give reasonable predictions of deflection provided care is taken in selecting section properties and due account is taken of the effects of cracking and creep. Detailed methods are given by Whittle[3.18].

3.7.2.1 *General*
The justification for a single load case of maximum design load on all spans or panels is given by Beeby[3.10]. Although it is a reasonable assumption for normal occupancy it cannot be rigorously proved. It is not considered valid for structures designed for storage where pattern loading may be a real possibility.

3.7.2.2 *Analysis*
It should be realised that although the equivalent frame method of analysis provides a reasonable set of moments and shear forces it will normally over-estimate the moments at the edge columns. The lateral distribution of moments at edges is normally very restricted as described in **3.7.4.2**.

3.7.2.3 *Division of flat slab structures into frames*
The division into longitudinal and transverse frames gives design moments in two directions at right-angles. These moments must be provided for in full, as otherwise equilibrium will not be satisfied. The loads in the columns can be assessed from either the longitudinal or the transverse frames and the assumptions of simple support as defined in **3.8.2.3** may be used if desired for internal columns where appropriate.

Where drops are used account should be taken of them in determining the section properties of the slab if they project more than $0.15\,l$ into the span.

3.7.2.4 *Frame analysis methods*
The frame method gives satisfactory results for most orthogonal grids. However whereas this method is suitable for analysis at the ultimate limit state it does not provide accurate predictions of deflections at service loads.

3.7.2.5 *Frame stiffness*

3.7.2.6 *Limitation of negative design moments*
This clause provides a check to ensure that static equilibrium is obtained. The value of h_c for the purposes of this clause should not exceed 1.5 times the size of the shorter side of a rectangular column.

3.7.2.7 *Simplified method for determining moments*
The coefficients given in Table 3.19 have been prepared taking due account of the necessary 20% downward redistribution of moments required under the single load case. The value of the effective shear force (**3.7.6**) when using these coefficients may be determined from the simplified factors 1.15 for internal columns, 1.25 for corner columns and edge columns bent about an axis parallel to the free edge and 1.4 for edge columns bent about an axis perpendicular to the free edge.

3.7.2.8 *Division of panels (except in the region of edge and corner columns)*
The definition of column and middle strips for rectangular panels has been altered with respect to CP110. This is as a result of work carried out by Regan[3.19]. For aspect ratios greater than 2 the centre section of the longer span tends to span one way and should be reinforced with nominal steel only in the direction of the short span. The lateral distribution of moments is discussed in more detail by Regan[3.19] and Whittle[3.18].

3.7.2.9 *Column strips between unlike panels*

3.7.2.10 *Division of moments between column and middle strips*
It should be noted that Table 3.21 does not give a suitable division of moments at edge columns. These areas require special attention as given in **3.7.4.2**.

3.7.3 Design of internal panels

3.7.3.1 *Column and middle strips*
A distinction should be made between the design of flat slabs with flat soffits and those with drops (or waffle slabs with solid areas around columns). The presence of the drop or solid area causes stress concentration at the outer corners. This affects the way in which the top reinforcement should be distributed to resist the negative moment in the column strip. The concentration of reinforcement provided by this clause should not apply in such situations and the reinforcement should be placed evenly across the column strip. Care should be taken to ensure that the top reinforcement extends over the corner of the drop or solid area to control cracking in this area.

3.7.3.2 *Curtailment of bars*

3.7.4 Design of edge panels

3.7.4.1 *Positive design moments in span and negative design moments over interior edges*

3.7.4.2 *Design moments transferable between slab and edge or corner columns*
Equation 24 gives a simplified formula providing a reasonable basis to assess the maximum moment of resistance of an edge joint. The reasons for restricting the effective width are given by Regan[3.19].

The value of b_e for a circular column may be taken as that for a square enclosing the circle.

If the equivalent frame method is used for determining the edge transfer moment this clause allows up to 50% redistribution. The reason for this is that this method is known to give higher moments of transfer than actually take place. Long discusses this in detail[3.20].

Where the simple coefficients given in Table 3.19 or the single load case in conjunction with the equivalent frame method of analysis are used, the moments and shear forces may be redistributed a further 30%. This is equivalent to approximately 50% redistribution of the elastic values from these methods.

In circumstances where, in spite of redistribution of the elastic moments to the limits given, they still exceed $M_{t,max}$ consideration should be given to altering the structural configuration. Otherwise flexural cracking in the slab close to the edge columns could become so excessive that it affects the shear capacity.

3.7.4.3 *Limitation of moment transfer*
Although the limitation on moment transfer is severe it is unlikely that much can be gained by torsion reinforcement in slabs with a depth less than 300mm. Regan[3.19] and Whittle[3.18] discuss this in more detail.

3.7.4.4 *Negative moments at free edge*
It should be noted that for normal situations the total transfer moment (slab/column) is

resisted by edge reinforcement in a narrow band (**3.7.4.2**). The remaining edge of the slab should be reinforced with nominal steel as described in this clause.

3.7.4.5 *Panels with marginal beams or walls*

3.7.5 Openings in panels

3.7.6 Effective shear forces in flat slabs
The equations given in this section which magnify the elastic shear differ from CP110. This results from work carried out by Regan[3.19] and Long [3.20]. In fact, equation 25 is a simplified version of those given by Regan and can be shown to give results within 2% of Regan's proposals. The enhancement factor given in CP110 ($1+12.5M/VL$) is reasonable for long spans with small columns. However for the more normal situations (up to 8m span) the current formulae which are based on the column width are more appropriate.

The use of the simplified factors (e.g. $1.15V_t$ etc) is reasonable where the spans do not differ by more than 25%. However, if the live to dead load ratio exceeds 1.00 then the more rigorous calculation should be made.

3.7.6.1 *General*
The calculations for effective shear given in this section apply to elastic methods of analysis. When using the single load case of maximum design load on all spans or panels simultaneously the value of V_{eff} should not be taken as less than $1.1V_t$ for the slab/internal column connections and $1.35V_t$ for the slab/edge columns bent about an axis perpendicular to the free edge.

3.7.6.2 *Shear stress at slab/internal column connections in flat slabs*
There may be occasions when the calculated value of V_{eff} exceeds the simplified value given for approximately equal spans. Consideration should be given to situations where the calculated value is likely to be larger and should be used. These will include:

(a) unequal loading of slab panels
(b) slabs where the difference in spans is more than 10%
(c) slabs where an edge slab/column connection cannot take the full elastic moment. This will cause the first interior column to have a higher moment.

3.7.6.3 *Shear stress at other slab-column connections*

3.7.6.4 *Maximum design shear stress at the column face*

3.7.7 Shear under concentrated loads

3.7.7.1 *Mode of punching failure*
A punching failure of a slab without shear reinforcement occurs when the tension in the concrete reaches its limit. The natural failure occurs on inclined faces of truncated cones or pyramids at an angle of about 35° to the horizontal. No theory of punching as yet is generally accepted and the Code recommendations are empirical, expressed in terms of nominal shear stresses along a control perimeter. The control perimeter is taken as rectangular in shape, $1.5d$ from the column or loaded area. The choice of perimeters is based on the use of the shear resistance values for single-way slabs together with convenient and simple geometric values.

3.7.7.2 *Maximum design shear capacity*
The Code recommendations are empirical and are expressed as a nominal shear stress at the face of the column or loaded area. The value of u_o is based on the size of a rectangle touching the loaded area. For a circular column this is a square of side equal to the diameter of the column. The failure mode associated with the maximum shear capacity is that of a diagonal compression strut failure. This may be considered to extend from the column face (or loaded area) to a perimeter $1.5d$ from the column.

3.7.7.3 *Calculation of design shear stress for a failure zone*
Equation 28 is an empirical formula which differs from that of CP110 which was expressed in terms of the full depth of slab rather than the effective depth. The reason for the change is to bring it in line with the calculation of shear stress for beams and single-way slabs which are both expressed in terms of effective depth.

3.7.7.4 *Shear capacity of a failure zone without shear reinforcement*
This clause allows an increase in v_c for perimeters closer than $1.5d$ from the face of column or loaded area. However this value should not exceed the maximum permitted value given in **3.7.7.2**.

Often a dilemma exists as to whether the bottom or top steel should be taken as the tensile reinforcement and from where its anchorage should be measured. If there is doubt then the bottom steel should be chosen. The required anchorage of the effective steel area is defined in Clause **1.2.3.5**. This explains that the reinforcement should extend beyond the failure zone considered by an effective depth or 12 times the diameter of the bar, whichever is greater. Each failure zone is $1.5d$ wide, corresponding to a notional failure line.

3.7.7.5 *Provision of shear reinforcement in a failure zone*
This clause includes a number of changes from CP110. The use of rectangular perimeters and zones is considered more convenient for placing shear reinforcement. Each shear perimeter checked is associated with a zone through which the failure plane is assumed to pass. The objective of providing shear reinforcement for a particular perimeter check is to ensure that the shear reinforcement is spread evenly over the associated zone and crosses the likely failure plane. In order to ensure that punching between the column (or loaded area) and the innermost shear perimeter is avoided this shear reinforcement should be placed not further than $0.5d$ from the face of the column.

3.7.7.6 *Design procedure*

3.7.7.7 *Modification of effective perimeter to allow for holes*
Where holes occur adjacent to one side of a column the reduction of shear perimeter may be more reasonably taken as a parallel projection of the hole on to the shear perimeter as shown in Figure H3.25.

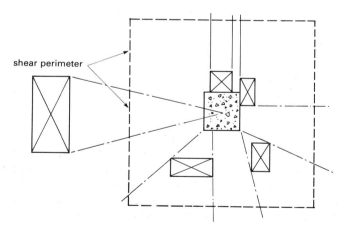

shear perimeter

Figure H3.25: Reduction of shear perimeter near holes.

3.7.7.8 *Effective perimeter close to a free edge*

3.7.8 Deflection of panels
When using Table 3.11 the value of M should be taken as the total bending moment calculated at mid-span for a panel.

3.7.9 Crack control in panels
See **3.12.11**. The only special point to note is that, if drops are used, the total depth of

the slab plus drop should be considered when deciding how the rules in **3.12.11.2.7** apply to the regions of the slab within the drops.

3.7.10 Design of columns in flat slab construction

3.8 Columns

3.8.1 General

In principle, columns would appear to be considerably more complex to design than beams due to the substantial number of extra variables which may require consideration. These are:

(a) Sections are subjected to combined moment and axial load rather than just moment.
(b) A considerable number of combinations of moment and axial load may be possible. These will frequently include cases giving biaxial bending.
(c) Bending of the column will lead to lateral deflections which, if significant, can affect the capacity of the column.

Fortunately, there are also a number of simplifying factors which reduce the complexity in most normal situations such as:

(a) Most columns are of rectangular cross-section and are designed as symmetrically reinforced. There are, indeed, very strong practical and behavioural reasons for employing symmetrically reinforced sections wherever possible.
(b) In many, if not most cases, only uniaxial bending need be considered. Except for lightly loaded columns, design for the maximum load plus maximum moment will be safe and usually not excessively conservative.
(c) The majority of columns are sufficiently stocky that deflections are not significant.
(d) Shear will generally not require consideration.
(e) Serviceability (deflections and cracking) will generally not require consideration.
(f) Since, in general, all sections of a column will contain the same reinforcement, the distribution of moments over the height of the column is rarely of importance, only the maximum values.

As a result of the above factors, design of most columns is a very simple matter. The fact that the Code has to provide rules for dealing with the less common, more complex situations should not be allowed to obscure this.

3.8.1.1 *Symbols*

3.8.1.2 *Size of columns*
Section **3.3**, and in particular Tables 3.4, 3.5 and Figure 3.2 give information which may influence the section dimension.

3.8.1.3 *Short and slender columns*
Slender columns are those where the deflection of the column under ultimate load conditions is sufficient significantly to influence the ultimate strength. Short or stocky columns are those where the deflection may be ignored. The limit of 10 for the slenderness ratio for unbraced structures is arbitrary as deflection has some influence on strength at all slendernesses. The situation is different for braced structures since (as will be discussed below), in braced structures the maximum moments induced by deflections occur at roughly mid-height of the column while the moments arising from normal frame action are greatest at top and bottom of the column. Studies have shown that for slenderness ratios less than 15, the moments arising from the frame action at the ends of the column will always give the critical design condition. Above 15, it becomes increasingly likely that the critical design condition will occur in the central region of the column.

3.8.1.4 *Plain concrete columns*
This clause was introduced in recognition of the fact that, if it is acceptable (and indeed normal) to design masonry columns without reinforcement, then it must be equally acceptable to design unreinforced concrete columns.

3.8.1.5 *Braced and unbraced columns*

This distinction is important in the treatment of slender columns. There are two basic deflected shapes which a column may take up, depending on the nature of the total structure.

If there are elements within the structure which are sufficiently stiff that they will effectively attract any lateral loads without significant deflection (e.g. groups of walls), then it can be assumed that there is no lateral displacement of the top of the column relative to the bottom and the deflected shape under ultimate load would appear as shown in Figure H3.26.

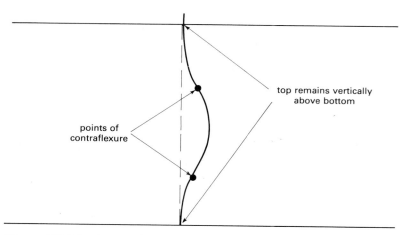

Figure H3.26: Assumed deformed shape of braced column.

Columns which deflect in this manner near failure are described as 'braced'.

If all the vertical members are relatively flexible so that significant sidesway may occur then the deflected shape near failure will take the alternative form shown in Figure H3.27. Columns which deflect in this manner are described as unbraced. Clearly in such a structure, all columns will deflect equally.

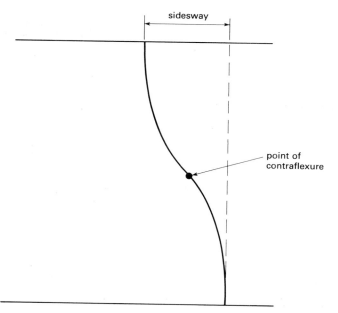

Figure H3.27: Assumed deformed shape of unbraced column.

3.8.1.6 *Effective height of a column*

The concept of effective height is used almost universally in dealing with the buckling of columns. The effective height is the height of a pinned ended strut which will have the same capacity as the column considered. The appropriate length follows from the deflected shape expected at failure. This is illustrated for braced and unbraced columns in Figure H3.28. It will be seen that, for a braced column, the effective length will always be less than or equal to the actual length, being shorter where the members connected top and bottom are stiffer. By contrast, the effective length of an unbraced column will always exceed the actual length. The effective length of a braced column with pinned ends or an unbraced column with rigid connections at both ends would be equal to the actual length. That for a cantilever with rigid connection at one end would be twice the actual height. Effective lengths of cantilever columns where some base rotation might occur will exceed twice the actual height.

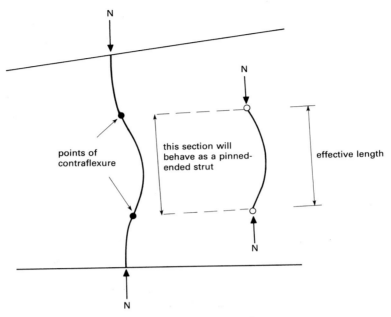

Figure H3.28 (a): Effective length concept for a braced column.

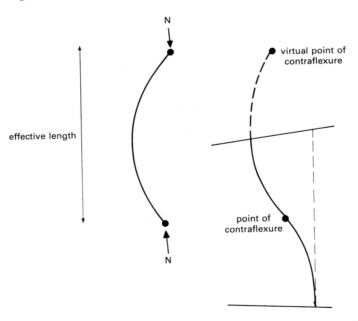

Figure H3.28 (b): Effective length concept for an unbraced column.

3.8.1.6.1 General. Effective lengths can be computed rigorously from elastic considerations but the process is complex and not justified in practice. Part 2 Section 2.5 gives approximate formulae. In this clause and **3.8.1.6.2**, a simplified method is given which leads to adequate estimates of effective length for most practical purposes.

3.8.1.6.2 End conditions. Tables 3.21 and 3.22 are based on the assumptions in Table H3.5.

Table H3.5 Assumed beam/column stiffnesses

End condition	Ratio α_c beam/column stiffness
1	0.5
2	1.5
3	3.0
4	7.0

Using these figures and the equations in Part 2 Section **2.5** gives the values for effective length in Tables 3.21 and 3.22.

An extensive discussion of the effective length of bridge piers is given in reference 3.21. This may be of value in special cases.

3.8.1.7 *Slenderness limits for columns*
This limit is simply considered to be the limit beyond which current knowledge should not be extrapolated.

3.8.1.8 *Slenderness of unbraced columns*
The additional limit applied here for cantilever columns will be seen to be effectively the same as the slenderness limit applied to cantilever beams in **3.4.1.6(b)**.

3.8.2 Moments and forces in columns

3.8.2.1 *Columns in monolithic frames designed to resist lateral forces. (Unbraced frames)*
This is simply to indicate that the simplified methods of assessing moments and forces which are permissible for braced frames should not be used for unbraced frames.

3.8.2.2 *Additional moments induced by deflection at ULS*
These will be discussed in the section on **3.8.3**.

3.8.2.3 *Columns in column-and-beam construction, or in monolithic braced structural frames*
This clause gives the simplified basis on which axial forces may be assessed. Moments should be obtained in accordance with **3.2.1.2** (though the clause omits stating this) unless it is reasonable to assume effectively axial loading.

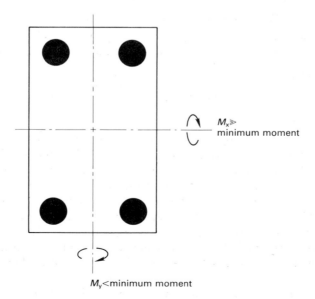

Figure H3.29: Problem situation for treatment of minimum moments.

3.8.2.4 *Minimum eccentricity*

It is impossible to guarantee that a column will be absolutely axially loaded: some moment will inevitably occur even if the calculations suggest otherwise. Hence it is prudent to allow for at least a minimum moment. The value chosen is arbitrary and, in fact, is less stringent than the rules imposed in many other countries.

The provision for biaxially bent sections actually introduces an element of ambiguity in some cases. The Code states that the minimum eccentricity only need be applied in one direction at a time. The immediate assumption one is tempted to make is that, for the case sketched in Figure H3.29, one should design for M_x about the major axis and the minimum eccentricity about the minor axis. However, common sense would suggest that this column would actually be considered to be uniaxially bent and the moment about the minor axis ignored. If this was done, since M_x exceeds the minimum moment, there would be no necessity to consider the minimum moment at all. It thus appears that the only logical way to interpret this clause is to check that the moment in at least one direction exceeds the minimum, otherwise the Code would be implying that all columns must be designed as biaxially bent.

3.8.3 Deflection induced moments in solid slender columns

These clauses have been derived from work by Cranston[3.22]. The logic behind them is as follows:

Consider, for simplicity, a pinned ended strut. Due to inevitable imperfections, this will deflect laterally under load. When the strut deflects, each section is subjected to a moment given by the deflection at that section multiplied by the vertical load. This moment causes a further increase in deflection and hence in moment. Under some conditions, this will lead to instability and a buckling failure: under lower loads, an equilibrium condition can be reached. For elastic materials, analysis of this situation leads to the classical Euler equation for the load capacity of slender struts. Reinforced concrete columns, especially close to collapse, are not elastic and it has been necessary to develop a more general approach to the problem. Furthermore, it is necessary to be able to deal with much more general problems than simply pinned ended struts. In its simplest terms, the method given in the Code can be derived as follows.

The curvature at the critical section in a strut at the moment of failure is obtainable from the basic assumptions for section behaviour. It will be given by

$$1/r_u = (\varepsilon_s - \varepsilon_c)/d = (0.0035 + \varepsilon_s)/d$$

Assuming a balanced section, ε_s will be given by $0.87 f_y/E_s$. For grade 460 steel this will be 0.002 and hence:

$$1/r_u = 0.0055/d$$

If the deflected shape of the column is assumed to follow a sine curve, then the deflection will be given by:

$$a_u = (l_e^2/\pi^2)(1/r_u) = (1/1800)(l_e/d)^2 d$$

Assuming the overall section depth is roughly 1.1 times the effective depth and allowing for the conservatism implicit in the derivation, this may be rewritten approximately as:

$$a_u = (1/2000)(l_e/h)^2 h$$

This will lead to a moment at the critical section of:

$$N.a_u = (N.h/2000)(l_e/h)^2$$

This analysis assumes a balanced section. For sections with greater axial loads than the balanced condition, the strain in the reinforcement near the least compressed face will be less than the yield strain. It will lie in the range $-0.0035 \leqslant \varepsilon_s \leqslant =0.002$, see Figure H3.30. This leads to the ultimate curvature being below that for a balanced section. This is allowed for by introducing a coefficient K such that the ultimate curvature is equal to the ultimate curvature for a balanced section multiplied by K. The expression used for K in the Code is empirical.

If the section of the strut is designed so that it can withstand this moment, then the strut will be stable under this condition and buckling failure will not occur under this load. In most columns one is not dealing with a pinned ended strut and the additional moment due to the ultimate deflection is added to the moments arising from normal frame action.

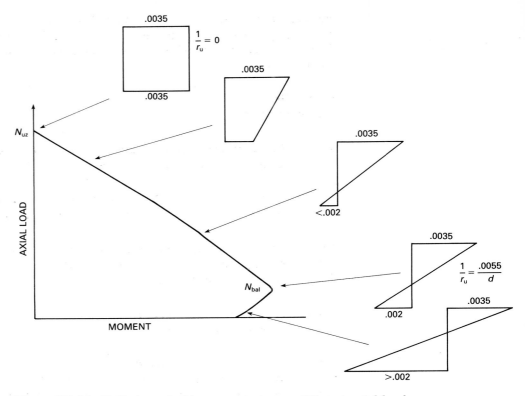

Figure H3.30: Variation of ultimate curvature at different axial loads.

It is not necessarily possible to predict exactly how a column will deflect and, ideally, one should consider the possibility of buckling about either axis. This will clearly involve considering biaxial bending. To avoid this for most common cases, the additional moment due to deflection is calculated on the basis of the smaller dimension of the columns. For

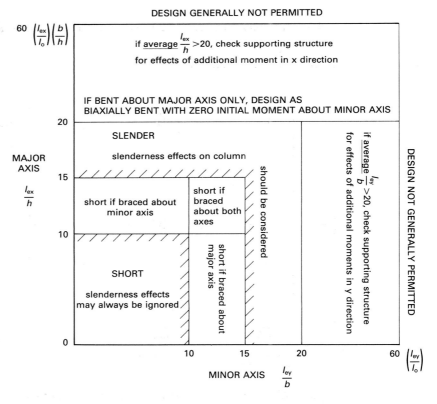

Figure H3.31: Interpretation of Clauses 3.8.1.7, 3.8.1.3, 3.8.2.2, 3.8.3.4 and 3.8.3.9.

uniaxially bent columns where $l_e/h<20$, this moment is applied in whichever direction the primary moments act, regardless of whether this is about the minor or major axis. This is a conservative approach and economies can occasionally be achieved by carrying out a biaxial design.

3.8.3.1 *Design*
See discussion above

3.8.3.2 *Design moments in braced columns bent about a single axis*
Figure 3.20 in the Code illustrates the provisions of this clause adequately.

3.8.3.3 *Slender columns bent about a single axis (major or minor)*
This simplified approach is dealt with at the end of the section on **3.8.3**.

3.8.3.4 *Columns where l_e/h exceeds 20, bent about their major axis*
In this case, the simplification used above becomes excessively conservative and a biaxial design will be more appropriate.

3.8.3.5 *Columns bent about their major axis*
The same comment applies as for **3.8.3.4**

3.8.3.6 *Slender columns bent about both axes*
Care needs to be taken here when the effective lengths about the two axes are very different or where the column is braced in one direction and unbraced in the other. Careful inspection of Figures 3.20 and 3.21 should indicate which moments should be combined with which in particular cases.

3.8.3.7 *Unbraced structures*

3.8.3.8 *Deflection of unbraced columns*
Equation 37 is a change from that given in CP110:1972. The approach in BS 8110 is the more correct.

3.8.3.9 *Additional moments on members attached to a slender column*

3.8.4 Design of column sections for ULS

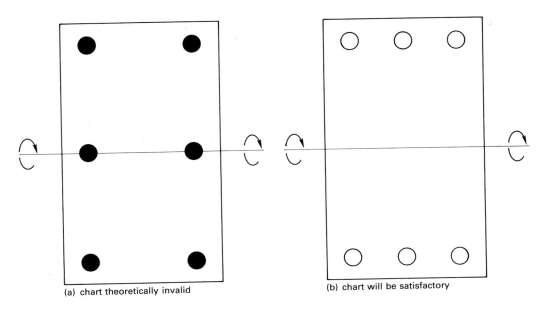

(a) chart theoretically invalid   (b) chart will be satisfactory

Figure H3.32: Validity of design charts for columns with reinforcement not concentrated in corners.

3.8.4.1 *Analysis of sections*

3.8.4.2 *Design charts for symmetrically-reinforced columns*
The design charts are drawn on the assumption that the reinforcement is concentrated close to the faces of the section. The charts are theoretically invalid if other arrangements of reinforcement are used, for example as shown in Figure H3.32.

Various methods have been suggested for enabling the charts to be used for this type of section but a reasonable approach is to establish an effective value for *d* by calculating the position of the centroid of the reinforcement in one half of the section (Figure H3.33). This value can then be used with the design charts in Part 3.

This approach is conservative but usually not excessively so.

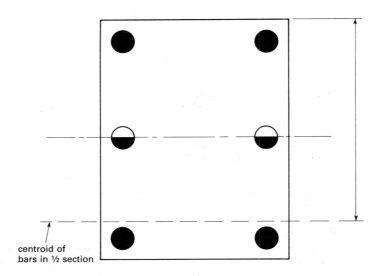

centroid of
bars in ½ section

Figure H3.33: Effective depth of a column section.

3.8.4.3 *Nominal eccentricity of short columns resisting moments and axial forces*
Equation 38 will be particularly appropriate where the column supports a rigid structure or very deep beams. A cross-section under pure axial load will, from the assumptions given in **3.4.4.1** carry an axial load of:

$$N = 0.45 f_{cu} A_c + 0.87 f_y A_{sc}$$

The reduction of approximately 10% built into equation 38 allows for the minimum eccentricity of 0.05 *h*.

3.8.4.4 *Short braced columns supporting an approximately symmetrical arrangement of beams*
Equation 39 contains a further reduction from equation 38 to cater for the moments which will arise from asymmetrical loading on symmetrical beams. Equation 39 should not be used for edge columns, unless the primary beams of the structure span parallel to the edge.

3.8.4.5 *Biaxial bending*
The method proposed in BS 8110 differs from that in CP110. The reason for the change is that, while the CP110 equation is probably technically superior, it cannot be used directly for design but only for checking a section which has already been detailed. The method in BS 8110 is adequate provided M_{ux}/bh^2 is not too different to M_{uy}/hb^2. Even in these circumstances a reasonable answer will be obtained if care is taken in the definition of *h'* and *b'*. It is suggested that, where the reinforcement is not concentrated in the corners, effective values of *h'* and *b'* are computed as suggested for *d* in the comments on **3.8.4.2** (Figure H3.33).

3.8.4.6 *Shear in columns*

3.8.5 Deflection of columns
This clause is concerned with the deflection under *service* loads, not the deflections discussed under **3.8.3** which is concerned with deflections at *ultimate* loads.

3.8.6 Crack control in columns

3.9 Walls

3.9.1 Symbols

3.9.2 Structural stability

3.9.2.1 *Overall stability*

3.9.2.2 *Overall stability of multi-storey buildings*
This clause is badly expressed. The intention is that lateral stability in any direction should not be provided solely by walls bending about their minor axes. Walls must be arranged to provide a stiff structure to resist the lateral loads.

3.9.2.3 *Forces in lateral supports*
This clause allows for possible 'out of plumb' of the structure or other unforeseen effects.

3.9.2.4 *Resistance to rotation of lateral supports*

3.9.3 Design of reinforced walls
Reinforced walls are effectively considered as a special case of reinforced columns. A reinforced wall has to contain at least 0.4% of vertical reinforcement, otherwise it must be treated as unreinforced. Much of the commentary on the column section (**3.8**) applies also to this section.

3.9.3.1 *Axial forces*

3.9.3.2 *Effective height*

3.9.3.2.1 *General.* For walls constructed monolithically with the surrounding structure, see **3.8.1.6** and the commentary on that clause.

3.9.3.2.2 *Simply-supported construction.* See **3.9.4.2**.

3.9.3.3 *Design transverse moments*

3.9.3.4 *In-plane moments*

3.9.3.5 *Arrangement of reinforcement for reinforced walls in tension*

3.9.3.6 *Stocky reinforced walls*
Stocky is identical to short.

3.9.3.6.1 *Stocky braced reinforced walls supporting approximately symmetrical arrangements of slabs.* As in the equivalent equation for columns, a notional allowance is included in the equation for small moments.

3.9.3.6.2 *Walls resisting transverse moments and uniformly distributed axial forces*

3.9.3.6.3 *Walls resisting in-plane moments and axial forces*

3.9.3.6.4 *Walls with axial forces and significant transverse and in-plane moments.* This clause gives a simplified approach to the complex problem of biaxial bending under ultimate conditions. Theoretically, the problem can be tackled from first principles using the assumptions of **3.3.5.1** but considerable complexity will be involved.

Where tension arises along the length of the wall, a simple strip foundation will not be sufficient unless it is designed to resist the resultant bending moments in the plane of the wall. Because of this, a solution using plain walls may be attractive.

3.9.3.7 Slender reinforced walls

3.9.3.7.1 Design procedure

3.9.3.7.2 Limits of slenderness

3.9.3.7.3 Transverse moments

3.9.4 Design of plain walls
Note the definition of plain walls given in **1.2.4.7**. Effectively, a plain wall is one with less than 0.4% vertical reinforcement: it may well contain some reinforcement for anti-crack or handling purposes. It may also be noted that where walls do not contain any reinforcement, the durability provisions of **6.2.4.2** rather than those of **3.3.5** would apply. Plain walls are intermediate between reinforced walls and masonry walls. Many of the provisions in BS 5628 might be considered to give useful guidance in particular cases. The handbook to that code could also be of value[3.23].

3.9.4.1 Axial forces
This follows the rules given for columns in **3.8.2.3**.

3.9.4.2 Effective height of unbraced plain concrete walls

3.9.4.3 Effective height of braced plain walls
The provisions of this clause are consistent with those in the Masonry Code (BS 5628:1978).

3.9.4.4 Limits of slenderness
The limit of 30 given here is slightly greater than that permitted in BS 5628 for masonry but generally less than that permitted for reinforced walls.

3.9.4.5 Minimum transverse eccentricity of forces
This clause follows the provisions for columns and reinforced walls.

3.9.4.6 In-plane eccentricity due to forces on a single wall

3.9.4.7 In-plane eccentricity due to horizontal forces on two or more parallel walls

3.9.4.8 Panels with shear connections

3.9.4.9 Eccentricity of loads from concrete floor or roof
The provision regarding common bearing areas restricts the maximum calculated eccentricity due to imposed load on the slabs to $h/6$ in internal walls.

Eccentricity of load in a braced wall by floor loading will arise as indicated in Figure H3.34(a), from which it will be seen that eccentricities at the top and bottom of the wall will be opposite in sign. Local cracking in the floor slabs will tend to reduce the eccentricities at both ends (Figure H3.34(b)). Precise evaluation of the eccentricity is impossible and so the simplification as sketched in Figure H3.34(c) is introduced. The cross-section at the top of the wall must be designed to resist the *total* load N_3 acting at the appropriate eccentricity.

Unbraced plain walls should be found only in single-storey construction. The procedure inherent in Figure H3.35 is suggested; effectively, cantilever action is being assumed to give the worst possible effect as regards the eccentricity calculation.

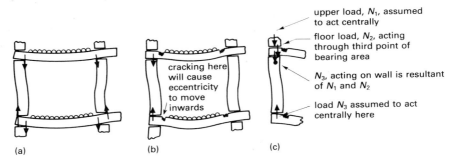

Figure H3.34: Eccentricity in braced walls.

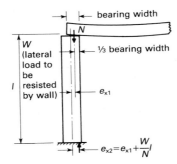

Figure H3.35: Eccentricity in a single-storey unbraced wall.

3.9.4.10 *Other eccentrically-applied loads*

3.9.4.11 *In-plane and transverse eccentricity of resultant force on an unbraced wall*

3.9.4.12 *Transverse eccentricity of resultant force on a braced wall*
See **3.9.4.9** above.

3.9.4.13 *Concentrated loads*
A much more detailed approach to concentrated loads is given in BS 5628 Clause 34. In awkward situations it could be worth using these clauses with γ_m taken as 2.25.

3.9.4.14 *Calculation of design load per unit length*
The intention of this clause is illustrated in Figure H3.36.

3.9.4.15 *Maximum unit axial loads for stocky braced plain walls*
The principles on which equations 43 to 46 are based are illustrated in Figure H3.37.

It will be seen that equation 43 follows directly from this Figure by considering equilibrium of vertical forces.

It is also worth noting that the stress on the concrete of $0.3f_{cu}$ corresponds to a γ_m factor for plain concrete of $1.5\times0.45/0.3=2.25$. This may be compared with the values given in BS 5628 of between 2.5 and 3.5, depending on control. It is logical to use a higher value of γ_m for plain concrete than for reinforced concrete since, in the case of reinforced concrete, both steel and concrete have to reach their design strength to precipitate failure whereas, with plain concrete, only the one material needs to reach its design strength. This has a higher probability of occurrence.

3.9.4.16 *Maximum design ultimate axial load for slender braced plain walls*
The additional eccentricity is assumed to occur near mid-height of the wall. Using the same assumption as for braced columns, the initial eccentricity at this level may be taken as $0.6\,e_x$. Substituting the total eccentricity $(0.6\,e_x+e_a)$ for e_x in equation 43 gives equation

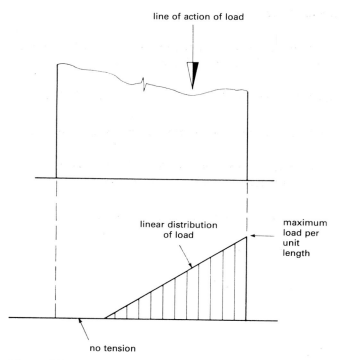

Figure H3.36: Load distribution along a wall.

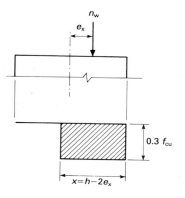

Figure H3.37: Stress block under ultimate conditions in plain wall.

44. Obviously, the condition at the top of the wall also needs checking; hence the requirement to check equation 43 as well.

3.9.4.17 *Maximum unit axial load for unbraced plain walls*
Equation 46 should read:

$$n_w \leqslant 0.3(h - 2(e_{x,2} + e_a))f_{cu}$$

3.9.4.18 *Shear strength*
This clause applies only to walls cast in situ. Where large panels with joints are used, the provisions of **5.3.7** must be applied.

Shears in plain walls arise from the change in bending moment down the wall. Where the ratio of effective height to thickness is 6 or more, the maximum shear that can possibly develop at right-angles to the plane of the wall will correspond to a change in eccentricity from $h/2$ at the top of the wall to $-h/2$ at the bottom. Thus, automatically, the shear is less than or equal to one-sixth of the axial load and for this reason need not be checked.

Where resistance to lateral load is being assessed under the stability requirements, adequate performance in shear may be assumed as long as the shear force is again not more than one-quarter of the axial load.

3.9.4.19 *Cracking of concrete*

3.9.4.20 *'Anticrack' reinforcement in external plain walls*
Refer to Table 3.4 for 'adequate cover'.

3.9.4.21 *'Anticrack' reinforcement in internal plain walls*

3.9.4.22 *Reinforcement around openings in plain walls*

3.9.4.23 *Reinforcement of plain walls for flexure*
This reinforcement is also 'anticrack' steel and not reinforcement for strength.

3.9.4.24 *Deflection of plain concrete walls*

3.9.4.24.1 *General*

3.9.4.24.2 *Shear walls*

3.10 Staircases

3.10.1 General

3.10.1.1 *Loading*

3.10.1.2 *Distribution of loading*

3.10.1.3 *Effective span of monolithic staircases without stringer beams*

3.10.1.4 *Effective span of simply-supported staircases without stringer beams*

3.10.1.5 *Depth of section*

3.10.2 Design of staircases

3.10.2.1 *Strength, deflection and crack control*

3.10.2.2 *Permissible span/effective depth ratio for staircases without stringer beams*
This clause makes allowance for some stiffening from the treads.

3.11 Bases

3.11.1 Symbols

3.11.2 Assumptions in the design of pad footings and pile caps

3.11.2.1 *General*
3.11 gives simple but safe rules for the design of individual wall and column bases. It does not refer to multiple column bases, rafts and other large scale foundation structures, which should be designed by taking due account of the ground conditions. For such structures reference to Part 2, Clause **2.2** may assist.

The assumptions of uniform and linearly varying soil pressures on bases are safe because the pressures will in fact tend to reduce towards the extremities of the base for cohesionless soils, and to be uniformly distributed in the case of cohesive soils.

3.11.2.2 *Critical section in design of an isolated pad footing*

3.11.2.3 *Pockets for precast members*

3.11.3 Design of pad footings

3.11.3.1 *Design moment on a vertical section taken completely across a pad footing*
The critical section is defined in **3.11.2.2**. The bending moments on such sections should be determined by summation of the moments arising from all external loads and reactions on one side of each critical section. In the longer direction of span, the moment so deduced may be assumed to be constant over the critical section, but across the shorter span, the moments tend to be greater opposite the column. The code includes an arbitrary rule for detailing the reinforcement accordingly (**3.11.3.2**).

Top reinforcement in pad footings is not normally required. Circumstances in which it should be considered include:

(a) when uplift is likely to occur
(b) where two or more columns use a single pad footing
(c) where control of surface cracking is essential.

3.11.3.2 *Distribution of reinforcement*

3.11.3.3 *Design shear*
It should be noted that although the critical section is assumed to be at the face of the column (**3.11.2.2**) an enhancement in design shear strength close to supports may also be applied in accordance with **3.4.5.8** and **3.4.5.10**. From these considerations the critical section for shear is more likely to be a distance d from the face of the column.

3.11.3.4 *Design shear strength near concentrated loads*
The following conditions are considered:

(a) shear along a vertical section extending across the full width of the base
(b) punching shear around the loaded area. Provided the column is placed near the centre of the footing V_{eff} may be taken as $1.15V_t$. Otherwise it should be determined from **3.7.6.3**.

3.11.4 Design of pile caps

3.11.4.1 *General*
It should be noted that one major difference between the results of using bending theory and truss analogy is the requirement for anchorage of the main tension reinforcement. Bending theory is likely to require only nominal anchorage of bars beyond the pile whereas a full anchorage length is required if truss analogy is required. In order to overcome this anomaly the following rules may be applied.

(a) if the distance from the column face to the critical section (Figure 3.23 of BS 8110, Part 1) is less than or equal to $0.6d$ then corbel design methods should be considered – see **5.2.7**. One requirement is that the tension reinforcement requires a full anchorage beyond the loaded area, in this case the pile
(b) if the distance from the column face to the critical section is $2d$ or more then a nominal anchorage beyond the pile of d or 12ϕ is all that is required
(c) if the distance lies between (a) and (b) then linear interpolation may be used

In assessing where the anchorage length should be measured from it may be assumed to be $\phi/5$ inside the outer limit of the pile.

3.11.4.2 *Truss method*

3.11.4.3 *Shear forces*
It should be noted that the critical section for shear may be less than $2d$ from the face of the column. The enhancement in shear resistance given in **3.4.5.8** then applies. Where more than one row of piles exists then two critical sections should be checked. One with the shear enhancement and one without is shown in Figure H3.38.

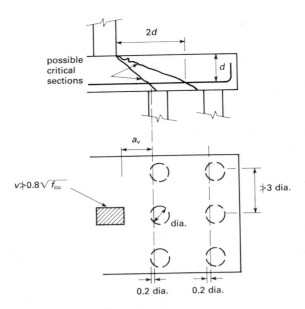

Figure H3.38: Shear in pile caps.

3.11.4.4 *Design shear resistance*

The requirement for an anchorage of the main reinforcement equal to the effective depth should be measured from the critical section as shown in Figure 3.23 of BS 8110, Part 1. This criterion may control the length of bars in situations where small diameter piles are used with shallow pile caps. Otherwise the criterion described in the explanatory notes for **3.11.4.1** will control.

3.11.4.5 *Punching shear*

When it is necessary to check punching shear on a perimeter as shown in Figure 3.23 it may be found that the distance from the column to the perimeter varies from one face to another. In such situations any enhancement factor allowed by **3.7.7.4** should only apply to the proportion of perimeter applicable.

Where the spacing of piles is large, punching shear on a perimeter 1.5d from the column may require checking.

3.12 Considerations affecting design details

This section of the Code provides information on a wide range of detailing aspects giving sensible values for the practical needs of detailing. However it does not set out methods of detailing. The complexity in deciding what detailing method should be used involves cost comparisons between materials and the labour to bend and fix the reinforcement. Often simple methods of bending and fixing reinforcement involve more material. It is considered that this is beyond the scope of the Code and reference should be made to other publications[3.4 and 3.24].

3.12.1 Permissible deviations

3.12.1.1 *General*

3.12.1.2 *Permissible deviations on member sizes*

Application of this clause will be a matter for judgement but nominal dimensions will generally be appropriate for designing members at least 125mm thick.

3.12.1.3 *Position of reinforcement*

3.12.1.4 *Permissible deviation on reinforcement fitting between two concrete faces*

Specified limits for the position of reinforcement are set out in **7.3**. These are summarized below.

Actual concrete cover	≮ nominal cover	−5mm
Actual concrete cover where reinforcement is located in relation to only one face of a member	≯ nominal cover	+5mm for bars up to and including 12mm diameter +10mm for bars over 12mm up to and including 25mm diameter +15mm for bars over 25mm diameter

Limits to the allowable deviation of the location of the reinforcement are required because:

(a) too large a negative tolerance will give durability problems

(b) too large a positive tolerance will give strength problems.

These limits need to accommodate the bending tolerance on reinforcement, which are specified in BS 4466 and quoted in the commentary on **7.3**; for bent bars up to 1000mm long, they are ±5mm. In addition when detailing reinforcing bars to fit between two concrete faces, the dimension to be shown on the schedule should be less than that derived from the nominal dimension by an amount dependent on the overall size of the concrete member; for a total concrete dimension of up to 1000mm, the amount may be assumed to be 10mm. Alternatively, the detailing method should allow the bars to be lapped and to slide to fit the dimension as built.

Where possible, it should be ensured that reinforcement on a tension face is positioned accurately with respect to that face; no reduction in effective depth need then be considered, nor will it be necessary, following the same approach as in **3.12.1.2**, to consider any reduction if the member thickness is at least 125mm.

3.12.1.5 *Accumulation of errors*

3.12.2 Joints

3.12.2.1 *Construction joints*
See **6.12**.

3.12.2.2 *Movement joints*
See **6.13** and Part 2, Section **8**.

3.12.3 Design of ties

3.12.3.1 *General*
Provided the recommendations of **3.1.4** have been followed, the requirements of **3.12.3** will normally ensure that a structure is robust for in situ reinforced concrete structures (Figure 3.1). Where precast concrete construction is involved care must be taken to ensure continuity of ties as described in **5.1.8**.

For many structures it will be found that reinforcement provided for the usual dead, imposed and wind loads will, with only minor additions and modifications, fulfil these tie requirements. In fact, normally designed in situ reinforced concrete structures detailed in accordance with the requirements of **3.12** other than for ties, will generally comply with the tie force requirements. Thus it is suggested that the structure be first proportioned for these usual loads and then a check carried out for tie forces. It should be noted that in meeting the requirements the tie reinforcement is assumed to act at its characteristic strength.

3.12.3.2 *Proportioning of ties*

3.12.3.3 *Continuity and anchorage of ties*

3.12.3.4 *Internal ties*

3.12.3.4.1 *Distribution and location.* Bars in internal ties may be assumed to be fully anchored to the peripheral tie if they are anchored around the outermost bars of the peripheral tie as for a link (**3.12.8.6**). Otherwise, the anchorage should be assessed from a plane passing through the centroid of the peripheral tie; the available anchorage length to anchor off the bar may be based on the characteristic bond stress as given in **3.12.8.4**, i.e. $f_{bu} \times 1.4$. Hence the required anchorage length will be 1.15/1.4 times the normal design anchorage length given in Table 3.29.

3.12.3.4.2 *Strength.* The strength requirement for ties is related to the number of storeys in the building. The philosophy behind this is that the consequences of collapse are generally more serious for high buildings; furthermore, simply because of their greater size, the probability of misuse or the occurrence of exceptional accidental loads is greater and the objective is to ensure that the risk is approximately the same for all heights.

3.12.3.5 *Peripheral ties*
It is important that the peripheral ties are adequately connected to both the vertical and horizontal ties. In many cases, it will be helpful for the whole of the peripheral tie to be arranged to lie along or outside the centre-line or median plane of the columns or walls respectively. In such cases, the internal ties will serve automatically as wall ties; where columns are involved, it may be assumed that all internal ties anchored to the peripheral tie within 1m on either side of the column centre-line form part of the column tie.

3.12.3.6 *Horizontal ties to columns and walls*

3.12.3.6.1 *General.* A further requirement for horizontal ties not included for internal or peripheral ties is that the tie force should not be less than 3% of the total design ultimate vertical load on the column or wall. This is likely to be the more critical for members in the lower storeys of high-rise buildings.

3.12.3.6.2 *Corner ties*

3.12.3.7 *Vertical ties (generally required in buildings of five or more storeys)*
Since the steel forming vertical ties in columns is tied together by stirrups there is little problem in connecting it to the horizontal tie. However, in the case of walls, reinforcement provided on the outer face will not usually be tied to the inner face. In such cases it may be necessary to provide links between the two layers at each floor level.

3.12.4 Reinforcement

3.12.4.1 *Groups of bars*

3.12.4.2 *Bar schedule dimensions*
For small precast units, the deductions plus allowances for cover may lead to steel not extending into support regions. It is suggested that for such units the flexural steel be carried right through to the end face with small projections through the stop end.

3.12.5 Minimum areas of reinforcement in members

3.12.5.1 *General*

3.12.5.2 *Symbols*

3.12.5.3 *Minimum percentages of reinforcement*
Tension reinforcement: The values given in Table 3.27 are based on the requirement

that the section can carry a higher load after cracking than before. The maximum tensile stress assumed in the concrete is 3N/mm^2.

Compression reinforcement: The minimum compression steel limit of 0.4% of the compression zone is new and a brief discussion of this is in order. In CP114, the minimum area of compression steel in columns is given as: "0.8% of the gross cross-sectional area of the column required to transmit all the loading . . .". This has traditionally been interpreted to mean:

$$A_{s.min}=0.008N/p_{cb}=0.0218N/f_{cu}$$

CP110 changed this to a minimum of 1% (without stating what it was 1% of) or, for lightly loaded members,

$$A_{s.min}=0.15N/f_y$$

Since any column requiring less than 1% of longitudinal steel could be classed as "lightly loaded", it could be argued that the second value always governed.

CP110 gave a limit of 0.4% for walls and this was justified on the basis of evidence[3.25] that the presence of reinforcement in walls reduces the strength of the surrounding concrete as placed. Under axial loading only, a plain concrete wall can actually resist *more* load than a corresponding wall with a small amount of main reinforcement.

As there seemed no consistency in any existing minimum reinforcement provisions, it was decided to adopt the 0.4% limit for all situations on the grounds that it was the only proposal for which a logical reason for such a limit was discoverable.

Care should be taken with small section columns as the minimum percentage rules can lead to impractical reinforcement details if not sensibly applied.

In normal circumstances 16mm diameter bars or larger should be used to ensure a robust cage. Smaller diameters should only be considered in short columns (less than 2.5m say) or where special measures are taken to ensure that the bars are fixed in position.

Lightly loaded columns where the section is large enough to resist the ultimate loads without the addition of reinforcement may be considered as plain concrete columns (**3.8.1.4**). These may be designed similarly to plain concrete walls (**3.9.4**). The minimum reinforcement required to control cracking (**3.9.4.19**) is 0.25% of the concrete cross-sectional area for steel grades 460 and above and 0.30% of the concrete cross-sectional area for steel grade 250.

Transverse reinforcement in flanges of flanged beams: The values given in Table 3.27 are half that required by CP110. The reduction appears reasonable when checked against recent research data. The statement in brackets at the bottom of Table 3.27 could be misleading. If this reinforcement was required just to resist horizontal shear then there would be little reason why it should not be placed in both the top and bottom of the flange. However the value has been reduced such that it would be wise for other reasons to place this amount of reinforcement close to the top of the flange (e.g. minimum tensile reinforcement, control of shrinkage cracks etc).

3.12.5.4 *Minimum size of bars in side face of beams to control cracking*

3.12.6 Maximum areas of reinforcement in members
These provisions give limits to what is normally practical from the point of view of placing concrete and steel fixing.

3.12.6.1 *Beams*

3.12.6.2 *Columns*

3.12.6.3 *Walls*

3.12.7 Containment of compression reinforcement
It has generally been considered prudent to tie compression bars into the section by means of links to stop them buckling out, either when yield commences or where longitudinal cracking might develop from any cause. Experimental work has not led to any clear definition of what minimum tying is really necessary so that rules given in

3.12.7.1 to **3.12.7.5** are essentially arbitrary and do no more than define accepted good practice.

3.12.7.1 *Diameter of links for containment of beam or column compression reinforcement*

3.12.7.2 *Arrangement of links for containment of beam or column compression reinforcement*

3.12.7.3 *Containment of compression reinforcement around periphery of circular column*

3.12.7.4 *Diameter of horizontal bars for support of small amounts of compression reinforcement in walls*

3.12.7.5 *Arrangement of links for containment of large amounts of compression reinforcement in walls*

The necessity for links in walls with more than 2% of steel will make for considerable practical difficulties. It is recommended that the cross-sectional area of the wall be increased to avoid this if at all possible.

3.12.8 Bond, anchorage, bearing, laps, joints, and bends in bars

3.12.8.1 *Avoidance of bond failure due to ultimate loads*

A significant change in BS 8110 from the provisions of CP110 and previous codes is the removal of the requirement for a check on local bond stresses. The local bond stress check was not often a critical factor in design but occasionally influenced the detailing of sections where high shears occurred in conjunction with low moments (simple supports and points of contraflexure). Contacts with designers suggested that many firms had always ignored this check without apparent ill effect. Furthermore, there were real doubts about the actual purpose of the check. When CP110 was being drafted the theory was put forward that it was a serviceability check against bond cracking but it seems highly unlikely that bond cracking would develop under service loads. Furthermore, the behaviour assumed for sections is that they are flexurally cracked. This is not true of the points where local bond would be checked so the hypothesis underlying the local bond check is invalid in just those areas where the check might have an effect. Thus, in the absence of any clear picture of what the check was intended to achieve, it seemed pointless to continue to require it.

3.12.8.2 *Anchorage bond stress*

The assumptions made in this and most other codes is highly simplistic as bond strength is a function of the ratio of cover to bar diameter and the amount of transverse steel as well as concrete strength and bar type. Reynolds[3.26], from tests on laps, gives a design formula for bond stress for a type 2 bar with no transverse shear as:

$$f_b = 0.2(0.5 + c/\phi)\sqrt{(f_{cu})}$$

For $c/\phi = 1$, this gives a value for β of 0.3. An allowance for nominal transverse steel will bring this to the Code value of 0.5; in any case, the coefficient of 0.2 in the equation gives a lower bound to all the data used to derive the formula plus a further allowance for a safety factor. It may also be noted that bond strength is markedly increased by the presence of transverse compression across the bar such as one would expect to be present at a support. From the practical point of view, however, it seemed an unnecessary refinement to attempt a more realistic treatment of anchorage bond since it would introduce considerable complications into design for little economic gain.

3.12.8.3 *Design anchorage bond stress*

3.12.8.4 *Values for design ultimate anchorage bond stress*

3.12.8.5 *Design ultimate anchorage bond stresses for fabric*

3.12.8.6 *Anchorage of links*

These values arise from experience and cannot be justified by calculation. It is believed that there is a misprint in (b) and that the continuation beyond the bend should be *four* times the bar size and not eight.

3.12.8.7 *Anchorage of welded fabric used as links*

3.12.8.8 *Anchorage of column starter bars in bases or pile caps*

The 'cover' to starters in bases or pile caps is very large and so, from the equation given above for bond stress, it will be seen that high bond strengths could be expected. While, for this case, there would be expected to be an upper limit to the value of c/ϕ which should be used in the equation, it was nevertheless believed that anchorage length would not be a limiting factor in the design of practical bases.

3.12.8.9 *Laps and joints*

A study carried out during the early stages of the revision process led to considerable concern about the provisions for laps as they had existed in previous British codes. Experimental evidence from Europe and America (e.g. references 3.26 and 3.27) suggested that, in limiting circumstances, the lap lengths given in CP110 could have factors of safety of less than 1.0. Studies of foreign codes suggested that, in some cases, many of these codes could require lap lengths of up to twice UK values. Against this, the Committee was not aware of any cases where laps had failed in practice. In drafting the revised clauses, the following factors were considered:

(a) the bond strength of bars cast near the top of members more than 300mm deep or so is significantly reduced due to settlement of the plastic concrete around the bar which leaves water filled lenses below the bar and sometimes cracks above the bar. The reduction is in the region of 20–40% for deformed bars

(b) closely spaced laps can lead to a plane of weakness within a section which can lead to a reduction in strength; corners are also a source of weakness (see Figure H3.39)

(c) bond increases with increasing ratio of cover to bar diameter (see above).

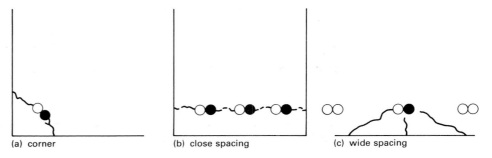

(a) corner   (b) close spacing   (c) wide spacing

Figure H3.39: Modes of lap failure.

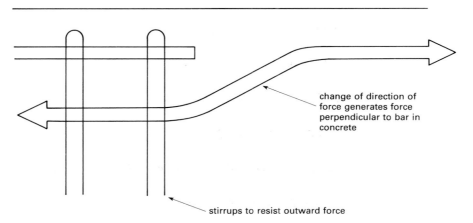

change of direction of force generates force perpendicular to bar in concrete

stirrups to resist outward force

Figure H3.40: Effect of joggled lap.

3.12.8.10 *Joints where imposed loading is predominantly cyclic*

3.12.8.11 *Minimum laps*

3.12.8.12 *Laps in beams and columns with limited cover*
The major considerations here are:

(a) as mentioned under **3.12.8.2** above, some allowance for transverse steel has been included in the bond stress formula

(b) 'joggles', frequently used at laps, are a source of major weakness and require the presence of stirrups for them to function. Figure H3.40 illustrates the actions of a joggle.

3.12.8.13 *Design of tension laps*
The logic behind these provisions has been discussed under **3.12.8.9** above. Table H3.6 attempts to clarify the intentions of the clause.

Table H3.6 Multiplying factors for lap length

		Tension lap lengths		
		Bars in top of section as cast with cover <2ø	Corner bars not in top of section with cover <2ø	Otherwise
Clear distance between laps	≥75mm and ≥6ø	$1.4l_b$ (48ø)	$1.4l_b$ (48ø)	$1.0l_b$ (34ø)
	Otherwise	$2.0l_b$ (68ø)	$1.4l_b$ (48ø)	$1.4l_b$ (48ø)

l_b=basic anchorage length, ø=bar size. Lap lengths for C30 concrete shown in brackets.

3.12.8.14 *Maximum amount of reinforcement in a layer including tension laps*
The logic behind this is discussed under **3.12.8.9** above.

3.12.8.15 *Design of compression laps*

3.12.8.16 *Butt joints*

3.12.8.16.1 *Bars in compression*

3.12.8.16.2 *Bars in tension*

3.12.8.17 *Welded joints in bars*

3.12.8.18 *Strength of welds*

3.12.8.19 *Design of shear strength of filler material in lap-joint welds*

3.12.8.20 *Design of welded lap joints*

3.12.8.21 *Limitations of length of weld in laps*

3.12.8.22 *Hooks and bends*

3.12.8.23 *Effective anchorage length of a hook or bend*

3.12.8.24 *Minimum radius of bends*

3.12.8.25 *Design bearing stress inside bends*
When a bar carrying tension is taken around a bend, compressive forces are generated in the concrete within the bend. The concrete within a bend is effectively subjected to a triaxial stress field, being restrained by the concrete on either side of the bend. Concrete in this situation can withstand very high stresses locally – much higher than those which can be carried by concrete in flexure. This is true provided that the average stress remains low. The provisions of this clause effectively allow higher local bearing stresses as the average stress reduces in the plane perpendicular to the plane of the bend. The equation is a rearranged version of that given in the most recent recommendations of the CEB[3.29].

3.12.9 Curtailment and anchorage of bars

3.12.9.1 *General*
It is necessary for a number of reasons to continue bars beyond where they are theoretically no longer required to resist bending

(i)   to allow for inaccuracies in the analysis. For example, the loading may well not be absolutely uniformly distributed, in which case the shape of the bending moment diagram will be different from that assumed
(ii) to allow for possible misplacement of the bars
(iii) in the presence of shear, diagonal cracks may form which, in the absence of stirrups, will cause the steel stress to be that corresponding to the moment at a section roughly an effective depth closer to the supports
(iv) cracks will occur at the points where the bars stop off and may well be of above average size. This may locally reduce the shear strength.

The minimum extension beyond the theoretical cut-off points of the greater of the effective depth or twelve times the bar size deals with points (i) to (iii) while the extra provisions guard against a reduction in shear strength. Provisions (c) and (e) control the size of the crack at the cut-off point and (d) ensures that there is a reserve of shear strength.

Clearly, no bar can be cut off less than an appropriate anchorage length from the last point where it is assumed to be fully stressed.

Condition (c) will be the easist to apply and is recommended for general use. Condition (d) will often apply in situations where low shear is present, e.g. in span regions of beams, where the trimming links automatically supply excess shear strength or in solid slabs. Condition (d) can be complied with by adding extra links but this is not recommended since apart from introducing extra shear calculations, more steel will be involved than if the main reinforcement is extended to comply with condition (c) or (e).

3.12.9.2 *Point at which a bar is no longer required*

3.12.9.3 *Curtailment of a large number of bars*

3.12.9.4 *Anchorage of bars at a simply-supported end of a member*
Condition (c), applicable to simply-supported ends of members, is intended to apply to small precast units. As already indicated in the commentary on tolerances, such units can have reinforcement extending right to the end face; a support width of 60mm is then theoretically feasible. Since the effect of misplacing steel can, in this instance, give a catastrophic reduction in strength, it is suggested that design is based on the most unfavourable configuration which can arise from tolerances.

When considering groups of bars extending to simple supports, the equivalent size of bar should be used.

3.12.10 Curtailment of reinforcement

This section provides simplified rules for common situations. The result should generally be conservative relative to application of the rules in **3.12.9.1**.

3.12.10.1 *General*

3.12.10.2 *Simplified rules for beams*

3.12.10.3 *Simplified rules for slabs*

3.12.10.3.1 *General*

3.12.10.3.2 *Curtailment of bars at end supports of slabs (where simple support has been assumed in assessment of moments)*

3.12.11 Spacing of reinforcement

3.12.11.1 *Minimum distance between bars*

The required minimum bar spacings are aimed primarily at allowing adequate room for the concrete to flow around the bars and at obtaining adequate compaction. With this in mind, the reasons behind the particular requirements, as illustrated in Figure H3.41, should be self-explanatory. Where an internal vibrator is to be used, room should be left between the top bars for its insertion. Generally, spacings wider than the minimum should be aimed at between top bars to allow the concrete to pass through easily. Bundling bars may be particularly useful in reducing congestion.

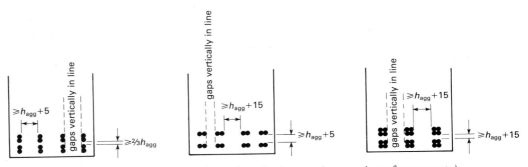

Figure H3.41: Minimum bar spacings (h_{agg} is the maximum size of aggregate).

The clause does not absolutely ban the use of spacings less than those recommended, but it should be noted that such spacing may impair the development of adequate bond strength. Very closely spaced bars may produce a plane of weakness along which bond failure by splitting may initiate. In the light of our present limited understanding of this form of bond failure, closer spacings should be avoided unless positive evidence of the efficiency of the particular arrangement exists.

3.12.11.2 *Maximum distance between bars in tension*

The maximum bar spacings are specified in order to limit cracking.

Part 2, Clause **3.8** gives the following equation for the calculation of the design surface crack width:

$$w_{cr} = \frac{3 a_{cr} \varepsilon_m}{1 + 2\left[(a_{cr} - c_{min})/(h - x) \right]}$$

where a_{cr} = distance from the point considered to the surface of the nearest longitudinal bar;

c_{min} = minimum cover to the longitudinal bar;

ε_m = average strain at the level considered;

w_{cr} = design surface crack width.

This equation has the property that, when the crack width is being considered directly over a bar (when $a_{cr} = c_{min}$) it reduces to:

$$w_{cr} = 3\,c_{min}\,\varepsilon_m \tag{3.4}$$

while, with increasing distance from a longitudinal bar $(a_{cr} \rightarrow \infty)$, the crack width approaches:

$$w_{cr} = 1.5(h-x)\,\varepsilon_m \tag{3.5}$$

From inspection of the equation, it can be seen that the crack width cannot exceed:

$$w_{cr} = 3a_{cr}\,\varepsilon_m \tag{3.6}$$

Except directly over bars or in beams where $(h-x)$ is greater than 20 times the cover, the calculated width will normally be much less than that given by equation 3.6.

Equation 8 in BS 8110 gives:

$$f_s = (5/8)f_y \times 1/\beta_b$$

Clearly, this can be converted to a strain by dividing by the modulus of elasticity of the steel. The maximum design surface crack width is given in Clause **3.2.4** in Part 2 as 0.3 mm. Substituting this for w_{cr} in equation 3.6 and substituting for strain from the relationship given above we get, after rearrangement:

$$a_{cr} \ngtr 32000\beta_b/f_y$$

The maximum calculated width will occur midway between bars. Therefore, as a_{cr} will be rather more than half the clear spacing between bars, it is reasonable to write:

$$\text{clear spacing} \ngtr 75000\beta_b/f_y$$

Table 3.30 in the Code derives from this formula.

Clearly, where more reinforcement is provided in the section than is required for the ultimate limit state, a wider spacing than is given by the Table could be used. A suitable value can be obtained by multiplying the spacings given in the Table by the ratio of the steel area provided to that required at ultimate.

3.12.11.2.1 *General*

3.12.11.2.2 *Bars of mixed size.* Where bars are being arranged in a section to control cracks, good practice would suggest that the sizes of bar in the section should not be too disparate – hence the limit on crack control bars to not less than 0.45 times the size of the largest bar. Also, very small bars mixed with larger ones could render invalid the assumptions on which Table 3.30 is based.

3.12.11.2.3 *Clear horizontal distance between bars in tension.* See notes above.

3.12.11.2.4 *Clear distance between bars in tension.* This is simply a slightly more rigorous approach than that in **3.12.11.2.3**.

3.12.11.2.5 *Clear distance between the corner of a beam and nearest longitudinal bar in tension*

3.12.11.2.6 *Bars near side faces of beams exceeding 750 mm overall depth.* This provision is intended to avoid the local yielding of bars in side faces.

This can lead to large cracks in the webs of such beams even where the crack widths at the level of the main steel are adequately controlled.

3.12.11.2.7 *Slabs.* If a member is sufficiently shallow that equation 3.6 gives a crack width of less than 0.3 mm, then flexural cracking cannot be excessive whatever the bar spacing. Further, the reduction in strain permitted in Part 2, Clause **3.8.3** to allow for tension stiffening has so far been ignored in formulating the bar-spacing rules. In slabs, where the steel percentage is usually small, this reduction can be very significant. For example, with 0.5% of high-strength steel, the reduction in strain will be roughly 50%.

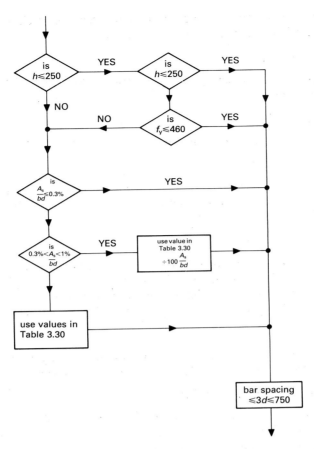

Figure H3.42: Maximum bar spacings in shallow members.

These factors have led to the rules for spacing of bars in slabs. For convenience, these provisions have been set out in the form of a flow chart in Figure H3.42.

In Table 3.30, the percentage redistribution to or from a section is the percentage difference between the ultimate moment used in the design to the moment obtained at the section from the elastic ultimate moment envelope. In terms of the parameters used in the equations above, the percentage redistribution in Table 3.30 is equal to $100(\beta_b - 1)$.

3.12.11.2.8 *Slabs where amount of redistribution is unknown*

3.12.11.2.9 *Spacing of shrinkage reinforcement*

REFERENCES

3.1 BEEBY, A.W. and TAYLOR, H.P.J. The use of simplified methods in CP110 – is rigour necessary? The Structural Engineer. Vol.56A, No.8. August 1978.

3.2 BEEBY, A.W. The analysis of beams in plane frames according to CP110. Wexham Springs, Cement and Concrete Association, October 1978. 34 pp. Development Report 1 (publication 44.001).

3.3 WOOD, R.H. The stability of tall buildings. Proceedings of the Institution of Civil Engineers. Vol.11. September 1958. pp.69-102.

3.4 THE CONCRETE SOCIETY and THE INSTITUTION OF STRUCTURAL ENGINEERS. Standard method of detailing structural concrete. London, The Institution of Structural Engineers, 1986.

3.5 CONSTRUCTION INDUSTRY RESEARCH AND INFORMATION ASSOCIATION. The design of deep beams in reinforced concrete. CIRIA Guide 2. 1977.

3.6 MARSHALL, W.T. A survey of the problem of lateral instability in reinforced concrete beams. Proceedings of the Institution of Civil Engineers. Vol.43. July 1969.

3.7 KRIZ, L.B. and RATHS, C.H. Connections in precast concrete structures – strength of corbels. Journal of Prestressed Concrete Institute. Vol.10, No.1. February 1965. pp.16-61.

3.8 MORROW, J. and VIEST, I.M. Shear strength of reinforced concrete frame members without web reinforcement. Journal of the American Concrete Institute. Proceedings Vol.53. March 1957. pp.833-869.

3.9 KANI, G.M.J. Basic facts concerning shear failure. Journal of the American Concrete Institute. Proceedings Vol.63, No.6. June 1966. pp.675-692.

3.10 SWANN, R.A. Experimental basis for a design method for rectangular reinforced concrete beams in torsion. London, Cement and Concrete Association, December 1970. 38pp. Technical Report 452 (Publication 42.452).

3.11 BEEBY, A.W. Modified proposals for controlling deflections by means of ratios of span to effective depth. London, Cement and Concrete Association, April 1971. 19pp. Technical Report 456 (Publication 42.456).

3.12 BEEBY, A.W. Span/effective depth ratios. Concrete. Vol.13, No.2. February 1979. pp.29-31.

3.13 BEAL, A.N. Span/depth ratios for concrete beams and slabs, The Structural Engineer, Vol.61A, No.4. April 1983. pp.121-123.

3.14 JOHANSEN, K.W. Yield-line formulae for slabs. London, Viewpoint Publications, 1972. (12.044)

3.15 HILLERBORG, A. Strip method of design. London, Viewpoint Publications, 1975. (12.067)

3.16 BEEBY, A.W. A proposal for changes to the basis for the design of slabs. Wexham Springs, Cement and Concrete Association, April 1982. 38pp. Technical Report 547 (Publication 42.547).

3.17 TAYLOR, R., HAYES, B. and MOHAMEDBHAI, G.T.G. Coefficients for the design of slabs by the yield-line theory. Concrete. Vol.3, No.5. May 1969. pp.171-172.

3.18 WHITTLE, R.T. Design of reinforced concrete flat slabs to BS 8110. London, Construction Industry Research and Information Association, September 1985. 48pp. Report 110.

3.19 REGAN, P.E. Behaviour of reinforced concrete flat slabs. London, 1981, Construction Industry Research and Information Association. 89pp. Report 89.

3.20 LONG, A.E., KIRK, D.W. and CLELAND, D.J. Moment transfer and the ultimate capacity of slab column structures. The Structural Engineer. Vol.56A, No.8. August 1978. pp.209-215.

3.21 JACKSON, P.A. The buckling of slender bridge piers and the effective height provisions of BS 5400: Part 4. Wexham Springs, Cement and Concrete Association, 1985. 18pp. Technical Report 561. (Publication 42.561).

3.22 CRANSTON, W.B. Analysis and design of reinforced concrete columns. London, Cement and Concrete Association, 1972. 54pp. Publication 41.020.

3.23 ROBERTS, J.J., TOVEY, A.K., CRANSTON, W.B. and BEEBY, A.W. Concrete masonry designer's handbook. London, Viewpoint Publications, 1983. 272pp. (13.024/27).

3.24 WHITTLE, R.T. Reinforcement detailing manual. London, Viewpoint Publications, 1981. 117pp. (12.085)

3.25 LARSSON, L.E. Bearing capacity of plain and reinforced concrete walls. Goteborg, Chalmers Tekniska Hoegskola, 1959. Doktorsavhandhingar. 248pp. No.19.

3.26 REYNOLDS, G. Bond strength of deformed bars in tension. Wexham Springs, Cement and Concrete Association, May 1982. 23pp. Technical Report 548.

3.27 BARTOS, P. (ed). Bond in concrete. London, Applied Science Publishers, 1982. 466pp.

3.28 AMERICAN CONCRETE INSTITUTE. Symposium on interaction between steel and concrete. Journal of the American Concrete Institute, Proceedings Vol.76, No.1. January 1979, No.2. February 1979.

3.29 CEB-FIP. Model Code for concrete structures. Paris, Comite Euro-International du Beton, April 1978. Bulletin d'Information N 124/125-E.

SECTION FOUR. DESIGN AND DETAILING: PRESTRESSED CONCRETE

4.1 Design basis

4.1.1 General

Section 4 contains methods for assessing compliance with the ultimate and serviceability limit state requirements given in 2.2 for prestressed concrete. The methods given are primarily concerned with the prestressing requirements and design of flexural members for prestressed concrete construction where the types of reinforcing steel and prestressing tendon covered in Sections 7 and 8 are used. These methods are general but, for particular applications, other ways of analysing and designing the structure or part of the structure may be more appropriate.

4.1.2 Alternative methods

This clause permits alternative methods to be used, firstly, because the Code itself gives very little guidance on the analysis and design of certain types of structural member, e.g. prestressed columns and slabs, and the engineer would have to consult the specialist literature for his method of design; and, secondly, because the technology of prestressing is still at the stage where new developments in techniques are taking place, and new materials are occasionally being introduced. These may be used provided that the engineer can satisfy himself that they are suitable for the purpose for which they are intended in complying with the criteria in Section 2.

4.1.3 Serviceability classification

It is the responsibility of the engineer to decide, or possibly the appropriate Authority or the client to specify, which class should be used for a particular set of circumstances; in taking this decision, such factors as the nature of the loading (static, dynamic, alternating, etc.), the relative magnitude of permanent and imposed loading and the environmental conditions should be considered. Equally, it is the responsibility of the engineer to choose the most appropriate class on economic and technical grounds.

Technically, a Class 2 design will give the best balance between ultimate, cracking and deflection requirements and this would be the class adopted for many structures; although tensile stresses are permitted under the design service loads, these are below the design tensile strength of the concrete and cracking will not normally occur. Where it is essential that the structure should not crack under serviceability conditions, a Class 1 design would be adopted.

A Class 3 design could be used where there is no particular requirement for the prevention of cracking under serviceability conditions, although generally this would imply that the cracks would not open under permanent loads. Class 3, or partially prestressed concrete, is an intermediate form of construction between fully prestressed concrete and reinforced concrete. Therefore, provided that the requirements of Section 2 are met, it could be considered for use in many cases where reinforced concrete might be used; for example, where construction depth is restricted, it can be used with advantage where an otherwise satisfactory reinforced concrete design cannot comply with the deflection requirements.

4.1.4 Critical limit state

All prestressed concrete members must satisfy the requirements of the ultimate and serviceability limit states. The shape of the cross-section is an important factor in obtaining a good balance between the ultimate and the serviceability requirements. An I section is normally suitable for Class 1 and 2 members and a T section is ideal for a simply supported Class 3 member.

In cases where the ultimate limit state in flexure is critical, ordinary untensioned reinforcement may be introduced to increase the moment of resistance. Some reinforcement is normally required for other purposes in members containing post-tensioned tendons and this may be utilised to increase both the resistance moment and the design hypothetical flexural tensile stress for Class 3 members. This approach is not practical for members containing pre-tensioned tendons and the alternative of tensioning an increased number of tendons to a lower stress level is not economically viable.

The recommended sequence of calculation for all members is as follows:

(a) stress limitations for serviceability (**4.3.4**) and at transfer (**4.3.5**)
(b) prestressing (**4.7**) and losses of prestress (**4.8** and **4.9**)
(c) ultimate limit state in flexure (**4.3.7**)
(d) ultimate limit state in shear (**4.3.8**)
(e) deflection calculations (**4.3.6**)
(f) transmission lengths (**4.10**), end blocks (**4.11**) and considerations affecting design details (**4.12**).

4.1.5 Durability and fire resistance
See **4.12.3**.

The fire resistance of a prestressed concrete structure is treated on an elemental basis i.e. a column, beam, slab, wall etc. The tables in this Code refer to widths or thicknesses of sections and the amount of cover necessary to tendons and secondary reinforcement.

Part 1 of the Code contains simplified tabular data for general use in ordinary prestressed concrete construction. Where the requirement of the design is not encompassed by the range of values given in the tables then the designer should refer to Part 2, Section **4** for a more detailed treatment.

4.1.6 Stability and other considerations
Although no specific recommendations are made on stability in Section **4**, a prestressed concrete structure, like any other, should comply with the requirements of **2.2.2**. This in effect means that the tie forces in **3.12.3** should be provided and, in precast concrete work, **5.1.8** will also apply.

4.1.7 Loads

4.1.7.1 *Load values*
Where it is necessary to consider the prestressing force as an applied load on the structure, γ_f should be taken as 1.0.

4.1.7.2 *Design load arrangements*

4.1.8 Strength of materials
See **3.1.7**, **6.3**, **7.1**, and **8.1**.

4.1.8.1 *Characteristic strength of concrete*

4.1.8.2 *Characteristic strength of steel*

4.2 Structures and structural frames

4.2.1 Analysis of structures
See **3.2.1**.

As for reinforced concrete, the forces and moments acting on a prestressed concrete structure will generally be calculated by using linear elastic analysis for the loads appropriate to both the ultimate and serviceability limit states.

If members are restrained or if the structure is statically indeterminate, then deformations of the structure may induce additional forces which should be considered for all limit states. The sequence of construction of the member, or of the structure as a whole, may also cause additional forces, e.g. due to successive prestressing in span-by-span construction or to the building of infill walls before beams have been fully stressed.

For the ultimate limit state, secondary or parasitic effects, induced in a statically indeterminate structure because support reactions change when prestress is applied, can be allowed for in the manner described below.

(a) the bending moments due to $1.0 G_k$ should be combined with the secondary moments due to prestress, due account being taken of the construction sequence
(b) the bending moment envelope due to $0.4G_k + 1.6Q_k$ and other relevant patterns of loading should be calculated
(c) this envelope should be added to the first bending moment diagram
(d) the resulting bending moment diagram may then be adjusted by redistributing moments as desired in accordance with **4.2.3**.

This method, in effect, does not put a safety factor on the secondary moments due to prestress.

4.2.2 Relative stiffness
See **2.5.2**.

4.2.3 Redistribution of moments

4.2.3.1 *General*
It is possible to design and detail critical sections in prestressed concrete so that complete redistribution of moments, as described in the commentary to **3.2.2**, can occur for the ultimate limit state; however, 20% redistribution is considered to be the upper limit consistent with good practice at the present time.

The conditions under which redistribution is allowed are very similar to those for reinforced concrete and the reasons for each of these given in the commentary to **3.2.2** may also be taken to apply.

A minor difference between reinforced and prestressed concrete is contained in condition (c) where no redistribution is permitted in prestressed concrete when the neutral axis depth exceeds 0.5 of the effective depth.

4.2.3.2 *Restriction in structures over four storeys where structural frame provides lateral stability*

4.3 Beams

4.3.1 General
See **3.4.1**.

4.3.2 Slender beams
Beams being lifted during erection may be extremely unstable compared with their final in-place condition. Particular attention should be given to the choice of the lifting method. Where it is considered necessary to check the stability of a beam during lifting, a realistic estimate of the initial imperfections has to be made to assess the lateral bending moment M_1, which should be limited to a value precluding cracking.

The two main imperfections likely to be present are the distance, a_1 (Figure H4.1), of the picking-up points from the minor axis, and the lateral bow, a_2. The centroid of the beam must hang vertically below the picking-up points so that, if the bow is parabolic, the angle of tilt due to the imperfections in a beam lifted at its ends is

$$\theta = (a_1 + 0.67a_2)/e$$

where e is the vertical distance between the picking up points and the centre of gravity of the beam (Figure H4.1).

The lateral bending moment at this stage is

$$M_2 = M_g\theta + N_L(a_1 + a_2)$$

The first term is the product of the dead load moment, M_g, and the angle of tilt, and the second term is the product of the longitudinal force in the beam due to the inclination of the lifting cables and the distance between the line of action of this force and the minor axis.

Even without the effects of buckling, this transverse bending moment can be embarrassingly high.

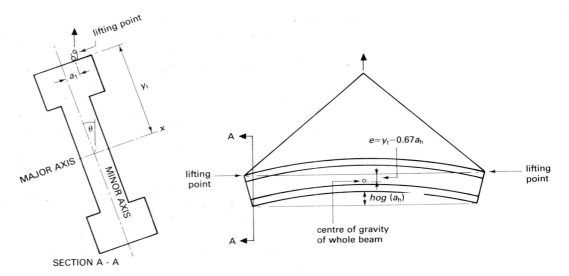

Figure H4.1: Notation used in calculations for slender beams.

The next stage of the check is to calculate the factor of safety γ_b of the beam as though it had no imperfections. This is required to calculate the buckling magnification factor on M_2. An extremely simple method of calculating γ_b has been suggested by Anderson[4.1] for beams with vertical lifting cables; thus

$$\gamma_b = e/a_{cent}$$

where a_{cent} is the vertical movement of the centroid of the whole beam due to self-weight if it were supported at the picking-up points with the minor axis horizontal. For beams lifted at their ends, a_{cent} can be taken as $0.64a_{mid}$ where a_{mid} is the maximum (mid-span) deflection of the beam similarly supported. The calculation required when inclined lifting cables are used is rather more complicated[4.2].

Finally, the lateral bending moment may be assessed[4.1] from

$$M_1 = M_2/(1 = 1/\gamma_b)$$

It has been assumed above that the beam does not twist as it buckles. However, the effect of neglecting twist is slight for typical structural concrete members. The importance of the various dimensions, particularly e, is obvious from the equations above. It is essential that the lifting points be rigidly fixed with respect to the beam so that there is no possibility of accidental side-slip. This would not only increase a_1 but would also cause an effective decrease in e.

In view of the sensitivity of M_1 to small errors in γ_b, γ_b should always be assessed conservatively and a value smaller than 2.0 should not be adopted.

A considerable amount of guesswork is involved in adopting values for a_1 and a_2. Because of this, and the lack of warning of impending collapse, personnel should be kept clear.

4.3.3 Continuous beams
See **4.2.1** and **4.2.3**.

4.3.4 Serviceability limit state for beams

4.3.4.1 *Section analysis*

4.3.4.2 *Compressive stresses in concrete*
The compressive stresses permitted in concrete at the serviceability limit state are based

on accepted practice. Creep is approximately linearly related to stress within this range, but would not necessarily be so for stresses which were a higher proportion of the characteristic strength; if higher stresses were adopted, there could be an appreciable increase in the loss of prestress.

4.3.4.3 *Flexural tensile stresses in concrete*

The allowable flexural tensile stresses given in Table 4.1 for Class 2 members are those that past practice has shown to be reasonable. Characteristic flexural tensile strengths for the concrete grades are not given in the Code but a value of approximately $0.6\sqrt{f_{cu}}$ is implied when a value of $\gamma_m = 1.3$ is taken into account (**2.4.6.2**).

Class 1 and 2 members behave elastically at this limit state; design based on elastic theory using the stresses given here will therefore be satisfactory. Class 3 members will be cracked at this limit state and should ideally be designed using elastic theory and cracked sections. In the absence of a generally accepted crack formula for prestressed concrete, design for this limit state is based on hypothetical flexural tensile stresses and uncracked sections. Research[4.3, 4.4] has shown that, in general, the limiting crack width criterion will not be infringed if the member is designed on the assumption that it is uncracked and if the hypothetical stresses given in Table 4.2 are not exceeded.

Research[4.5] has also indicated that the crack widths in members with imperfect bond and in deep members are related to the depth of the section. As the hypothetical flexural tensile stresses are based on a study of structures in service and on the tests reported in reference 4.3, it is necessary to reduce the stresses in beams with depths greater than 400mm as these were outside the scope of the test data. Table 4.3 gives depth factors that should be used when designing beams of depth other than 400mm.

Research[4.5] also indicates that it is feasible to extend the methods given in Section **3** of Part 2, to predict both crack widths and deformations in partially prestressed (Class 3) members.

In considering the limiting tensile stress for each class of member, the engineer should remember that cracking due to shrinkage and thermal effects can occur, for example, because of inadequate curing before the member is stressed or of late removal of moulds; this will impair the tensile strength of the concrete after stressing and should be either prevented by proper supervision or allowed for in the design by reducing the tensile stress level.

4.3.5 Stress limitations at transfer for beams

4.3.5.1 *Design compressive stresses*

In accordance with accepted practice, the concrete strength at transfer should be assessed by tests on cubes cured, as far as possible, under the same conditions as the concrete in the member.

4.3.5.2 *Design tensile stresses in flexure*

A small tensile stress is permitted at transfer in Class 1 members. This may be used to advantage in the ends of simply supported pre-tensioned members with straight tendons; although this stress (reduced somewhat by loss of prestress) is still present under service load conditions, it is unlikely to be significant and may be ignored in design.

Fairly high tensile stresses are allowed for Class 2 and Class 3 members; in the span these will be cancelled by compressive stresses due to dead and imposed loading. At the ends of members, consideration should be given in certain circumstances to providing some additional reinforcement, particularly if there is any risk of cracking due to shrinkage. **4.3.5.2**(c) suggests that the section should then be analysed as a cracked section. An approximate method is as follows.

A Class 3 beam is shown in Figure H4.2, which shows the type of additional reinforcement that might be required to prevent failure at the end of the member under prestress. The design approach would be to calculate the stress distribution and in particular the tensile force (T), using elastic theory and the concrete section properties, and to add enough reinforcement at the top of the member to carry this force; this is not the same as a true cracked section analysis as no account is taken of strain compatibility. As this is to avoid failure, it is suggested that the force so calculated be

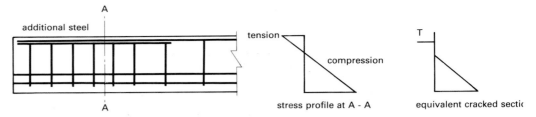

Figure H4.2: Conditions at end of a Class 3 beam.

multiplied by, say, 1.2 to allow for possible accidental overstress and then to design the reinforcement on the assumption that it is acting at $0.87f_y$. This reinforcement would have to be adequately anchored.

4.3.6 Deflection of beams

4.3.6.1 *General*
Prestressed concrete members are unlikely to display excessive sag but it may be necessary to limit the deflections that occur after the installation of finishes and partitions in some cases. Guidance on limiting values of deflection and suitable levels of permanent load is given in **3.2** and **3.3** of Part 2.

4.3.6.2 *Method of calculation*
The calculation of the deflections of Class 1 and Class 2 members is simple compared with that for reinforced concrete members, as such members should not be cracked under service loads. This being so, it can be assumed that the whole concrete section behaves elastically. Long-term effects may be estimated by employing an effective elastic modulus which allows for creep.

The effective elastic modulus for computing the deflection at the end of a particular period relative to that at the beginning can be obtained from the relationship

$E_{eff}=E_c/(1+\phi)$

where E_{eff} is the effective elastic modulus for the period considered
E_c is the instantaneous elastic modulus at the beginning of the period considered
ϕ is the creep coefficient for the period considered.

Values for the instantaneous elastic modulus and for the creep coefficient can be obtained from **7.2** and **7.3** respectively of Part 2.

Deflections for members of constant section can be calculated by using simple elastic relationships such as

$a=Kl^2 M/E_{eff}I$

in which a = deflection
K = a constant depending on the shape of the bending moment diagram
l = effective span
M = moment at appropriate position
I = second moment of area of section.

Values of K and M for many common shapes of bending moment diagram can be obtained from Table 3.1 of Part 2.

When computing deflections, it must be remembered that the prestress causes a deflection because it applies a moment to the beam at any section equal to the prestressing force multiplied by the eccentricity of the force at that section. The prestress may produce a shape of bending moment diagram for which deflection coefficients cannot easily be obtained. In this case, the component of the deflection due to the prestress will have to be computed by using some form of numerical integration technique. Such techniques may also be required where non-prismatic members are used.

It should be noted that, owing to the action of the prestress, the deflection may be either upward or downward, depending on the particular case considered. A simple example will show how, in contrast to reinforced concrete, the most critical condition for deflection may not be that obtaining after all creep has occurred. Consider a beam with prestress such that the deflection under permanent loads is upward. With time, this

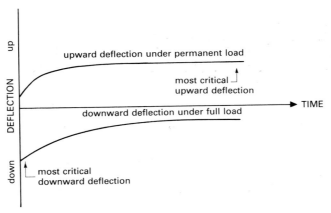

Figure H4.3: Significance of type of loading on the relation between deflection and time.

upward deflection may increase. This being so, any downward deflection under the full imposed load will decrease with time. The most critical condition for downward deflection will therefore be the application of full imposed load at the earliest possible moment when the minimum amount of upward creep has occurred. (See Figure H4.3.)

Deflections can never be calculated with precision; the elastic modulus, creep and shrinkage behaviour of the concrete, loading history, environment, construction timetable etc., are all variable and largely unpredictable in advance. If deflections are likely to be critical, it is perhaps more realistic to assess upper and lower bounds due to likely extremes of the important parameters and to allow in design for this possible range of behaviour. This is particularly relevant in precast prestressed units which are subsequently incorporated into a structure at indeterminate ages.

Class 3 members are designed to be cracked under full imposed load. However, provided that the hypothetical flexural tensile stresses given in **4.3.4.3** are used, the probability that the structure will contain open cracks under its normal loading is low. Further, the possible deviation from the uncracked behaviour is not large, and so little error will be involved in assuming the whole section to be acting and in calculating the deflection as for Class 1 and Class 2 members[4.5].

4.3.7 Ultimate limit state for beams in flexure

In most cases, Class 1 and Class 2 members already complying with the requirements of the serviceability limit state will require only a check at this limit state and should comply without modification. Class 3 members may require the addition of ordinary untensioned reinforcement in order to increase the resistance moment of the section.

4.3.7.1 *Section analysis*

Three methods are available for the analysis of prestressed concrete sections in flexure. These are:

1. The section may be analysed in accordance with assumptions (a) to (f) by using the stress-strain curves given in Figures 2.1, 2.2 and 2.3 for concrete, reinforcement and tendons respectively.
2. The section may be analysed in accordance with assumptions (a) to (f) by using the rectangular stress block described in assumption (b) for concrete and the stress-strain curves given in Figures 2.2 and 2.3 for reinforcement and tendons respectively.
3. The section may be designed in accordance with **4.3.7.3** and **4.3.7.4** by using design formulae and Table 4.4.

Methods 1 and 2, for which a typical section, stress distribution and strain profile are shown in Figure H4.4, are applicable to sections of any shape with any distribution of tendons and reinforcement. The analysis normally involves a trial and error approach, using strain compatibility, in order to determine the neutral axis depth for which the forces acting on the section are in equilibrium, as follows:

1. Assume a value for the neutral axis depth x and draw a strain profile by taking a value of 0.0035 at the extreme compression fibre.
2. Calculate the corresponding strain at the level of the tendons and add to this the

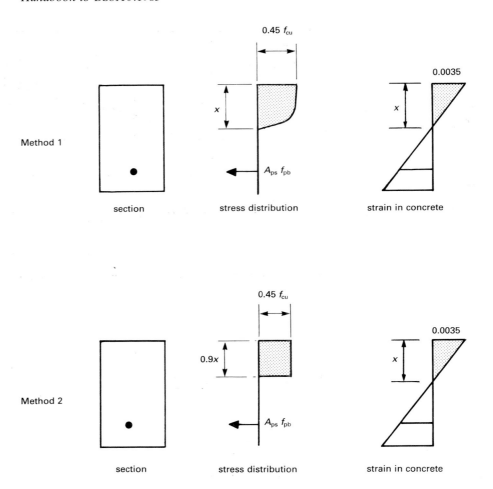

Figure H4.4: Design of prestressed concrete sections in flexure.

    prestrain in the tendons after all losses have occurred. Where appropriate, also calculate the strain at the level of the reinforcement.

3.   Determine the stresses in the reinforcement and the tendons from Figures 2.2 and 2.3 respectively and calculate the corresponding forces.

4.   Calculate the force in the concrete in the compression zone and compare this with the total force in the reinforcement and tendons.

5.   Modify the neutral axis depth and repeat steps 1 to 4 until equilibrium of forces is obtained.

6.   Take moments about a convenient position, such as the neutral axis, for all the forces acting on the section.

Methods 1 and 2 will give very similar answers with method 2 being easier to apply, particularly for sections with non-rectangular compresion zones. Method 3, which is directly applicable to sections with rectangular compression zones only, will give approximately the same answer as methods 1 and 2 in this case.

4.3.7.3 *Design formulae*

An approximate method for obtaining the resistance moment of sections, in which the tendons are effectively concentrated at one position in the tension zone, has been derived in accordance with assumptions (a) to (f). The design stress-strain curve for a high strength tendon ($f_{pu}=1860\text{N/mm}^2$, $E_s=195\text{kN/mm}^2$) has been used and the non-dimensional stress terms are slightly conservative for lower strength tendons. The method uses the rectangular stress block for the concrete and is directly applicable to sections that are rectangular for a depth (from the compression face) of not less than $0.9x$, where x is the neutral axis depth.

For a beam containing bonded tendons, equation 51 may be rewritten in a form that is suitable for plotting graphically, as follows:

$$M_u/(f_{cu}bd^2)=0.87\ [(f_{pu}A_{ps})/(f_{cu}bd)]\ [(f_{pb})/(0.87f_{pu})]\ (1-0.45x/d)$$

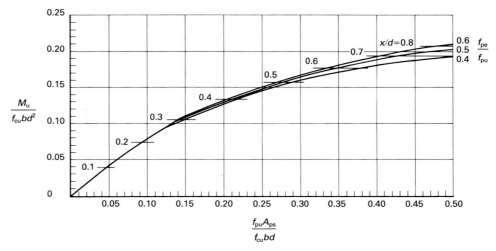

Figure H4.5: Design chart for prestressed rectangular beams (bonded tendon).

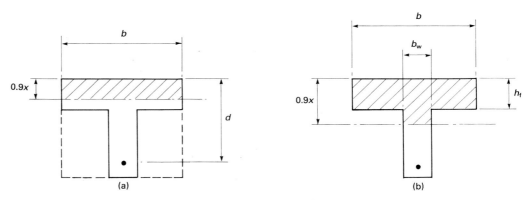

Figure H4.6: Design of T beams for flexure.

Using the values of $f_{pb}/0.87f_{pu}$ and x/d given in Table 4.4, a graph of $M_u/f_{cu}bd^2$ against $f_{pu}A_{ps}/f_{cu}bd$ may be produced as shown in Figure H4.5.

For a flanged section in which the flange thickness $h_f \geqslant 0.9x$, the equation or the graph may be used by taking the width of the section as the flange width b, as shown in Figure H4.6(a). Where $h_f < 0.9x$, as shown in Figure 4.6(b), the forces acting on the section may be equated to provide:

$$A_{ps}f_{pb} = 0.45\, f_{cu}[(b-b_w)h_f + 0.9b_w x]$$

which may be rewritten in the following form:

$$f_{pb}/0.87f_{pu} = 0.52\, [(f_{cu}b_w d)/(A_{ps}f_{pu})]\, [(b/b_w - 1)h_f/d + 0.9x/d]$$

This linear relationship between $f_{pb}/0.87f_{pu}$ and x/d may be plotted graphically, together with the appropriate relationship given in Table 4.4, as shown in Figure H4.7. The intersection of the two relationships gives the values of $f_{pb}/0.87f_{pu}$ and x/d to be used in equation 51 with an appropriate value of d_n. Alternatively, M_u may be calculated from:

$$M_u = 0.45f_{cu}\, [(b-b_w)h_f\, (d-0.5h_f) + 0.9b_w x(d-0.45x)]$$

For a beam containing unbonded tendons, equation 52 has been developed from the results of tests in which the stress in the tendons and the length of the zone of inelasticity in the concrete were both determined[4.6, 4.7].

The beam is considered to develop both elastic and inelastic zones and the length of the inelastic zone is taken to be $10x$. The extension of the concrete at the level of the tendons is assumed to be negligible in the elastic zones and the extension in the inelastic zone is assumed to be taken up uniformly over the length l of the tendon. Thus, the total strain ε_{pb} in the tendons is given by:

$$\varepsilon_{pb} = \varepsilon_{pe} + 0.0035\, [(d-x)/x]\, (10x/l)$$

$$= \varepsilon_{pe} + 0.0035(d/l)(1-x/d)$$

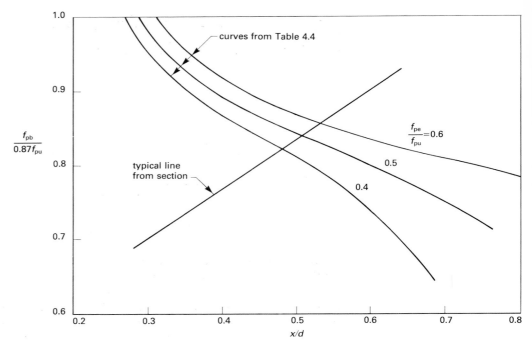

Figure H4.7: Treatment of flanged section where $H_f=0.9x$.

The corresponding stress in the tendons is then given by

$$f_{pb} = f_{pe}+(0.035E_s) \, (d/l)(1-x/d) \leq 0.7f_{pu}$$

The neutral axis depth may be determined by equating the forces acting on the section which, for a section with a rectangular compression zone, provides:

$$A_{ps}f_{pb} = 0.45f_{cu}b \, (0.9x)$$

This may be rewritten in the form of equation 53 and substituted in the expression for f_{pb} to give:

$$f_{pb} = f_{pe}+(0.035E_s)(d/l) \, [1-2.47((f_{pu}A_{ps})/(f_{cu}bd))(f_{pb}/f_{pu})] \leq 0.7f_{pu}$$

Equation 52 is then obtained by putting $E_s = 200kN/mm^2$ and, as an approximation, $f_{pb}/f_{pu} = 0.7$ in the last term.

4.3.7.4 *Allowance for additional reinforcement in the tension zone*
This approximate method for taking account of additional reinforcement in the tension zone will generally under-estimate the contribution of the reinforcement. A more rigorous strain compatibility analysis would allow the full design strength of a grade 460 steel to be utilised for all values of $x \leq 0.636d$, for example.

4.3.8 Design shear resistance of beams

4.3.8.1 *Symbols*

4.3.8.2 *Maximum design shear stress*
A limit on the maximum shear force carried by a member is necessary in order to stop the diagonal thrusts in the web of the member crushing the concrete. When the web has holes for ducts and these holes are not grouted after stressing, or when designing in the constructional phase for post-tensioned grouted construction, the minimum web width should be used. Even after grouting, the grouted section may cause spalling of the concrete on either side of the duct.

Information on this problem may be obtained from reference 4.8. The conclusions from this work are that, for grouted ducts, only the concrete and one-third of the duct width should be considered for the check on maximum shear, as noted for symbol b_v.

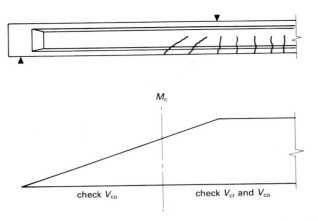

Figure H4.8: Prestressed beam showing zones for shear.

4.3.8.3 *Calculation of design shear resistance*

At the ultimate limit state, the member will have zones that are cracked in flexure and others that are not; the behaviour in each zone has characteristic features that require different design methods. Figure H4.8 shows a prestressed concrete beam under load, together with its bending moment diagram; the zones where the bending moment is less than the cracking moment should be designed so that the shear force carried by the beam is less than V_{co}; the zones where the bending moment is greater than the cracking moment should be designed to ensure that the shear force carried by the beam is less than V_{cr}. The nature of equation 55 ensures that, where the bending moment is less than the cracking moment, V_{cr} is always greater than V. It is therefore necessary to check only for V_{co} in these zones. Elsewhere, either V_{co} or V_{cr} may be critical and the section must be designed for the worst case. This procedure applies for all members. In each case, two sets of calculations must be made. A flow chart is shown in Figure H4.9.

A more complete description of the derivation of these clauses is given in reference 4.9.

4.3.8.4 *Sections uncracked in flexure*

In the zone of the beam that is uncracked in flexure, shear cracks may occur in the web as shown in Figure H4.10. V_{co} is calculated to see that the shear force is not high enough to cause failure by an extension of these cracks through the beam.

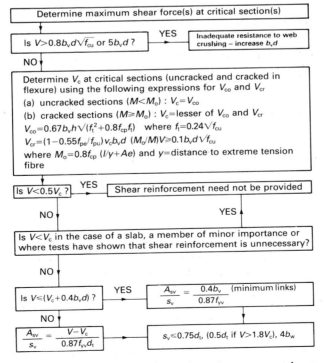

Figure H4.9: Flow chart for shear in prestressed concrete.

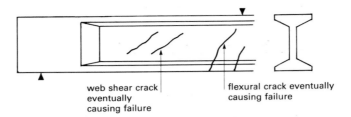

Figure H4.10: Prestressed beam with possible shear failure.

The principal tensile stress at the centroid of the section is limited to $0.24\sqrt{f_{cu}}$.
If the principal tensile stress is taken as positive, elastic theory gives:

$$-f_t = [(f_{cp}+f_{cy})/2] - \sqrt{[(f_{cp}-f_{cy})^2/4+f_v^2]}$$

where $f_v = V_{co} \, S/Ib_v$
S = the first moment of area about the centroidal axis of the part of the section to one side of the axis
I = second moment of area of the section
f_{cy} = compressive stress normal to the longitudinal axis.

These equations may be rearranged to give:

$$V_{co} = (Ib_v/S)\sqrt{(f_t^2+f_tf_{cp}+f_tf_{cy}+f_{cp}f_{cy})}$$

Assuming f_{cy} to be negligible gives

$$V_{co} = (Ib_v/S)\sqrt{(f_t^2+f_tf_{cp})}$$

For a rectangular section $Ib_v/S = 0.67b_vh$, and substituting this into the previous equation gives:

$$V_{co} = 0.67b_vh\sqrt{(f_t^2+f_tf_{cp})}$$

The prestress f_{cp} has a dominant effect on the value of V_{co} and, as partial safety factors have been incorporated in the values of f_t, an additional factor of 0.8 has been applied to f_{cp}. This now gives equation 54:

$$V_{co} = 0.67b_vh\sqrt{(f_t^2+0.8f_tf_{cp})}$$

For I, T and L sections $Ib_v/S>0.67b_vh$, so that the expression above is slightly conservative. However, for such sections, the point of maximum principal tensile stress is not at the centroid but at the junction between the web and flange; the simplification of checking only at the centroid of the section is therefore slightly unsafe in this case. The two effects cancel out giving a reasonable, simple method for checking all types of section.

Table 4.5 is a solution of equation 54 for given values of the prestress at the centroidal axis of the beam and of f_{cu} and may be used instead of equation 54.

If a beam has deflected tendons, the bending moment imposed on it by the tendons is as shown in Figure H4.11(a). This compares with the moment applied if the tendons were straight (Figure H4.11(b)).

For a beam with deflected or draped tendons, a shear is applied at the ends equal to the rate of change of moment or, more simply, the tendon force resolved vertically. This shear force should be subtracted from, or added to, the imposed shear where appropriate, before V_{co} is compared with the imposed shear.

When additional tendons are added to provide a vertical prestress, then the web cracking force, V_{co}, will be increased. This effect may be considered by modifying equation 54 to include the vertical prestress.

$$V_{co} = 0.67b_vh\sqrt{(f_t^2+0.8f_{cp}f_t+0.8f_tf_v+0.64f_{cp}f_v)}$$

where f_v is the vertical prestress.

Hence $V_{co} = 0.67b_vh\sqrt{[f_t^2+0.8f_t(f_{cp}+f_v+0.8f_{cp}f_v/f_t)]}$ and Table 4.5 may be used if $(f_{cp}+f_v+0.8f_{cp}f_v/f_t)$ is substituted for f_{cp}. If the prestressing tendons applying the vertical prestress are vertical, then no external moment is applied to the beam and the vertical force carried by the tendons cannot be subtracted from the shear force. If the tendons are inclined as in Figure H4.12 then, as in the case of deflected longitudinal tendons, an external moment and shear are applied to the member and the latter may be subtracted from or added to the external shear force where appropriate.

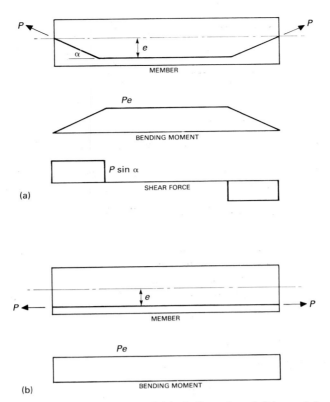

Figure H4.11: Effects of (a) *deflected and* (b) *straight tendons in sections uncracked in flexure.*

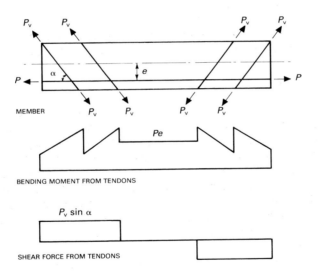

Figure H4.12: Theoretical effect of inclined tendons in sections uncracked in flexure.

Shear failure occurs along the plane on which the principal tension acts and the inclination of this plane to the beam axis varies with the prestress. A method for determining the position of the critical section near the end of a pre-tensioned member, with due allowance for the development of the prestress, is given in reference 4.10. A simplification of this method is shown in Figure H4.13.

4.3.8.5 *Sections cracked in flexure*
In the zone of a beam that is cracked in flexure, a crack may become inclined and eventually cause failure (Figure H4.10). A check on the value of V_{cr} is needed to make sure that this does not occur. The position of this crack varies, but tests indicate that a crack at a distance of half the effective depth from the point of maximum moment is usually the one that causes failure. A large number of tests have been carried out[4.11, 4.12]

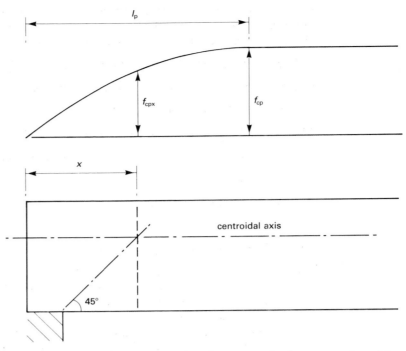

Figure H4.13: Critical section for shear at end of a pre-tensioned beam.

and, from these, a lower bound to the ultimate shear cracking load may be drawn. The expression for this lower bound is

$$V_{cr} = 0.037b_v d\sqrt{(f_{cu})} + M_c/(M/V - d/2)$$

where M_c is the cracking moment.

Thus, the shear force at which the cracks extend is equal to the shear force present when the section is at its cracking moment plus a constant. The value of the constant depends on the tensile strength of the concrete. The expression may, conservatively, be simplified to:

$$V_{cr} = 0.037b_v d\sqrt{(f_{cu})} + M_c V/M$$

This formula in itself would be an adequate code design formula except that it is appropriate only for members similar to those tested in the experimental investigations mentioned previously. The tests were carried out on members which had high prestress levels (over $0.5f_{pu}$) and this formula is therefore not directly applicable to members which may have very low prestress levels. As there was no appropriate experimental evidence available, the formula was modified so that it was dependent on prestress. The modified formula in the Code gives a linear relationship between the reinforced concrete shear clauses, if the prestress is zero, to the formula above, if the prestress if $0.6f_{pu}$.

The modification was carried out in the following way:

$$V_{cr} = A + B$$

where A depends on material strength and could be likened to the shear calculated from the v_c values in **3.4.5**.

B is the shear force to crack the member.

If A is changed to give the v_c values, modified by prestress, and B is zero when the prestress is zero, the two shear design methods would fit, i.e.

$$V_{cr} = [1 - n(f_{pe}/f_{pu})]\, v_c b_v d + M_o V/M$$

Now, if both f_{pe}, the effective prestress, and M_o, the moment to cause zero stress in the concrete at the extreme tension fibre, are zero, the formula should give the same result as the reinforced concrete design method,

$$V = v_c b_v d$$

Expanding the formula,

$$V_{cr} = 0.037b_v d\sqrt{(f_{cu})} + 0.37(I/ya_v)\sqrt{(f_{cu})} + M_o V/M$$

This is the same as the formula where $0.37\sqrt{(f_{cu})}$ is the tensile strength of the concrete and a_v is the lever arm of the cracking moment. Since the value of a_v in practice is $4h$ where shear is likely to be a problem, we obtain:

$$V_{cr}/b_v d = 0.037\sqrt{(f_{cu})}+[(0.37h)/(24d)]\sqrt{(f_{cu})}+M_o V/Mb_v d$$

By assuming that h/d is unity – a conservative assumption – and substituting $f_{cu} = 50$

$$V_{cr}/b_v d = 0.26+0.11+M_o V/Mb_v d$$

When $f_{pe} = 0.6f_{pu}$, n should be such that $(1-0.6n)v_c = 0.37 \text{N/mm}^2$

If we take an average value of v_c as 0.55 (for 0.5% steel), than

$$1-0.6n = 0.67$$

Therefore $n = 0.33/0.6 = 0.55$

and so

$$V_{cr} = [1-0.55(f_{pe}/f_{pu})]v_c b_v d+M_o V/M \qquad \text{(equation 55)}$$

If a beam has deflected tendons in a region where it is cracked in flexure, the tendon will apply an external shear to the beam in a way that was described in the previous section. Figure H4.14 shows a typical case. There is some experimental evidence[4.13] which shows that the ultimate strength of beams is reduced because the main tendons are not near the tension face and are unable to restrain cracking. Inclined cracking therefore occurs earlier than if the tendon were straight, giving a corresponding decrease in the ultimate load. It is therefore necessary to add the shear from the inclined tendon where it increases the imposed shear and to ignore it in other cases.

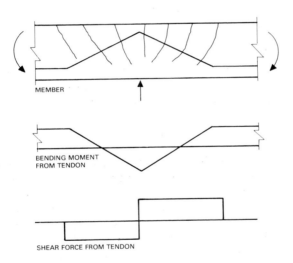

MEMBER

BENDING MOMENT
FROM TENDON

SHEAR FORCE FROM TENDON

Figure H4.14: Theoretical effect of deflected tendons in sections cracked in flexure.

4.3.8.6 *Cases not requiring shear reinforcement*
When the shear force V is less than $0.5V_c$, there is no need for shear reinforcement as the factor of safety is very high. There is no evidence of trouble due to the omission of minimum reinforcement in many joists, lintels and members of minor importance.

4.3.8.7 *Shear reinforcement where V does not exceed $V_c+0.4b_v d$*
In this case, minimum reinforcement is required as for reinforced concrete. Test evidence shows that the provision of minimum shear reinforcement can add considerably to the strength of prestressed concrete beams and ensure a more ductile failure.

4.3.8.8 *Shear reinforcement where V exceeds $V_c+0.4b_v d$*
In this case, more than the minimum reinforcement is required.

4.3.8.9 *Arrangement of shear reinforcement*

4.3.8.10 *Spacing of shear reinforcement*

4.3.9 Torsion

Torsion in prestressed concrete may generally be treated in the same way as for reinforced concrete. There are, however, certain differences in behaviour.

Cracking may not be acceptable under serviceability conditions. In this case, the principal tensile stress due to prestress, flexure, shear and torsion calculated from the characteristic loads and deformations should not exceed $0.24\sqrt{(f_{cu})}$ at any location (including the flexural tensile fibres). Full elasticity should be assumed in the analysis both of the structure and of the sections in these calculations.

4.4 Slabs

4.4.1 General

4.4.2 Flat slabs

References 4.14 and 4.15 contain recommendations for the analysis and design of flat slabs containing bonded or unbonded tendons. The punching resistance of a prestressed concrete slab is greater than that of an ordinary reinforced concrete slab with a similar area of flexural steel and this is allowed for, in references 4.14 and 4.15, by considering the area of the tendons A_{ps} to be replaced by an equivalent area of ordinary reinforcement $A_{ps}f_{pu}/410$. A more logical approach[4.16] is to calculate the punching resistance as for an ordinary reinforced concrete slab, using the actual area of the tendons, and to add this to the decompression load; i.e. the load required to annul the effect of the prestress in terms of the stress at the extreme fibres put into tension by the applied loading. These approaches implicitly assume the tendons to be bonded and the response to loads beyond the decompression level to be the same as that of ordinary reinforced concrete. If unbonded tendons are used, the response is less favourable and the punching resistance is typically reduced by about 10%[4.16].

4.5 Columns

For short columns under axial load, there is little justification for prestressing, except for handling. In this context, prestressing could be used to advantage in concrete piles or possibly in precast columns, designed for axial load, to cover erection stresses and to cater for any unexpected eccentric loading. Generally, a low level of prestress will deal with these problems and this clause allows prestressed columns having a mean stress due to prestress of less than 2.0N/mm^2 to be designed as reinforced columns.

The Code makes no specific recommendations for the design of prestressed columns with a mean pre-compression greater than 2.0N/mm^2. In this case, it is suggested that the additional moment approach given in **3.8.3** be applied directly with the cross-section being designed as a prestressed concrete section. Numerous methods have been proposed for the analysis of prestressed columns[4.17–4.19]; generally, these are similar in principle to the approach given in **3.8** for reinforced concrete columns. Experimental work has been carried out on prestressed columns with slenderness ratios of up to 30 under short-term loading[4.20, 4.21] and under various levels of long-term loading[4.22].

4.6 Tension members

4.7 Prestressing

4.7.1 Maximum initial prestress

4.7.2 Deflected tendons in pre-tensioning systems

4.8 Loss of prestress, other than friction losses

4.8.1 General

An assessment of the loss of prestress that can occur at various stages in the life of a prestressed member is an essential part of the design calculations, particularly for satisfying the serviceability limit states; errors in calculating losses are unlikely to seriously affect the ultimate resistance of the member. It is often necessary to calculate only those losses which occur at transfer and to assess the total loss, so that both the initial and final stress conditions in the member can be calculated; however, for certain cases, particularly composite construction, it may be necessary to calculate losses at an intermediate stage.

The values given in this clause for assessing loss of prestress due to various causes are necessarily general and approximate. This should be remembered when making design calculations; excessive accuracy is unnecessary, as the assumptions on which the various methods are based will not be completely realized in practice. For example, it should be borne in mind that, in practice, the prestressing force may be altered by the imposed loads and by the varying climate to which the member is subjected. Only rarely will it be possible to assess this variation accurately but if, for example, the engineer knows that part of the imposed load will be permanent and will be applied early in the life of the member, he should modify the calculations in the following clauses accordingly.

Where new materials are used or where there are special design conditions, the engineer may depart from the recommended values, but he must ensure that these new values are based on adequate experimental evidence.

Thermal curing is often used to accelerate the hardening of concrete, particularly for the manufacture of precast elements containing pre-tensioned tendons. This can have a significant effect on the losses of prestress due to relaxation of the steel tendons and the elastic deformation and subsequent shrinkage and creep of the concrete. Steam curing, for example, often results in reduced shrinkage and creep effects[4.23]. In addition, the relaxation of the steel is accelerated during the period between tensioning and transfer with a corresponding reduction in the stress applied to the concrete at transfer[4.24].

4.8.2 Relaxation of steel

4.8.2.1 *General*

The treatment during manufacture and the subsequent conditions of service have an important influence on the performance of prestressing steel in structures. The extent of the variation in relaxation for similar straightened wire is illustrated in Figure H4.15(a), which shows data for two types of cold-drawn wire of 5mm diameter. Wire H was straightened by a roller-type straightener and subsequently heat-treated at a moderately elevated temperature (relaxation class 1). Wire E was straightened by a final pass through a die under tension at a moderately elevated temperature (relaxation class 2).

The test period for obtaining data in relaxation tests at constant strain has been set at 1000h and the effect on relaxation of longer test periods is also shown in Figure

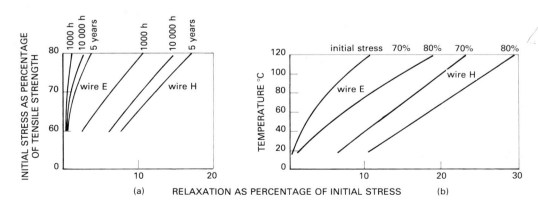

Figure H4.15: Effect of (a) *time and* (b) *temperature on the relaxation of 5mm diameter wire at various levels of stress.*

H4.15(a). The strain in the prestressing tendons does not remain constant during the life of a structure but reduces with time, owing to creep and shrinkage of the concrete. In the case of pre-tensioning, there is also a reduction at transfer owing to the elastic deformation of the concrete. An allowance for the effects of these strain reductions has been made in the long-term relaxation factors given in Table 4.6.

4.8.2.2 *The 1000h relaxation value*
The certified values should be obtained from the manufacturers. However, in the absence of this information, the maximum values specified in the appropriate British Standard should be used. See Table 8.1.

4.8.2.3 *Abnormal relaxation losses*
When structures are likely to be at temperatures above normal, the loss of prestress due to relaxation of the steel will be greater, and Figure H4.15(b) gives the results of 1000 h tests at various temperatures. For steels with a tensile strength from $1540N/mm^2$ to $1700N/mm^2$, the increase in the loss due to relaxation above that at 20°C may be taken as $1.8N/mm^2$ per degC for an initial stress of 70% of the characteristic strength, and $2.6N/mm^2$ per degC for an initial stress of 80% of the characteristic strength. These values appear to be less influenced by the manufacturing process than do the values for relaxation at 20°C.

Where large lateral forces may be applied to the tendon, relaxation losses will again be higher than normal. These loads may be imposed on the tendon by a change in the cable profile or because of the method employed for gripping the tendon; losses under these circumstances can only be determined by tests which simulate accurately the precise conditions that will occur during the actual construction.

References 4.25–4.30 should prove useful in assessing relaxation loss under special conditions.

4.8.3 Elastic deformation of concrete

4.8.3.1 *General*
The modulus of elasticity of concrete depends significantly on the type and source of aggregate but it will generally be sufficient to use a mean value taken from Table 7.2 of Part 2. In using the table, $f_{cu,28}$ may be replaced by f_{ci} to obtain a value for E_{ci}. The modulus of elasticity of the tendons may be obtained from Figure 2.3 of Part 1. When the tendons are spread over the cross-section, the stresses in the adjacent concrete could be determined separately for each tendon but it is generally sufficient to consider them as concentrated at their centroid.

4.8.3.2 *Pre-tensioning*
For pre-tensioning, the average loss of prestress in the tendons due to elastic shortening is given by $(E_s/E_{ci})f_{co,p}$, where $f_{co,p}$ is the initial stress in the concrete, adjacent to the centroid of the tendons, due to the prestress only.

The actual stress in the concrete and the tendons will be modified by the self-weight stresses which will vary along the length of the member. These stresses will depend to some extent on practical considerations such as the method of release and the adherence of the concrete to the mould and, subsequently, on the methods of handling and stacking. The self-weight stresses need to be considered when checking the initial stress conditions in the concrete.

4.8.3.3 *Post-tensioning*
For post-tensioning, the stressing of any tendon or group of tendons causes a loss of prestress due to elastic shortening in any other tendon that has already been stressed and anchored. The effect is progressive and the overall loss depends upon the number of stressing operations. For a small number of operations (there is no loss for a single operation), the loss can be assessed at each stage and summed. Generally, however, the overall effect may be adequately assessed by taking the average loss of prestress in the tendons due to elastic shortening as $0.5(E_s/E_{ci})f_{co,av}$, where $f_{co,av}$ is the initial stress in the concrete, adjacent to the centroid of the tendons, averaged along the length of the

tendons. In this case it is appropriate to consider the actual stress in the concrete due to the combined effects of prestress and self-weight (and any other permanent loads that are applied at transfer).

4.8.4 Shrinkage of concrete

The loss of prestress in the tendons due to shrinkage of the concrete is given by $E_s\varepsilon_{cs}$ where ε_{cs} is the shrinkage for the period considered.

The drying shrinkage of plain concrete depends mainly upon the relative humidity of the air surrounding the concrete, the surface area from which moisture can be lost relative to the volume of concrete and the mix proportions. The shrinkage of the concrete is increased if aggregates with a high moisture movement or a low modulus of elasticity are used. Concrete for prestressing requires the use of good quality aggregates and a mix with a low water/cement ratio and the shrinkage values given in this clause are adequate for most design purposes.

Where necessary, an estimate of the drying shrinkage may be obtained from Figure 7.2 of Part 2 for normal-weight concrete containing good quality aggregates. Figure 7.2 relates to concrete of normal workability, made without water reducing admixtures, where the original water content is about 190 litres/m^3. The shrinkage may be modified in proportion to the original water content for values in the range 150 litres/m^3 to 230 litres/m^3. For post-tensioning, in cases where a considerable delay is anticipated between the placing of the concrete and the application of the prestress, allowance may be made for the shrinkage that will take place prior to transfer on the basis of the ambient relative humidity during that period.

4.8.5 Creep of concrete

4.8.5.1 *General*

On the assumption that creep is proportional to the initial stress in the concrete, the average loss of prestress in the tendons due to creep of the concrete is given by

$$E_s\varepsilon_{cc} \quad E_s(\phi/E_{ci})f_{co}$$

where ε_{cc} is the creep strain in the concrete for the period considered

ϕ is a creep coefficient for the period considered

f_{co} is the initial stress in the concrete, adjacent to the centroid of the tendons, due to the combined effects of prestress and self-weight. For bonded tendons, the stress should be taken at the section under consideration. For unbonded tendons, the stress should be averaged along the length of the tendons.

4.8.5.2 *Specific creep strain*

The creep of plain concrete under sustained stress consists fundamentally of a 'basic creep' that develops under conditions of no moisture change (sealed condition) and an additional 'drying creep' that responds to environmental influences in the same way as drying shrinkage. The influence of the type and source of aggregate is illustrated in Figure H4.16. Further information on the significant factors affecting creep, including the age of loading, may be obtained from references 4.31–4.33.

The stress in the concrete at the centroid of the tendons does not remain constant during the life of the structure but reduces with time, owing to the combined effects of relaxation of the steel and shrinkage and creep of the concrete. An approximate allowance for these effects could be made by considering a stress that is the mean of the initial and the final values, due to the combined effects of prestress and self-weight. However, in the simplified approach adopted in this clause, an allowance for the effect of the reducing stress has been included in the values given for the creep coefficient. These values take account of the age of loading but, somewhat illogically, the values given for UK outdoor exposure are allowed also for indoor exposure for Class 1 and Class 2 members.

Where necessary, the creep coefficient may be estimated from Figure 7.1 of Part 2. In this case, it will be appropriate to allow for the effect of the reducing stress in the concrete owing to the loss of prestress. In some cases, it may also be appropriate to take account of stress reductions due to the application of superimposed dead load and/or part of the imposed load.

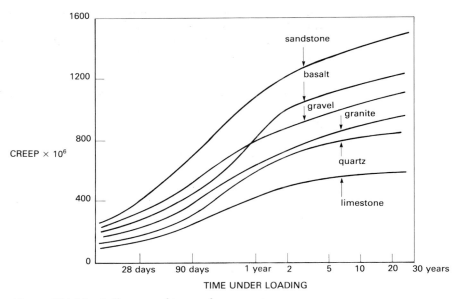

Figure H4.16: Influence of type of aggregate on creep.

4.8.6 Draw-in during anchorage

With wedge-anchorage systems, a loss of prestress occurs in the tendons as a result of the draw-in of the anchorage components at lock-off. In the case of pre-tensioned tendons, the 'loss' is normally offset by 'over-extending' the tendons during the tensioning operation. With post-tensioned tendons it is possible, in some cases, to 'recover the loss' by re-fitting the jack using a special bearing foot to encircle the anchorage. Shims are then inserted under the anchorage whilst holding the tendon at the required stressing force. Normally, this is not a viable procedure and the loss due to draw-in of the anchorage components should be allowed for in the design calculations. Typical values for the draw-in for a particular anchorage system can be obtained from the manufacturers.

The movement of the tendon due to draw-in during anchorage causes a reversal of the friction that develops in the duct during tensioning (**4.9.3** and **4.9.4**). For long tendons, the movement due to draw-in is taken up over a limited length of tendon with the greatest loss of prestress occurring immediately behind the anchorage.

4.9 Loss of prestress due to friction

4.9.1 General

Attention is drawn to **8.7.5.4** which indicates the required correlation between measured load and extension. Friction losses can be reduced under certain conditions by stressing from both ends, by over-stressing and then reducing the anchorage force, by vibrating the tendon or beam during tensioning or by using a water-soluble oil in the duct (provided that this does not affect bond after grouting and, hence, the ultimate strength of the member).

For long-span prestressed beams, low-friction saddles or deviators may be used at changes in direction of the tendons; the tendons are generally straight between the saddles and may be external to the section, in which case they pass through ducts only near the anchorages. Under these circumstances the loss of prestress due to friction may be radically different from that indicated in this clause. The coefficient of friction at the saddles will depend on the type of tendon and its surface condition, on the type of deviator, and on whether or not any lubricant has been used. It has been reported, for example, that the coefficient of friction when 28mm diameter strands were deflected through an angle of 1 in 10 was of the order of 0.08. Generally, the major part of the loss due to friction occurs in the ducts near the ends of the tendons. Losses due to friction under these conditions are best determined from tests.

4.9.2 Friction in jack and anchorage

The friction in the jack and anchorage will vary with the prestressing system but is rarely a matter of concern for the designer, since the supplier will provide a jack that is calibrated to give a specified force at the duct side of the anchorage. However, it is important to remember that this calibration will be based on the assumption that the equipment is well-maintained and that the anchorages and ducts are properly aligned; otherwise, the losses could be much higher.

4.9.3 Friction in the duct due to unintentional variation from the specified profile

4.9.3.1 *General*

4.9.3.2 *Calculation of force*

4.9.3.3 *Profile coefficient*
The value of K can vary considerably in practice depending mainly on the type of duct and the method of support but also, to a lesser extent, on the ratio of duct size to tendon size and on workmanship.

4.9.4 Friction due to curvature of tendons

4.9.4.1 *General*

4.9.4.2 *Calculation of force*
The duct profile normally comprises a series of parabolic curves, with common tangent points where reversals of curvature occur, and short straight lengths leading to the anchorages. It is useful to replace x/r_{ps} by α, where α is the total angular change in radians to the position at distance x from the jack. In this case, equations 58 and 59 may be combined to give $P_x = P_o e^{-(Kx+\mu\alpha)}$.

If $(Kx+\mu\alpha) \leqslant 0.2$, the equation may be simplified to the linear form $P_x = P_o[1-(Kx+\mu\alpha)]$ where $P_o(Kx+\mu\alpha)$ represents the combined loss due to friction in the duct.

4.9.4.3 *Coefficient of friction*
The physical condition of the tendon and the duct is important, i.e. whether or not heavy rusting or any sharp local distortions to the sheath are present. As indicated, it is possible to reduce the stated values if special precautions are taken and if the values used are based on tests; references 4.34–4.37 contain test data on both the coefficient of friction and the profile coefficient for a wide range of practical cases.

4.9.5 Lubricants

4.10 Transmission lengths in pre-tensioned members

4.10.1 General

4.10.2 Factors affecting the transmission length
Transverse reinforcement will be necessary in the ends of pre-tensioned members to satisfy the requirements of **4.12.7**. In addition, if the beam is to be supported within the transmission length, extra reinforcement will be required to carry shear; this should be designed in accordance with **4.3.8**. Generally, it is good design practice to be slightly conservative in assessing the transmission length and the necessary transverse reinforcement, particularly if the prestressed member is to be used in a composite construction where the reinforcement will help in dealing with additional shear due to differential shrinkage (**5.4.6.4**).

4.10.3 Assessment of transmission length
The recommended values for wire are based on both site and laboratory measurements[4.38]. For strand[4.39, 4.40], values based on laboratory measurements have been increased to allow for variations that occur in practice.

4.11 End blocks in post-tensioned members

4.11.1 General

When concentrated forces are applied to the ends of members, large bursting forces are induced for a distance along the member until the longitudinal stress profile becomes linear. These bursting forces are usually concentrated in the zone between $0.2y_o$ and $2y_o$ of the end of the member, where $2y_o$ is the side dimension of the end block.

This force has been considered in the past both theoretically and experimentally. The theories consider possible ways in which the longitudinal stress varies along the member and derive the bursting stress as the accompanying outward stress component. The experimental methods usually involve the analysis of measured surface strains and these have suggested that bursting stresses are slightly higher than the theories propose. Both approaches agree that the major variable is the ratio of the side of the loaded area to the side of the end block. Table 4.7, which gives the design bursting forces, is therefore a compromise between the various methods of end block design and gives values that are between the theoretical and experimental conclusions.

References 4.41 and 4.42 compare the various theories and the results of an experimental investigation into the problem. No detailed experimental investigations have been carried out on the anchorage of very large tendons.

When bearing plates are grouped together, a suitable design approach is to treat the area immediately beneath each end plate as a separate end block and then to link these blocks together. This method of considering the end of the member as a number of symmetrically loaded prisms is presented in references 4.42 and 4.43. When anchorages are eccentrically located on the end of the member, it is possible to have high tensile stresses on the loaded area of the member and these may cause spalling. This subject is discussed in reference 4.44.

Distributions of both bursting and spalling stresses, determined by a finite element procedure, for axial, eccentric and multiple anchorages on rectangular and I-section beams are shown in references 4.45 and 4.46. Guidance on the design of end blocks is contained in reference 4.47.

4.11.2 Serviceability limit state

The basis of the design is to use the tendon jacking load and to carry all bursting tensile forces on reinforcement acting at a design stress that is limited to control cracking.

In the past, some design has been based entirely on the results of the experimental investigations of the problem and, in conjunction with this, designers have used the higher experimental forces with the concrete carrying some of the bursting tensile force to reduce the net amount of reinforcement. These methods could still be used, but tension should not be carried in the concrete if the bursting forces are obtained from Table 4.7; nor should any theoretical approach to the problem that does not consider the compatibility of transverse strains between the concrete and the end block reinforcement be used.

4.11.3 Ultimate limit state

With unbonded tendons, over-loading at an early stage before any significant loss of prestress has occurred could result in a force greater than the jacking load. The use of the characteristic tendon force ensures an adequate partial safety factor.

4.12 Considerations affecting design details

4.12.1 General

The detailing rules for reinforcement are contained in **3.12** and, with the exception of **3.12.5** and **3.12.11**, these should be applied whenever reinforcement is used in prestressed concrete members. The rules given here are additional and relate particularly to prestressing tendons.

4.12.2 Limitations on area of prestressing tendons

When a beam cracks, tension previously carried by both the steel and the concrete is now carried by the steel alone. If the percentage of steel is very low, the steel may not be capable of carrying this additional force and may yield or rupture, causing immediate failure. A minimum amount of steel is therefore required to ensure that the beam is capable of carrying load after cracking and so provide a visual warning of possible failure ans some measure of ductility.

If a beam has a very high steel percentage, failure will also be less ductile as the strength of the beam will depend on the concrete and failure will not be caused by yield of the steel; failure could possibly occur before any cracking has taken place, but this is unlikely because of the design methods adopted in **4.3.4** and **4.3.7**. This safeguard is particularly relevant to composite construction, where the prestressed unit might fail in this way during erection or construction before the in situ concrete is placed.

The design ultimate moment of resistance should be not less than:

$$M_u = (f_{cpy}+0.6\sqrt{f_{cu}})I/y$$

where f_{cpy} is the prestress in the concrete at the extreme tension fibre at a distance y from the centroid of the section of second moment of area I.

4.12.3 Cover to prestressing tendons

The recommendations on cover in relation to durability and fire resistance requirements are similar to those for reinforced concrete in **3.3.4** to **3.3.6**; in practice, it will often be requirements of fire resistance rather than durability that will control the cover to be provided.

4.12.3.1 *Bonded tendons*

4.12.3.1.1 *General*

4.12.3.1.2 *Cover against corrosion.* The exposure conditions defined in Table 3.2 are used as the basis for Table 4.8, which is essentially Table 3.4 with the minimum cement content taken not less than 300kg/m³. This limit reflects the importance of the cement content in protecting the steel, and the somewhat greater sensitivity of prestressing tendons to the effects of corrosion, due to their generally small cross-section and high stress level. See also the commentary on **6.2**.

4.12.3.1.3 *Cover as fire protection.* Table 4.9 gives nominal covers to all steel to meet specified periods of fire resistance. The format is similar to Table 3.5 for reinforced concrete and the covers relate specifically to the minimum widths and thicknesses given in Figure 3.2. See also the commentary on **3.3.6** regarding covers and anti-spalling measures.

4.12.3.2 *Tendons in ducts*

4.12.3.3 *External tendons*

It should be noted that the cover added to external tendons will not in fact be put into compression by prestress. Some compression may be induced later owing to creep and shrinkage but this may not always be enough to offset the tensile strains due to imposed loading. It is essential therefore that cover provided in this context be thoroughly compacted and that this concrete be anchored to the prestressed member (preferably by reinforcement). The positioning of the tendons and the shape of the cross-section should be so arranged that the influence of any transverse cracking or longitudinal splitting is kept to a minimum.

4.12.3.4 *Curved tendons*

4.12.4 Spacing of prestressing tendons

4.12.4.1 *General*

The layout of prestressing tendons should be such that the concrete can be easily placed

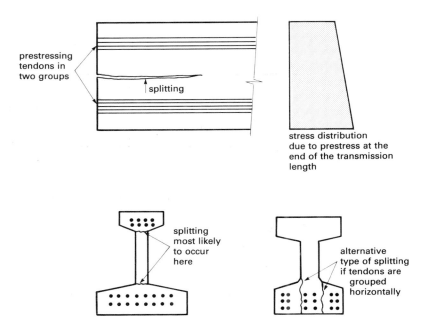

Figure H4.17: Splitting at ends of pre-tensioned beams.

and thoroughly compacted. No general rules can be formulated because the layout will depend very much on the type of section and on the amount of transverse reinforcement provided; it will also depend to some extent on the method used for vibrating the concrete and on the type of tendon and anchorage system used.

4.12.4.2 *Bonded tendons*

Where straight tendons are grouped some distance apart in pre-tensioned members, tension may develop at the end of the beams between the groups of tendons as the pre-compression spreads out from being a series of point loads on the end of the beam to give a linear stress distribution across the section at the end of the transmission zone. Figure H4.17 shows the areas where splitting is possible, the most likely spot being at any change of cross-section in the depth of the member. Under these circumstances, stirrups or helices should be used to contain the tendons at the end of the beam and to prevent splitting from developing. This reinforcement should be designed in accordance with the specialist literature[4.48 and 4.49] and provided over a distance along the beam at least equal to the total depth of the beam.

4.12.4.3 *Tendons in ducts*

4.12.4.4 *Curved tendons*

4.12.5 **Curved tendons**

4.12.5.1 *General*

The type of action visualized in this clause is illustrated in Figure H4.18(a). There may also be a risk of the side cover spalling in very narrow webs and of the bottom cover spalling off where tendons run close and approximately parallel to the soffit of slabs. The manufacturers of most post-tensioning systems specify cover and spacing requirements for their tendons and ducts and these should be regarded as minima.

In general, where a number of prestressing tendons in the same plane are curved in that plane, the innermost tendon should be stressed and grouted first. Where this is not possible, such as in statically indeterminate structures, then it may be necessary to anchor the tendon back into the compression zone (as shown in Figure H4.18(b)) for highly curved tendons. Consideration could also be given to providing helical reinforcement to carry tensile stresses between the ducts.

The recommendations in **4.12.5.2** to **4.12.5.4** are taken from reference 4.50. Further research data and suggested design rules are given in reference 4.51.

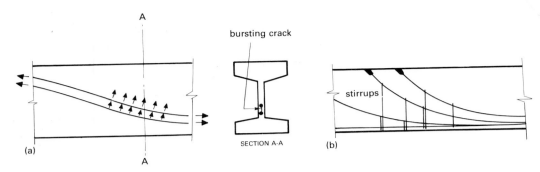

Figure H4.18: Bursting stresses from tendons with high curvature.

4.12.5.2 *Cover*

4.12.5.3 *Spacing*

4.12.5.4 *Special measures to reduce spacing of ducts*

4.12.6 Longitudinal reinforcement in prestressed concrete beams

4.12.7 Links in prestressed concrete beams

This clause catalogues the various situations in prestressed concrete design where transverse reinforcement is required. The design and detailing of links for shear considerations is governed by **4.3.8.7** to **4.3.8.10**. If a pre-tensioned member is supported near its ends, such that a considerable proportion of the transmission length (as determined from **4.10.3**) is within the span, the transmission length could be designed as a reinforced concrete section in accordance with **3.4.5** as a conservative alternative to the approach given in **4.3.8.4**. The requirement for links to resist longitudinal splitting forces at the ends of pre-tensioned members is dealt with in the commentary to **4.12.4.2**.

4.12.8 Shock loading

As in reinforced concrete, the provision of transverse steel in major structural members is considered to be good practice, irrespective of shear requirements and this is especially so if the member has to resist shock loading. In general, for this situation, minimum reinforcement requirements should be in accordance with **3.12.5.3**. In post-tensioned members, the ducts should be grouted.

REFERENCES

4.1 ANDERSON, A.R. Lateral stability of long prestressed concrete beams. Journal of the Prestressed Concrete Institute. Vol.16, No.3. May-June 1971. pp.7-9. See also discussion by SWANN, R.A. Vol.16, No.6. November-December 1971. pp.85-87.

4.2 SWANN, R.A. The lateral buckling of concrete beams lifted by cables. The Structural Engineer. Vol.44, No.1. January 1966. pp.21-33.

4.3 BATES, S.C.C. Some experimental data relating to the design of prestressed concrete. Parts 1, 2 & 3. Civil Engineering and Public Works Review. Vol. 53, No.627. September 1958. pp.1010-1012. Vol.53, No.628. October 1958. pp.1958-1961 and Vol.53, No.629. November 1958. pp.1280-1284.

4.4 ABELES, P.W. Partial prestressing and its suitability for limit state design. The Structural Engineer. Vol.49, No.2. February 1971. pp.67-86.

4.5 BEEBY, A.W., KEYDER, E. and TAYLOR, H.P.J. Cracking and deformation in partially prestressed concrete beams. London, Cement and Concrete Association, January 1972. 26pp. Publication 42.465.

4.6 PANNELL, F.N. The ultimate moment of resistance of unbonded prestressed concrete beams. Magazine of Concrete Research. Vol.21, No.66. March 1969. pp.43-54.

4.7 PANNELL, F.N. and TAM, A. The ultimate moment of resistance of unbonded partially prestressed reinforced concrete beams. Magazine of Concrete Research. Vol.28, No.97. December 1976. pp.203-208.

4.8 LEONHARDT, F. Abminderung der Tragfahigkeit des Betons infolge stabformiger, rechtwinklig zur Druckrichtung angerdraehte Einlagen. pp.71-78. KNITTEL, G. and KUPFER, H. eds. Stahlbetonbau: Berichte aus Forschung und Praxis. Berlin, Wilhelm Ernst & Sohn, 1969. Festschrift Ruesch.

4.9 REYNOLDS, G.C. revised by CLARKE, J.L. and TAYLOR, H.P.J. Shear provisions for prestressed concrete in the Unified Code CP110 : 1972. London, Cement and Concrete Association, October 1974. 16pp. Publication 42.500.

4.10 BUILDING REGULATIONS ADVISORY COMMITTEE. Report by Sub-Committee P (high alumina cement concrete), BRAC (75) P40, Appendix K. 1975.

4.11 HAWKINS, N.M. The shear provision of AS CA 35 – SAA Code for prestressed concrete. Institution of Engineers Australia, Civil Engineering Transactions. Vol.CE6, No.2. September 1964. pp.103-116, and University of Sydney, Department of Civil Engineering 1964. 46pp. LS6681.

4.12 SOZEN, M.A. and HAWKINS, N.M. Shear and diagonal tension. Discussion of a paper by ACI-ASCE Committee 326. Proceedings of the American Concrete Institute. Vol.59, No.9. September 1962. pp.1341-1347.

4.13 MACGREGOR, J.G., SOZEN, M.A. and SIESS, C.P. Effect of draped reinforcement on behavior of prestressed concrete beams. Proceedings of the American Concrete Institute. Vol.57, No.6. December 1960. pp.649-678.

4.14 THE CONCRETE SOCIETY. Flat slabs in post-tensioned concrete with particular regard to the use of unbonded tendons – design recommendations. Concrete Society Technical Report No.17. 1979. 16pp.

4.15 THE CONCRETE SOCIETY. Post-tensioned flat-slab design Handbook. Concrete Society Technical Report No.25. 1984. 44pp.

4.16 REGAN, P.E. The punching resistance of prestressed concrete slabs. Proceedings of the Institution of Civil Engineers, Part 2. Vol.79. December 1985. pp.657-680.

4.17 BENNETT, E.W. The design of prestressed members subjected to axial force and bending. Concrete and Constructional Engineering. Vol.61, No.8. August 1966. pp.267-274.

4.18 ZIA, P. and MOREADITH, F.L. Ultimate load capacity of prestressed concrete columns. Proceedings of the American Concrete Institute. Vol.63, No.7. July 1966. pp.767-788.

4.19 BROWN, K.J. The ultimate load-carrying capacity of prestressed concrete columns under direct and eccentric loading. Civil Engineering and Public Works Review. Vol.60, No.705. April 1965. pp.539-541. Vol.60, No.706. May 1965. pp.683-687. Vol.60, No.707. June 1965. pp.841-845.

4.20 BROWN, H.R. and HALL, A.S. Tests on slender prestressed concrete columns. Detroit, American Concrete Institute, 1965. pp.192-204. SP-13.

4.21 ARONI, S. Slender prestressed concrete columns. Proceedings of the American Society of Civil Engineers. Vol.94, No.ST4. April 1968. pp.875-904.

4.22 CEDERWALL, K., ELFGREN, L. and LOSBERG, A. Prestressed concrete columns under short-time and long-time loading. Goteborg, Chalmers University of Technology, 1970. 16pp. Publication 70:3.

4.23 KIRKBRIDE, T.W. Review of accelerated curing procedures. Precast Concrete. Vol.2, No.2. February 1971. pp.93-106.

4.24 FEDERATION INTERNATIONALE DE LA PRECONTRAINTE. Acceleration of concrete hardening by thermal curing. FIP Guide to Good Practice. 1982. 16pp.

4.25 BANNISTER, J.L. Steel reinforcement and tendons for structural concrete. Part 2: tendons for prestressed concrete. Concrete. Vol.2, No.8. pp.333-342. August 1968.

4.26 BATE, S.C.C., CORSON, R.H. and JEFFS, A.T. Prestressing nuclear pressure vessels. Engineering. Vol.197, No.5111.3. April 1964. pp.492-495. Also Building Research Station Current Paper, Engineering series 12, 1964. 6pp.

4.27 BATE, S.C.C. and CORSON, R.H. Effect of temperature on prestressing wires. Conference on prestressed concrete pressure vessels, London, March 1967. London, Institution of Civil Engineers, 1968. pp.237-240. Paper No.21.

4.28 CAHILL, T. and BRANCH, G.D. Long-term relaxation behaviour of stabilized prestressing wires and strands. Conference on prestressed concrete pressure vessels, London, March 1967. London, Institution of Civil Engineers, 1968. pp.219-228. Paper No.19.

4.29 ABRAMS, M.S. and CRUZ, C.R. The behaviour at high temperature of steel strand for prestressed concrete. Journal of the PCA Research and Development Laboratories. Vol.3, No.3. September 1961. pp.8-19.

4.30 BANNISTER, J.L. Steel reinforcement and tendons for structural concrete. The Consulting Engineer. Vol.35, No.2. February 1971. pp.80-90.

4.31 NEVILLE, A.M. Creep of concrete: plain, reinforced and prestressed. Amsterdam, North-Holland Publishing Company, 1970. 622pp.

4.32 EVANS, R.H. and KONG, F.K. Estimation of creep of concrete in reinforced concrete and prestressed concrete design. Civil Engineering and Public Works Review. Vol.61, No.718. May 1966. pp.593-596.

4.33 THE CONCRETE SOCIETY. The creep of structural concrete. Concrete Society Technical Paper, No.101. 1973. 47pp.

4.34 COOLEY, E.H. Friction in post-tensioned prestressing systems. London, Cement and Concrete Association, 1953. 37pp. Publication 41.001.

4.35 WYATT, K.J. Measurement of friction in corrugated curved prestressing ducts. Sydney, Commonwealth Experimental Building Station, 1964. 17pp. Technical Record 52:75:322.

4.36 COMMISSIE VOOR UITVOERING VAN RESEARCH INGESTELD DOOR DE BETONVERENIGING. Frictional losses in prestressing tendons, (in Dutch). The Hague, 1968. 61pp. Report No.30.

4.37 INSTITUTION OF CIVIL ENGINEERS. Conference on prestressed concrete pressure vessels, London, March 1967. London, Institution of Civil Engineers, 1968. Group E: Properties of materials (Prestressing tendons). Papers 22-27. pp.251-300.

4.38 BASE, G.D. An investigation of the transmission length in pre-tensioned concrete. London,

Cement and Concrete Association, 1958. 29pp. Publication 41.005.

4.39 BASE, G.D. An investigation of the use of strand in pre-tensioned prestressed concrete beams. London, Cement and Concrete Association, 1961. 12pp. Publication 41.011.

4.40 MAYFIELD, B., DAVIES, G. and KONG, F.K. Some tests on the transmission length and ultimate strength of pre-tensioned concrete beams incorporating Dyform strand. Magazine of Concrete Research. Vol.22, No.73. December 1970. pp.219-226.

4.41 ZIELINSKI, J. and ROWE, R.E. An investigation of the stress distribution in the anchorage zones of post-tensioned concrete members. London, Cement and Concrete Association, 1960. 32pp. Publication 41.009.

4.42 ZIELINSKI, J. and ROWE, R.E. The stress distribution associated with groups of anchorages in post-tensioned concrete members. London, Cement and Concrete Association, 1962. 39pp. Publication 41.013.

4.43 GUYON, Y. Prestressed concrete. New York, John Wiley & Sons Inc, 1960. Vol.1. 559pp. Vol.2. 741pp.

4.44 LENSCHOW, R.J. and SOZEN, M.A. Practical analysis of the anchorage zone problem in prestressed beams. Journal of the American Concrete Institute. Vol.62, No.11. November 1965. pp.1421-1439.

4.45 YETTRAM, A.L. and ROBBINS, K. Anchorage zone stresses in post-tensioned members of uniform rectangular section. Magazine of Concrete Research. Vol.21, No.67. June 1969. pp.103-112.

4.46 YETTRAM, A.L. and ROBBINS, K. Anchorage zone stresses in post-tensioned uniform members with eccentric and multiple anchorages. Magazine of Concrete Research. Vol.22, No.73. December 1970. pp.209-218.

4.47 CONSTRUCTION INDUSTRY RESEARCH AND INFORMATION ASSOCIATION. A guide to the design of anchor blocks for post-tensioned prestressed concrete members. CIRIA Guide 1. June 1976. 34pp.

4.48 ARTHUR, P.D. and GANGULI, S. Tests on end-zone stresses in pre-tensioned concrete I beams. Magazine of Concrete Research. Vol.17, No.51. June 1965, pp.85-96.

4.49 KRISHNAMURTHY, D. Design of end zone reinforcement to control horizontal cracking in pre-tensioned concrete members at transfer. Indian Concrete Journal. Vol.47, September and October 1973, pp.346-351 and 379-385.

4.50 DEPARTMENT OF THE ENVIRONMENT. Prestressed concrete curved tendons. London, Department of the Environment, August 1969. 3pp. Interim Memorandum (Bridges) IM2.

4.51 McLEISH, A. Bursting stresses due to prestressing tendons in curved ducts. Proceedings of the Institution of Civil Engineers, Part.2. Vol.79, September 1985. pp.605-615.

SECTION FIVE. DESIGN AND DETAILING: PRECAST AND COMPOSITE CONSTRUCTION

5.1 Design basis and stability provisions

5.1.1 General

5.1.2 Basis for design

5.1.3 Handling stresses

5.1.4 Compatibility

5.1.5 Anchorage at supports

5.1.6 Joints for movement

5.1.7 Stability

This section is emphasised because, often, precast units designed by one engineer are incorporated into a structure designed by another. It is most likely that the engineer in the chain of authority closer to the eventual client will have responsibility for the overall stability of the structure.

The requirements of **3.1.4** with regard to the provision of tie forces, the importance of the layout of the structure in plan, and the possible protection of those members vital to stability apply equally to precast and composite concrete construction. The detailing rules of **3.12** should be used whenever appropriate; **5.3.4** gives some additional rules for anchoring and lapping bars more relevant to the special problems presented by precast construction.

Bars which are used to provide the tie forces required in **3.12.3** should be positioned and detailed so that they have the necessary cover to enable their full strength to be developed. If ties are to be provided by lapped bars in narrow spaces between precast units, attention should be paid to the requirements of **5.1.8.2**. In complying with the vertical tie requirements, lifting and levelling bolts may be used to form part of this effectively uninterrupted tie.

For buildings supported by plain concrete walls, the vertical tie requirements are satisfied if the tie is able to carry the dead and live load from the floor above.

Where this is not so, or where in any structure of five or more storeys the requirements of **3.12.3.7** are not met, Section **2.6** of Part 2 permits an alternative approach to design. This is the 'alternative path' approach, where, for each storey in turn, the notional removal of any single vertical load-bearing member is considered, and the structure checked to ensure that the loads can still be carried by catenary, cantilever or some other form of structural action. Any building component that is normally not load-bearing may be taken into account and the γ_m values should be taken as 1.3 for concrete and 1.0 for reinforcement. There are limitless possibilities here over the range of types of structure (and their usage) covered by this Code and the value of the loading is left to the discretion of the engineer; in general, all permanent loads would be considered and some fraction of imposed loading – this will depend on usage and special consideration may have to be given to warehouses, plant rooms, etc. **2.4.3.2** gives some advice on this subject. Only rarely will it be necessary to consider debris loading, because of the relative magnitudes of the safety factors for normal and exceptional loads and also because of the tie force requirements.

The 'alternative path' method outlined above will be the most appropriate for precast concrete structures made of load-bearing concrete panels. For this reason, a definition is given of what constitutes a single load-bearing element. This involves the further necessity to define a 'lateral support' in **2.6.3.2.2** of Part 2: this may be either a substantial partition at right-angles to the wall being considered and tied into it or, alternatively, a narrow width of the wall itself which has been locally stiffened and is capable of resisting a specified horizontal force.

2.6 of Part 2 introduces a second alternative design approach, again only for the situation where **3.12.3.7** is not complied with. Instead of a vital structural member being considered to be rendered ineffective, it is proposed that the design is satifactory if the member can resist a pressure of 34kN/m^2, the γ factors being as described for the alternative path approach. This approach is therefore attempting to quantify the effects due to exceptional loading, but at the same time a minimum tying together has still to be provided since **3.12.3** must be complied with. In practice, this will generally be the most appropriate alternative approach for columns in framed structures.

It should be realised that only in exceptional cases will structures require other than the provision of ties. Key elements defined in clause **2.2.2.2** will be identified from a study of the structural scheme and **2.2.2.2(d)** makes it clear that in most circumstances vertical tying of the structure will be the normal design solution.

Key elements will only be met in those structures where there is an exceptional and unavoidable tendency for more than the local area around the element to collapse in the event of accident.

5.1.8 Stability ties
These may be located in any part of the structure providing that they interact properly.

5.1.8.1 *Ties generally*

5.1.8.2 *Continuity of ties*
The categories (a) to (d) give guidance on how ties are to be provided. Other methods may be developed but the important principle is that the tie should be provided in an identifiable *positive* way.

5.1.8.3 *Anchorage in tall structures*
This requires that in buildings of five or more storeys *all* precast members must be anchored to the tied part of the structure. This is to avoid excessive debris loading in the event of an accident.

5.1.8.4 *Avoidance of eccentricity*
This is to ensure that, in the case of accident, ties which have to straighten do not allow units to fall from bearings.

5.1.9 Durability
In this respect, connections should be robust and should be filled with good quality grout or well compacted connection concrete. The provision of caps or seals to sensitive connections on the periphery of a structure should also be considered.

In preparing the design, detailing and specification for connections, the difficulty of achieving on site the intended quality in relation to dimensions and in situ concrete should be taken into account.

5.2 Precast concrete construction

5.2.1 Framed structures and continuous beams
It is in general more difficult to provide full moment continuity in precast concrete construction than in in situ structures but, where this is to be the basis of design, then the procedures given in Sections **3** and **4** in the Code may be adopted, including the redistribution of moments. Redistribution may be particularly useful in reducing design moments at connections.

5.2.2 Slabs

5.2.2.1 *Design of slabs*
Again the basis for analysis and design of precast slabs should be that given in Section **3** or **4** as appropriate.

5.2.2.2 *Concentrated loads on slabs without reinforced topping*
This clause makes empirical recommendations on the width of a slab (perhaps made up

of a number of precast units) which can be considered to be helping to resist concentrated loads, including line loads from partitions in the direction of the span. The type of partition will have a considerable influence on the way the load is distributed transversely across the slab; moreover, the type and width of the precast units and the connection between them can have a considerable influence. A limited amount of testing has been carried out on a range of standard floor units and generally this has shown that the actual transverse distribution can be defined accurately by means of the load distribution or grillage analysis for bridge decks, which are in common use in this country. If, in a particular case, a more accurate assessment is required than is given by this clause, references 5.1,, 5.2 and 5.3 should be consulted.

Many manufacturers will have results from load tests on their units in structures and these should be available for guidance.

5.2.2.3 *Concentrated loads on slabs with reinforced topping*
The comments to **5.2.2.2** apply here also.

5.2.2.4 *Slabs carrying concentrated loads*

5.2.3 Bearings for precast members
The definitions in **1.2.5** are important and have specific meanings when used in the following clauses.

5.2.3.1 *General*
This section comes from the work of a Committee of the Institution of Structural Engineers[5.4]. The clauses do not require that there is a definite check on the provision of overlap of reinforcement (a); it is clearly impossible in bearings on brickwork etc. The use of the clauses will however give overlap where it is appropriate to be provided.

5.2.3.2 *Calculation of net bearing width of non-isolated members*
When assessing the effect of potential rotation, the restraint and support of the supporting member should be considered when assessing its likely rotation.

5.2.3.3 *Effective bearing length*
Figure 5.4 is in error in that the vertical dimension in the lower part of the figure is shown as bearing width when it should show bearing length, see definition **1.2.5.5**.

5.2.3.4 *Design ultimate bearing stress*
The requirement to rely upon the weaker of the bearing surfaces is clearly important if the bearing length of the supported member is similar to the available length for bearing of the supporting member and vice-versa. Where for example one member is narrow with respect to the other, higher bearing stresses in the wider member, subject to test or the provisions of reinforcement to prevent bursting, based on clause **4.11** in Part 1, will be appropriate.

Higher bearing stresses than $0.8f_{cu}$ may be used when justified by tests. References 5.5 – 5.9 provide data on bearing stresses.

5.2.3.5 *Net bearing width of isolated members*

5.2.3.6 *Detailing for simple bearing*
This refers forward to Clauses **5.2.3.7** and **5.2.4.**

5.2.3.7 *Allowances for effects of spalling at supports*
Plastic load shedding packs are now available which reduce the effects of the problem described in **5.2.3.7.4**.

5.2.4 Allowance for construction inaccuracies

5.2.5 Bearings transmitting compressive forces from above

5.2.6 Other forces at bearings

5.2.6.1 *Horizontal forces at bearing*
Particular attention should be placed on the detailing of both supporting and supported member. Continuity reinforcement must be anchored to both members in such a way as to avoid planes of weakness away from the support. It should be realised that the provision of tensile restraint will render both supporting and supported member prone to tension cracking. Reinforcement should be provided to minimise crack widths in this regard since it can be a serious cause of failure if proper provision to control and distribute cracks is not made.

It will often be sufficient, instead of providing a full sliding bearing (a), to provide a flexible bearing which allows sufficient capability to move laterally.

5.2.6.2 *Rotation at bearing of flexural members*
The use of suitable elastic bearing materials will do much to distribute and smooth out the bearing stresses.

5.2.7 Concrete corbels

5.2.7.1 *General*

5.2.7.2 *Design*
The essence of the design method recommended for a corbel is the assumption that it behaves as a simple strut-and-tie system, as indicated in Figure H5.1 for loads appropriate to the ultimate limit state. So that it can function in this way, it is first necessary to eliminate the possibility of a shear failure and **5.2.7** suggests that the total depth of the corbel (h) be determined from shear considerations in accordance with **3.4.5.8**. The corbel width (b) will normally be determined from practical considerations and the size of the bearing plate transmitting the ultimate load (V_u) to the corbel should then be calculated by using a bearing stress not greater than $0.8f_{cu}$, as suggested in **5.2.3.4**, provided that it may be shown that the horizontal force at the bearing is low (less than $0.1\ V_u$).

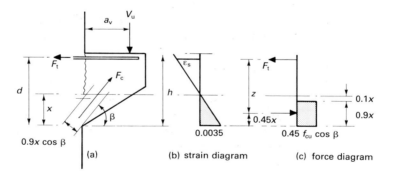

Figure H5.1: Design basis for corbels (5.2.7.2).

The requirements of **5.2.7** for the proportioning of the corbel and the detailing of the reinforcement are illustrated in Figure H5.2. Of the three methods shown for anchoring the main tension steel (A_{st}) at the outer face of the corbel, that in diagram (a) is the most efficient technically. It also has some practical advantages in that the ratio a_v/d is higher than for the other two methods where the requirements of **3.12.8.24** regarding the minimum radii of bends have to be met for the main tension steel.

For higher a_v/d ratios, design will be controlled principally by flexure at section A-A (Figure H5.1). Particular attention has to be paid to the occurrence of horizontal forces at the bearing, since these can considerably reduce the corbel strength; this problem is discussed and dealt with in reference 5.10.

5.2.7.2.1 *Simplifying assumptions*

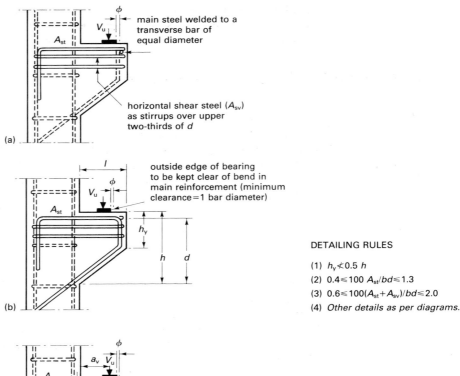

DETAILING RULES

(1) $h_y \not< 0.5\, h$

(2) $0.4 \leqslant 100\, A_{st}/bd \leqslant 1.3$

(3) $0.6 \leqslant 100(A_{st} + A_{sv})/bd \leqslant 2.0$

(4) *Other details as per diagrams.*

Figure H5.2: Possible methods of anchoring main tension reinforcement in corbels.

5.2.7.2.2 *Reinforcement anchorage*

5.2.7.2.3 *Shear reinforcement*

5.2.7.2.4 *Resistance to applied horizontal force*

5.2.8 Continuous concrete nibs

Reference 5.11 has a considerable amount of information on the reinforcement of nibs. The designer often has to consider the strength of continuous nibs supporting regularly or irregularly spaced discrete loads, e.g. from double tees. In this condition, a global case, supposing failure of the complete nib in bending and shear, as well as local bending and shear failure modes beneath the discrete loads, should be considered.

5.2.8.1 *General*
See above.

5.2.8.2 *Area of tension reinforcement*
See above.

5.2.8.3 *Position of tension reinforcement*
See above.

5.2.8.4 *Design shear resistance*

5.2.8.5 *Links in the member from which the nib projects*
This "hang up steel" is important and should also be considered in any design where primary beams are loaded away from supports by secondary beams.

5.3 Structural connections between precast units

5.3.1 General
It is necessary to consider all aspects of joint requirements at an early stage in design. Note the emphasis placed on the need to consider both strength and stability during the construction and erection stages. Several failures have occurred in precast concrete construction in the past, because of lack of consideration of the erection procedure prevailing on site.

5.3.2. Design of connection

5.3.2.1 *Methods*
The use of tests will be quite common. It is difficult to justify all the design requirements of joints, anchorage, bursting, bearing, etc., with the design data currently available. In many cases, compliance with these data will result in a cumbersome and heavy design. Although it is not commonly thought necessary, the same degree of attention given to the analysis in detail of in situ connections, e.g. beam to column joints, will give similar difficulties of justification. A test justification will be of great assistance in proving the correct interaction of the internal member force lines.

5.3.2.2 *Manufacturing and construction*
A designer familiar with the processes and techniques of precasting will consider the points mentioned in the clause. Advice should, in other cases, be sought from an experienced manufacturer or, at the tender stage, his input should be welcomed. Reference 5.12 gives many simple tips for good detailing.

5.3.2.3 *Design for protection*
See **5.1.9**.

5.3.3 Instructions to site
The strength and stability of precast concrete structures generally depend very much on the connections and on the way they are made; mention has already been made of the influence that workmanship and tolerances can have on strength. It is vital, therefore, that clear and detailed instructions, preferably on the drawings, are passed from the designer to the manufacturer and erector to ensure that the joints are adequately made. Instructions should also be passed on with regard to the various factors mentioned in **5.3.2**.

5.3.4 Continuity of reinforcement

5.3.4.1 *General*
The engineer's attention is drawn to the necessity to establish clearly what function is expected from each joint generally and, in this particular case, what is the function of the reinforcement through the joint; i.e. is it to provide full moment continuity, or partial continuity in helping to control cracking and deflection, or simply part of the tie force requirements of **5.1.8**. Various acceptable ways of achieving continuity are listed; these are covered in detail in subsequent clauses, but in general it should be noted that the detailing rules contained in **3.12** should be obeyed.

5.3.4.2 *Lapping of bars*
For flexural members where continuity of reinforcement is required through a joint between precast floor slabs or beams, the most common details are illustrated in Figure H5.3. For details (a) and (b), **5.3.4.2** states that the lap requirements of **3.12.8** should be satisfied. The biggest problem here is that vertical links will be required in the support

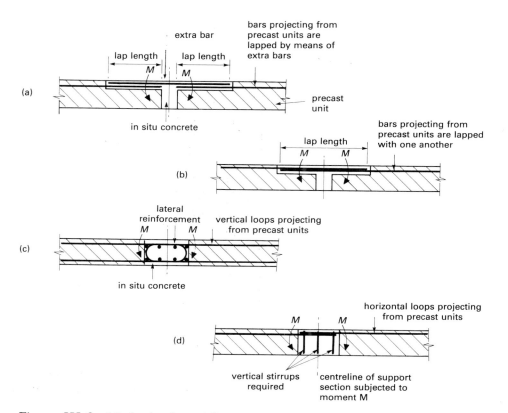

Figure H5.3: Methods of providing continuity of reinforcement for precast floors and beams.

zone generally and the main reinforcement must be contained within these; this can create practical problems on site in achieving the required lap lengths, as these links will be cast into the precast units.

Details (c) and (d) show in general terms the more popular alternative solution of achieving continuity of reinforcement through loops. In general, detail (c) is preferable to (d) both on technical and practical grounds (see reference 5.13). The bearing stresses inside the loops have to be limited in accordance with **3.12.8.25**. To comply with these bearing stresses under the ultimate loads, empirical rules based on test data are given in Figure H5.4 for proportioning vertical loops in flextural zones such as those shown in Figure H5.3. If h_o is less than 14 ϕ, straight portions should be added to the loops to transfer some of the tension force in the bars by bond. Lateral reinforcement of the type idealized in Figure H5.3(c) should be provided through the loops, and a loop from one precast unit should generally be adjacent to a similar loop from the other unit, i.e. the loops should not be too staggered across the width of the joint. There is no clear evidence that the presence of lateral reinforcement in the form of dowels, as shown in Figure H5.3(c), enhances bearing capacity by more than about 15–20%, but it should be included in any case, partly to comply with **5.1.7** and to ensure more ductile behaviour near failure.

It is necessary to roughen the sides of substantial grout pockets into which reinforcement is to be embedded; this is to guard against the tendency of the grout to shrink away from the sides of the pocket; an example of where this would be necessary is shown in

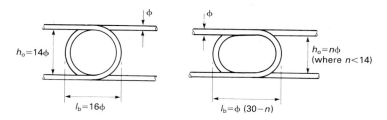

Figure H5.4: Empirical detailing rules for achieving continuity of reinforcement with vertical loop bars.

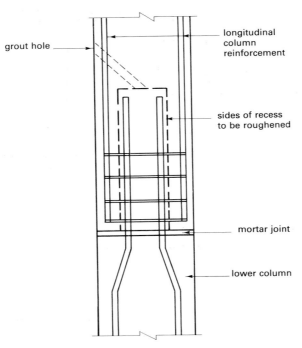

Figure H5.5: Example of where a grout recess would need its sides roughened (a joint between two large columns subject to mainly axial load).

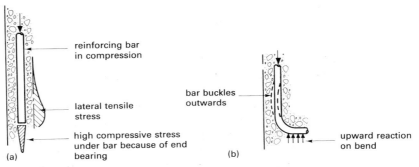

Figure H5.6: Problems at ends of compression bars (a) *stress distribution in concrete,* (b) *effect of bending or hooking compression bars.*

Figure H5.5. A point to note from Figure H5.5 is the way in which the longitudinal bars have been detailed at the end of the column. There is some test evidence to indicate that the load transfer mechanism between bars in compression and the surrounding concrete is partly by bond and partly by end bearing[5.14]. This causes high compressive stresses immediately under the bar and lateral tensile stresses which can lead to vertical splitting (Figure H5.6). The problem is made worse if the compression bar is hooked or bent (Figure H5.6) because this increases the tendency for the bar to buckle outwards. The best solution is that adopted in Figure H5.8; this problem is dealt with in considerable detail in reference 5.14.

5.3.4.3 *Reinforcement grouted into aperture*
Figure H5.5 gives an example where a tension capacity may need to be considered, to comply for example with the tie requirements of **3.12.3.7**.

5.3.4.4 *Overlapping reinforcement loops*
See **5.3.4.2**.

5.3.4.5 *Sleeving*
The two types of sleeving permitted by **5.3.4.5** are shown schematically in Figure H5.7. Research has been carried out on the type (1) sleeve, whose principal advantage is the

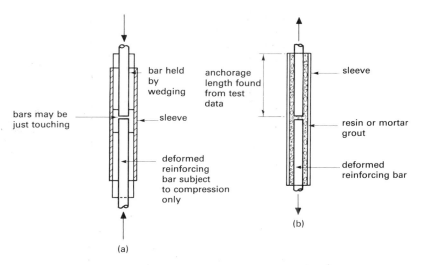

Figure H5.7: Types of connection referred to in 5.3.4.5 – (a) compression sleeve,
(b) compression and tension sleeve.

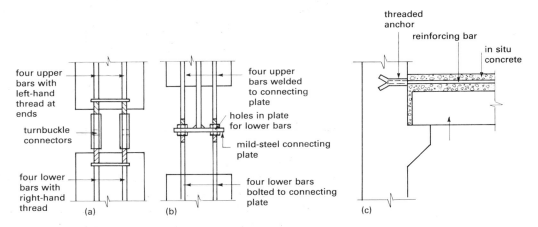

Figure H5.8: Examples of types of threading referred to in 5.3.4.6.

low anchorage length achieved by some resin mortars (see references 5.16 and 5.17); the design of this type of connection can be carried out only by referring to the test data [5.13 and 5.15–5.18]. However, the fire resistance requirement may preclude the use of resin mortars. Commercial mechanical splices of type (2) are currently available, all of them backed by test data. The manufacturer's instructions and the recommendations of **5.3.4.5** should be followed carefully in designing both types of connection.

5.3.4.6 Threading of reinforcement

Examples of the three methods referred to in this clause for using threaded bars are shown in Figure H5.8. The first two methods (parts (a) and (b) respectively of Figure H5.8) are generally used for joining precast columns, where they have the practical advantage of getting the units off the crane quickly. Tests have been carried out to study the strength of this type of connection when the columns are subjected to axial loads[5.15].

These are by no means the only methods of joining precast columns. Threaded anchorages can obviously be used in a wide range of situations in precast concrete work; Figure H5.8 merely shows one possible application. In general, the strength of such a special connection should be determined by tests and by reference to Clause **3.12.8.16.2**.

5.3.4.7 Strength of threaded couplings

See above.

5.3.4.8 Welding of bars

Some useful information on particular uses of welding in precast concrete work generally can be found in references 5.19–5.21.

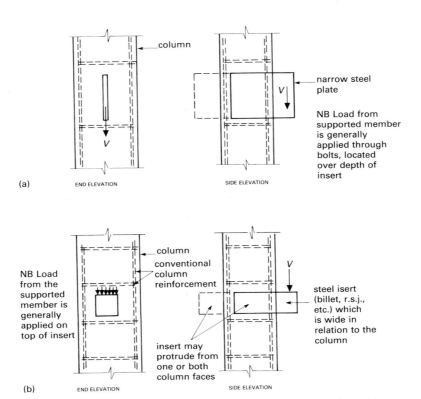

Figure H5.9: Basic types of connection using structural steel inserts.

5.3.5 Connections other than those involving continuity of reinforcement

5.3.5.1 *Joints with structural steel inserts*

A clear distinction has to be drawn at the design stage between the two basic types of possible connection. These are illustrated in Figure H5.9 which shows a narrow plate embedded in a column, to which a smaller plate in the end of the supported beam will be bolted or otherwise connected. In considering the design of this connection, it is best to refer to the specialist literature (notably reference 5.22); the behaviour is somewhat analogous to the behaviour of end blocks with low y_{po}/y_o ratios, in that it is dominated by the tendency of the narrow steel plate to split the column. However, it has been shown[5.22] that an end block approach is not very successful for design as the strength is also influenced by shrinkage effects at the bottom of the plate and by the precise location of transverse links in the column.

The behaviour of the more common type of connection shown in Figure H5.9 (b) is controlled by distribution of bearing stresses underneath the steel insert. An excellent general treatment of the design problems associated with this type of connection is given in reference 5.23 which is based on American design practice and on certain simplifying assumptions. If the insert protrudes from two opposite sides of the column and the imposed loads on each side are equal, design is relatively simple, since **5.2.3.4** permits a uniform bearing stress of up to $0.8 f_{cu}$ under the ultimate loads. Consideration should be given to the loads imposed on the concrete in the column from the structure above the joint and, if designing to the upper stress limitation, the provision of additional column links immediately beneath the steel insert should also be considered.

The rigorous design of a single steel insert of the type shown in Figure H5.9 (b) can be complex because the distribution of bearing stress in the concrete under the insert is not known. However, a simple design solution can be obtained from the assumed force system shown in Figure H5.10 where the bearing stresses are taken to be uniform along the lengths l_2 and l_3. The values of V_u, l_1, (from **5.3.5.1**) and b (from practical considerations) will be known initially and l_2 may be calculated from:

$$l_2 = \frac{V_u}{b_1 \times 0.8 f_{cu}}$$

This enables the steel insert to be designed (i.e. h_1 to be determined) to resist a

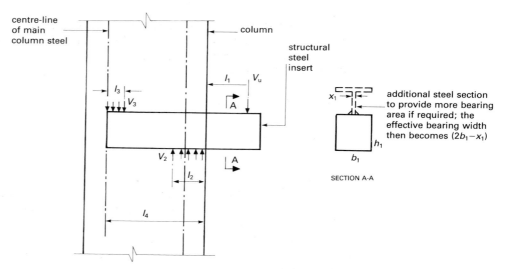

Figure H5.10: Force system for design of single steel inserts for columns.

moment equal to $V_u(l_1+l_2)$; shear at the column face would also require checking. It is then necessary to calculate V_3 and l_3. This may be done by taking moments about the line of action of V_2, thus:

$$0.8f_{cu}b_1l_3(l_4-1/2\ l_2-1/2\ l_3)=V_u\ (l_1+1/2\ l_2)$$

This gives a quadratic equation in terms of l_3. The design may then be considered satisfactory if $l_2<0.6(l_4-1/2\ l_3)$, i.e. if the bearing stress areas do not overlap. Note that, in lightly loaded columns, it may be necessary to provide the tying-down force V_3 by welding vertical reinforcing bars to the steel insert and anchoring them in the column underneath. The width b will generally be governed by practical considerations; i.e. it must fit inside the column reinforcement cage and allow the concrete to be placed and compacted and the width should not exceed one-third of the column width. If there is then insufficient bearing area to satisfy the inequality given above, additional bearing may be provided by welding on additional steel sections as shown in Figure H5.10 (Section A-A).

In practice, many types of structural steel insert can be used and each should be considered carefully in the light of the above general comments. It is considered that, with many of these, higher bearing stresses could be carried successfully, especially if additional column links were provided.

A common design problem is that of a billet protruding from each side of a column carrying different loads on each side. This would occur if spans are not equal on each side of the column. In this case the stiffness of the insert is of importance and the design

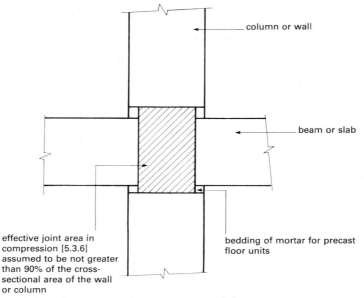

Figure H5.11: Effective joint area for compression joints (5.3.6).

120

problem becomes statically indeterminate. Very stiff inserts will carry the load in bearing with a variable but linear stress across the column, like a pad foundation. Flexible billets may impose vertical bearing stresses in the upward direction in the centre of the column. More research is required in this area and design should have experimental backing.

5.3.5.2 *Resin adhesives*

5.3.5.3 *Other types*

5.3.6 Joints transmitting mainly compression

The strength of this type of connection may be assessed by the methods given in **3.8** or **3.9** as appropriate, provided that a reduced effective area is assumed for the joint. The reduced area, assessed in accordance with sub-clause (a), is illustrated in Figure H5.11. Where the precast floor units intrude well into the joint and sub-clause (a) becomes restrictive, then sub-clause (b) comes into operation, but only where the floor or beam units are solid over the bearing area.

A detailed study of the factors influencing the strength and behaviour of horizontal joints in compression is given in references 5.14 and 5.24.

In designing horizontal joints at the top and bottom of walls or columns, **3.9.4.18** makes no specific recommendations with regard to forces acting at right-angles to the wall. It is suggested that there is no need to check the resistance of such joints to lateral forces provided that the calculated horizontal shear is less than 25% of the normal compressive force acting on the joint. Where this is not so, it will be necessary to consider the design of the joint in accordance with the provision of **5.3.7 (d)**.

5.3.7 Joints transmitting shear

In precast concrete construction usually involving the use of fairly wide floor or wall slabs, the design concept for the structure as a whole may be such that a number of these slabs may be required to act together to transmit forces in the plane of the units in the direction of their span: one of the examples quoted in the clause is that of floor units acting as a wind girder in transmitting lateral loads acting on the sides of a building back to an in situ concrete core designed specifically to carry these.

To achieve this full diaphragm action it is necessary to design the joints between the units to carry shear forces acting in the plane of the units themselves. Five alternative methods of design are given in **5.3.7**, one of which must be followed. The methods are presented in order of increasing shear resistance requirements; precast units with smooth surfaces and no reinforcement across the joint between them are allowed to transmit only very small shear forces [sub-clause (a)]. In sub-clause (c), steel provided from considerations of stability may be considered to be sufficient to prevent separation of the units. If reinforcement is provided so that it can develop its design strength, high shears can be carried [sub-clause (d)]; in this case, too, account may be taken of any normal compressive force acting on the joint, thus giving a modified value for F_b. The design method presented in sub-clause (d) is based on the 'shear-friction hypothesis' developed by Mast[5.25] which is a design method capable of providing a conservative solution to a number of apparently different problems in designing structural joints for precast concrete construction. For example, Mast has developed it for use in designing concrete corbels and also for the horizontal shear connection problem in composite T-beams.

5.4 Composite concrete construction

5.4.1 General

This section applies to flexural members consisting of precast concrete units acting together with in situ concrete to carry the imposed loads. The essential requirement, therefore, is that the two concretes should act as one effective section; if this can be achieved, then the resulting composite section may be designed in accordance with the requirements of Section **3** or **4** as appropriate. **5.4** therefore gives the necessary *additional* requirements to ensure composite action and also deals with those special problems that can arise because the two concretes are cast at different times. However, only general recommendations can be made, as the types of composite section can vary a great deal in practice.

5.4.2 Analysis and design of composite concrete structures and members

5.4.3 Effects of construction methods
It is important to bear in mind the need to pass appropriate instructions to site (**5.3.3**).

5.4.4 Relative stiffness of members
This can be of significance in situations where concrete is poured as a structural infill or topping between and on precast units.

5.4.5 Assessment of strengths of sections of precast pre-tensioned units designed as continuous members
On many occasions the support section will be designed as reinforced to carry hogging moments. In this situation, prestress may be ignored in the compression zone at the ultimate limit state. If no redistribution of moment is carried out, it is likely that at the serviceability limit state the compressive stresses are low, spalling will not occur and creep will be low. Such a section will not need a concrete stress check at the serviceability limit state. If compressive stresses are high, i.e. the transmission length may be short compared with the span, some debonding of prestressing tendons may be necessary. In any event it is important to recognise the problems discussed in the commentary to **5.2.6.1**.

5.4.6 Serviceability limit states

5.4.6.1 *Serviceability*

5.4.6.1.1 *General*

5.4.6.1.2 *Prestressed precast units.*
The starting point in designing a prestressed concrete member will generally be the serviceability limit state involving the use of permissible compressive stresses as given in **4.3.4.2**. Provided it can be shown that failure would be of the under-reinforced type, **5.4.6.1.2** allows an increase in these stresses of up to 50%; this applies particularly to the situation where the prestressed unit is unpropped. This means that the maximum compressive stress under all loads can be permitted to reach a value of $0.5f_{cu}$. As a substantial proportion of this stress will be due to permanent loads, it is suggested that this enhanced stress should be used with caution and for particular situations where the detrimental effects due to possible excessive creep will be less severe. It has been common practice in bridge design in recent years to apply this enhancement allowance as shown in Figure H5.12. For those situations shown in Figure H5.12 (a), the full stress value of $0.5f_{cu}$ could be used; in Figure H5.12 (b) a 25%

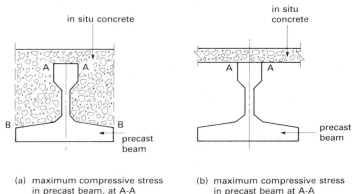

(a) maximum compressive stress in precast beam, at A-A is $0.5 f_{cu}$

(b) maximum compressive stress in precast beam at A-A is $0.42 f_{cu}$

Figure H5.12: Suggested enhanced compressive stress values in composite beams for different forms of construction.

increase of up to $0.42f_{cu}$ is suggested. For other intermediate cases the level of stress allowed should depend mainly on the amount of lateral restraint provided to the compression flange of the precast beam by the in situ concrete.

5.4.6.2 *Tension in in situ concrete*

5.4.6.2.1 *Prestressed precast units in direct contact with in situ concrete.* The presence of a prestressed flange on the tension side of added concrete (as at B-B in Figure H5.12 (a)) considerably retards the formation of cracking of that concrete. The stress levels given in Table 5.4 should ensure that no significant flexural cracking due to the imposed loads will have occurred in the in situ concrete at level B-B in Figure H5.12 (a) and therefore the two concretes should continue to act as one composite section. The tensile stresses given in Table 5.4 may be increased by up to 50% (provided that the permissible tensile stress in the prestressed concrete beam is reduced by the same numerical amount) and therefore more prestress is required; this recognises the fact that the greater the level of prestress at the contact surface, the greater is the apparent enhancement to the tensile strain capacity of the added concrete.

5.4.6.2.2 *Prestressed precast units not in direct contact with in situ concrete.* For the situation illustrated in Figure H5.12 (b) the in situ concrete top flange should be treated strictly as a reinforced concrete section subjected to any local transverse bending and designed in accordance with **3.4.7**.

5.4.6.3 *Tension in prestressed precast units*

This is of relevance if the prestressed unit has thin exposed webs where cracks could be a visual or durability problem. So long as reinforcement is provided in the units or in the composite infill, tension in prestressed units is less of a problem in construction of the type shown in Figure H5.12 (a).

Where continuity for live loading is achieved by placing reinforcement in the in situ concrete top flange and designing the support section to be reinforced, this will certainly induce tensile stresses in the top of the prestressed beams (A-A in Figure H5.13) under the service loads and **5.4.6.3** suggests that these stresses be limited in accordance with **4.3.4**. Even if a full allowance is made for transmission length and loss of prestress, this may be rather restrictive in design if straight tendons are used. It would not seem unreasonable, for the type of section in Figure H5.12 (a) only, to treat the ends of these prestressed units as being Class 3 under full service loading, as any cracking will be limited by the requirements of **3.4.7** for the support section and will be remote from the prestressing tendons; if this suggestion is adopted, it should apply only to a length on either side of the support centre-line approximately equal to twice the overall section depth at the supports. Another solution to this problem would be to taper the top surface of the prestressed unit towards the support.

5.4.6.4 *Differential shrinkage*

5.4.6.4.1 *General.* If an in situ concrete floor slab is cast on an older precast unit, the two concretes tend to shrink at different rates, because much of the creep and shrinkage strain in the precast member will have taken place before the connection is made. The effect of this is to induce secondary stresses in the composite section as a whole, the most critical of which is likely to be the tensile stress induced in the bottom of the precast

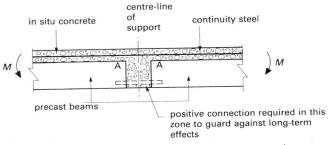

Figure H5.13: Continuity in composite construction.

unit, which could be important if the section is designed right up to the limiting stresses in **4.3.4.3**.

As suggested in **5.4.6.4.1** these effects are not generally of great significance in most practical cases for simply-supported members. They are likely to be worse if the precast unit is prestressed, where the stress in the top fibre (i.e. at the interface) due to prestress is near zero, because the greatest differential strain movement between the two concretes will occur in this circumstance. It is suggested that, even then, these effects require investigation only if there is a difference of more than one strength grade between the two concretes and if the time interval between casting the precast unit and placing the in situ concrete is more than about 8 weeks. The type of composite cross-section most susceptible to these effects is the composite T-beam illustrated in Figure H5.12 (b).

5.4.6.4.2 *Calculation of tensile stress.* A method for evaluating differential shrinkage effects is given in reference 5.26 which also gives some indication of how the differential shrinkage coefficient, referred to in **5.4.6.4.2**, can be evaluated for design purposes for various types of section. Further information is given in reference 5.27.

5.4.6.4.3 *Approximate value of differential shrinkage coefficient for building in a normal environment.* See above.

5.4.7 Ultimate limit state

This section is a major departure in BS 8110 when compared with the previous method of shear connection design. The method of CP110 was based on elastic section analysis and was thought appropriate therefore for the serviceability loadings.

This new method involves the forces acting at the ultimate limit state as this is the appropriate limit state for the mechanism. The intention was not to make any change with respect to safety factors and this and the old CP 110 method were intended to produce similar results.

Reference 5.28 provides full details of the source of the new design method.

5.4.7.1 *Horizontal shear force due to design ultimate loads*

The analytical method requires a different approach depending on the position of the compression zone relative to the plane under consideration. There may be occasions where the plane under consideration is so low in the tension zone that **5.4.7.1 (a)** is very conservative. In those cases, only the tension carried across the plane in shear needs to be considered.

5.4.7.2 *Average horizontal design shear stress*

The definitions in Table 5.5 are intended to represent real practical surfaces rather than idealised and unrepresentative surfaces mentioned in previous codes. The as cast or as extruded finishes are deliberately introduced to cover the finish produced by slip form or extrusion machines now commonly used to produce prestressed slab units.

In bridge construction the term "rough as cast" is often used to describe surfaces at the top of the conventional cast where the vibrator is removed leaving a very rough surface with large aggregate particles on the surface. Where bridge beams with this finish are incorporated into buildings, the horizontal stresses from the roughest category in Table 5.5 are appropriate.

5.4.7.3 *Nominal links*

5.4.7.4 *Links in excess of minimum*

5.4.7.5 *Vertical shear*

5.4.7.5.1 *General.* Reinforced concrete composite members may be designed by using **3.4.5** and, as long as there is adequate longitudinal shear connection between the concretes, the gross section may be used in the design.

The design of prestressed concrete composite members is a little more complicated

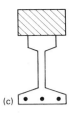

Figure H5.14: Composite sections considered in designing for shear (5.4.7) – (a) original member, (b) with composite infill, (c) with composite topping.

than the design of non-composite prestressed concrete members and the simplified methods in **4.3.8** do not necessarily apply.

The assessment of V_{co}, the shear capacity of a member uncracked in flexure, in **4.3.8** assumes that the member carries all the shear in its web and that the critical point of maximum principal tensile stress is at the centroid. In composite construction, it is ideally necessary to check all possible critical sections and to ensure that the principal tensile stress of all the structural concrete in the member is less than the permitted value of $0.24\sqrt{f_{cu}}$. When in situ concrete is placed between precast prestressed concrete members, the precast concrete provides restraint to the infill and increases its capacity to carry tension. In these cases, therefore, it is generally considered satisfactory to check only the principal tensile stress in the precast concrete. For most practical cases, it will be found that the precast part of the composite section is capable of carrying all the ultimate shear load, and this is all that the Code requires. Further complete checks, on the composite section as a whole, will be required only if the ratio of imposed loading to dead loading is exceptionally high.

The shear force at which flexure–shear cracks form, V_{cr}, may also be calculated by using **4.3.8**. It is necessary to consider each composite section on its merits when deciding how much of it is resisting shear. Figure H5.14 (a) shows an original precast prestressed member that is incorporated into a composite member in two ways: in Figure H5.14 (b) it has composite infill and in Figure H5.14 (c) it has composite topping. In (b), the infill concrete may crack before the original member and the post-cracking shear strength of the infill may not necessarily add to the gross shear strength of the member.

It is therefore wise to make some reduction in the infill concrete shear in calculating flexure–shear strength, the amount of the reduction depending on whether the infill is restrained between precast members or restrained by reinforcement cast into the precast member.

When the composite member has a structural topping, as in Figure H5.14 (c), the flexure–shear capacity, V_{cr}, may be calculated by using the gross section depth and the web width of the original member because, in this case, the additional concrete has been placed in an area where it can add to the shear strength of the member.

5.4.7.5.2 *In situ concrete between precast prestressed units.* See above.

5.4.8 Differential shrinkage between added concrete and precast members

5.4.9 Thickness of structural topping

5.4.10 Workmanship

REFERENCES

5.1 SOMERVILLE, G. Some loading tests on double-T floor units. London, Cement and Concrete Association, July 1965. Technical Report 391. 15 pp.

5.2 SPARKE, A.N. Distribution tests on hollow box precast floors. Civil Engineering and Public Works Review. Vol.62, No.726. January 1966. pp.83-86.

5.3 LAGUE, D.J. Load distribution tests on precast prestressed hollow-core slab construction. Journal of the Prestressed Concrete Institute. Vol.16, No.6. November-December 1971. pp.10-18.

5.4 INSTITUTION OF STRUCTURAL ENGINEERS. Structural joints in precast concrete. London. 56 pp. 1978.

5.5 WILLIAMS A. The bearing capacity of concrete loaded over a limited area. Cement and Concrete Association. 1979. Technical Report 526. 70pp.

5.6 HAWKINS, N.M. The bearing strength of concrete loaded through rigid plates. Magazine of Concrete Research. Vol.20, No.62. March 1968. pp.31-40.

5.7 HAWKINS, N.M. The bearing strength of concrete loaded through flexible plates. Magazine of Concrete Research. Vol.20,, No.63. June 1968. pp.95-102.

5.8 KRIZ, L.B. and RATHS, C.H. Connections in precast concrete structures – bearing strength of column heads. Journal of the Prestressed Concrete Institute. Vol.8, No.6. December 1963. pp.45-75.

5.9 GERGELEY, P. and SOZEN, M.A. Design of anchorage zone reinforcement in prestressed concrete beams. Journal of the Prestressed Concrete Institute. Vol.12, No.2. April 1967. pp.63-75.

5.10 SOMERVILLE, G. The behaviour and design of reinforced concrete corbels. London. Cement and Concrete Association, August 1972. Technical Report 472. 12pp.

5.11 CLARKE, J.L. Behaviour and design of small nibs. Cement and Concrete Association, 1976. Technical Report 512. 8 pp.

5.12 RICHARDSON, J.G. Precast concrete production. Viewpoint Publications, 1973. 232 pp.

5.13 FRANZ, G. The connexion of precast elements with loops. Proceedings of a symposium on design philosophy and its application to precast concrete, London, 1967. London, Cement and Concrete Association, 1968. pp.63-66.

5.14 SOMERVILLE, G. Horizontal compression joints in precast concrete frame structures. Thesis submitted to the City University for the degree of PhD, December 1971. 196 pp.

5.15 SOMERVILLE, G. and BURHOUSE, P. Test on joints between precast concrete members. Garston, Building Research Station, 1966. Current papers Engineering series 45. 18 pp.

5.16 IGONIN, L.A. Glued joints for reinforcing bars and precast reinforced concrete units. London, Civil Engineering Research Association, 1965. CERA Translation No. 1, 16 pp.

5.17 MARKESTAD, A. and JOHANSEN, K. Jointing reinforcing steel with resin mortars. Nordisk Betong. Vol. 14, No. 1. 1970. pp.79-93.

5.18 IVEY, D.L. Fatigue of grouted sleeve reinforcing bar splices. Proceedings of the American Society of Civil Engineers. Vol.94, No.ST1, January 1968. pp.199-210,

5.19 TOPRAC, A.A. and THOMPSON, J.N. Welding between precast concrete units. Journal of the Prestressed Concrete Institute. Vol.8, No.3, June 1963. pp.14-29.

5.20 LEBEL, L.M. and KNYAZHEVICH, M.G. Investigations of joints of precast reinforced concrete slabs. Beton i Zhelezobeton. No.2. 1969. pp.82-85. Translated from the Russian. Garston, Building Research Station, May 1970. Library Communication 983. 7 pp.

5.21 HANSON, N.W. and CONNER, H.W. Seismic resistance of reinforced concrete beam-column joints. Proceedings of the American Society of Civil Engineers. Vol.93, No.ST5. October 1967. pp.533-560.

5.22 HOLMES, M. and POSNER, C.D. Factors affecting the strength of steel plate connections between precast concrete elements. The Structural Engineer. Vol.48, No.10. October 1970. pp.399-406.

5.23 PRESTRESSED CONCRETE INSTITUTE. Design handbook – precast and prestressed concrete. Chicago, Third Edition, 1985. 528 pp.

5.24 INTERNATIONAL COUNCIL FOR BUILDING RESEARCH STUDIES AND DOCUMENTATION (CIB). Proceedings on an international symposium on bearing walls, Warsaw 1969. Oslo, Norwegian Building Research Institute, 1970. 15 pp.

5.25 MAST, R.F. Auxiliary reinforcement in concrete connections. Proceedings of the American Society of Civil Engineers. Vol. 94, No.ST6. June 1968. pp.1485-1504.

5.26 KAJFASZ, S., SOMERVILLE, G. and ROWE, R.E. An investigation of the behaviour of composite concrete beams. London, Cement and Concrete Association, November 1963. Research Report 15. 44 pp.

5.27 BIRKELAND, H.W. Differential shrinkage in composite beams. Proceedings of the American Concrete Institute. Vol.56, No.11. May 1960, pp.1123-1136.

5.28 FEDERATION INTERNATIONALE DE LA PRECONTRAINTE. Shear at the interface of precast and in situ concrete. FIP, Wexham Springs, Slough. 1982. 31 pp.

SECTION SIX. CONCRETE: MATERIALS, SPECIFICATION AND CONSTRUCTION

6.1 Constituent materials of concrete

6.1.1 Choice and approval of materials

As with CP110, one of the basic principles of this Code continues to be that the Engineer must decide the essential factors to be specified, ideally in terms of readily measurable parameters or attributes required for the work (e.g. pumpability, freedom from bleeding etc). The concrete producer is then left with the greatest freedom possible to design the concrete mix to satisfy these requirements. The concrete producer will usually have more knowledge of the local materials, quality of cement, type and gradings of the aggregate, etc and hence should be in a good position to provide concrete having the desired performance characteristics.

Whilst making a clear preference for materials complying with, or selected from, a British Standard, the Code does allow the use of non-standard materials particularly where there are possible technical and cost benefits. However, with all materials, the Code emphasises the need for satisfactory data on their suitability and for assurance of quality control. The performance of concrete made with non-standard or unfamiliar materials and their suitability may be established on the basis of previous data, past experience or specific tests. Wherever possible, certificates of compliance with British or other clearly defined standards should be provided by the material supplier.

Unfamiliar materials or combinations of materials may produce concrete whose properties differ considerably from those with conventional materials. For example concretes containing ground granulated blastfurnace slag (ggbfs) or pulverized-fuel ash (pfa) have longer finishing times, which may be an advantage or a disadvantage.

6.1.1.1 Design

6.1.1.2 Materials

6.1.2 Cements, ground granulated blastfurnace slags and pulverized-fuel ashes

The British Standard *Glossary of building and civil engineering terms*, BS 6100:1984, defines Portland cement as "active hydraulic binder based on ground Portland cement clinker" and indicates that Portland cement is a general term for the various forms of Portland cement. In particular BS 12 covers the main ones, OPC and RHPC, BS 4027 covers SRPC and BS 1370 covers Low heat PC. In all these, no addition other than of gypsum or one agreed grinding aid (i.e. propylene glycol) is permitted. The next category of Portland cements covers Portland-blastfurnace cement (BS 146) and the corresponding Low heat Portland-blastfurnace cement (BS 4246) and Portland pfa cement (BS 6588). These cements are 'blended hydraulic cements' according to the definitions given in the respective British Standards and in the Glossary, BS 6100. However, it should be noted that they may be manufactured either by blending of the components or by intergrinding.

The materials themselves (i.e. pfa and ggbfs) are covered by British Standards viz: BS 3892: Part 1 for pfa and BS 6699:1986 for ggbfs. The only other cement permitted in BS 8110 is Supersulphated cement to BS 4248, which is not available in the UK.

In recent years, the potential advantages in some circumstances of combining Portland cement with either ggbfs or pfa have come to be realised. The recent amendments of BS 5328 have defined cement as a hydraulic binder which can be

(a) hydraulic cement that is an active hydraulic binder formed by grinding clinker to BS 12, BS1370 or BS 4027,

or

(b) hydraulic binder, manufactured by a controlled process in which Portland cement clinker or Portland cement is combined in specific proportions with a latent hydraulic binder consisting of pfa or ggbfs, to BS 6588, BS 146 or BS 4246, according to the latent hydraulic binder used, or

(c) hydraulic binder, manufactured in the concrete mixer by combining Portland cement to BS 12 with a latent hydraulic binder consisting of pfa to BS 3892:Part 1 or ggbfs to BS 6699, complying with the general requirements for proportions and properties given in BS 6588, BS 146 or BS 4246 according to the latent hydraulic binder used.

In line with this, the cements in BS 8110 are defined in terms of three categories as:

(1) Portland cement including ordinary, rapid hardening, low heat and sulphate-resisting (**6.1.2.1**(a));
(2) Cements containing ggbfs BS 146 and BS 4246 and cement containing pfa BS 6588 (**6.1.2.1**(b)). The availability of these cements varies throughout the UK;
(3) Combinations of Portland cement and ggbfs or pfa (**6.1.2.1**(d)).

The third category which permits combinations of Portland cements and ggbfs and pfa at the mixer (mixer-blends) is a new departure and care must be taken to ensure that such mixer-blends produce equivalent concretes to those made with the corresponding blended cements. When using mixer-blends the following principles apply:

(i) The relevant British Standard for blended cement should be used as the basis for comparison;
(ii) The mixer-blend combinations should generally be based on BS 12 cement;
(iii) The ggbfs and pfa should comply with appropriate British Standards:
BS 3892 Pulverized-fuel ash Part 1: Specification for pulverized-fuel ash for use as a cementitious component in structural concrete.
BS 6699:1986 Specification for ground granulated blastfurnace slag for use with Portland cement.
(iv) It is permitted in **6.2.4.3** to replace Portland cement with at least an equal weight of ggbfs or pfa. The cementing efficiences of these materials may be lower and **3.3.5.5** states that the total mass of Portland cement plus ggbfs or pfa may need to be increased to achieve a specified strength;
(v) Confirmation must be provided that combinations of cements and ggbfs or pfa conform with the properties of the corresponding blended cement.

Satisfactory performance can be judged either by tests of the combinations against the relevant blended cement standard or other performance tests in concrete.

There are many test data available on the use of ggbfs or pfa in concrete but care must be taken that where previous data are relied upon, the same materials and proportions are currently being used.

Certification procedures for the percentage of ggbfs and pfa which are now being provided by the suppliers of these materials along the following lines may provide an acceptable mechanism of confirmation:

"When blended in the combination $(100-X)\%$ BS 12 Portland cement and $X\%$ ggbfs (or pfa) complying with BS (. . .), the results confirm that for the period (. . .), the proportions and properties of this combination were in compliance with the physical and chemical requirements of BS (. . .), as determined in accordance with this procedure."

The performance, and particularly the durability, of concrete made with these materials can be considered as being equal to that of Portland cement concrete provided that the ggbfs or pfa concrete complies with the same grade as would be achieved by the Portland cement concrete (**3.3.5.5**). In order to obtain concrete of equal strength at 28 days, it may be necessary to increase the total mass of Portland cement+ggbfs or pfa compared with the mass of Portland cement in the concrete.

The properties of fresh and green blended hydraulic cement concretes are different from Portland cement concretes and construction practices may have to be modified to take these differences into account[6.1].

The use of the appropriate type of cement or ggbfs or pfa can assist in producing concrete with special properties related to durability as shown in Table H6.1.

Table H6.1 Concrete characteristics requiring the use of special cements, or ggbfs, or pfa

Property of concrete	Consider the use of cement to British Standard or the use of ggbfs or pfa	Further information
Early strength development	RHPC to BS 12 Ultra-high early strength Portland cement	–
Low heat evolution	BS 1370 BS 4246 BS 146 BS 6588 Combinations of OPC to BS 12 and ggbfs or pfa	–
Improved resistance to sulphate attack	BS 4027 BS 4248 Combinations of OPC to BS 12 and ggbfs, 70%–90% or pfa, 25%–40%	see **6.2.3.3** BRE Digest 250
Improved resistance to alkali-silica reaction	Use low alkali cement (less than 0.6% equivalent Na_2O) Combinations of OPC to BS 12 and ggbfs, at least 50% or pfa, at least 30%	see **6.2.5.4** BRE Digest 258 see references 6.1, 6.2, 6.3, 6.4

6.1.2.1 *General*

6.1.2.2 *Properties of concrete made with cements containing ggbfs or pfa*

6.1.2.3 *Combinations of cements and ggbfs or pfa*

6.1.2.3.1 *Proportions and production*

6.1.2.3.2 *Performance and suitability for purpose*

6.1.2.4 *Cements for sulphate-resisting concrete*
This clause reflects the fact that if a proportion of SRPC is replaced with an equal weight of pfa, the sulphate resistance of the resulting concrete may be reduced. However if the higher minimum cement and maximum water/cement ratio of the OPC (BS 12)/pfa combination is adopted, an SRPC(BS 4027)/pfa mix should give adequate durability.

6.1.2.5 *Cements for low heat concrete*

6.1.3 Aggregates

6.1.3.1 *General*
The aggregates covered by the Code comprise all types of materials classified in terms of their density as:

Normal-weight (particle density 2000–3000kg/m^3)
Lightweight (particle density less than 2000kg/m^3)
Heavyweight (particle density greater than 3000kg/m^3)

6.1.3.2 *Aggregate specifications*
Wherever possible the Code prefers aggregates complying with the appropriate British Standard but other materals may be used provided there are satisfactory data on the properties of concrete made with them.
Here again, the emphasis is on 'performance in concrete'. For example suitable gradings

are not laid down; the requirement being that the overall grading should be such as to produce concrete of the required workability and finishability which can be placed and properly compacted into position without the use of excessive mixing water and resultant 'bleeding'.

Where necessary, special aggregate characteristics can be defined by reference to the appropriate British Standard or other authoritative documents as shown in Table H6.2.

Table H6.2 Choice or limitation of aggregate characteristics

Aggregate characteristics	Choice or limitations		Further information
Nominal maximum size	20mm	Suitable for most uses	
	40mm	Thick or lightly reinforced sections	
	10, 14mm	Thin or heavily reinforced sections	
Grading	Variations from relevant BS accommodated by concrete mix design		BS 5328
	Separate fine and coarse aggregate for strength grade C20 and above		
Shell content	Accommodated in concrete mix design		BS 882
Flakiness	Dependent on aggregate type and concrete grade		BS 882
Dimensional change	Higher initial drying shrinkage with high moisture movement aggregates (e.g. Scottish dolorites or whinstones)		BRE Digest 35
Fire resistance	For high degrees of fire resistance, limestones or lightweight aggregates may be needed		BS 8110 Pt. 2 Section 4
Wear resistance	Heavy duty grade aggregate for industrial floors		BS 882
Density	Special aggregates required for high or low density concretes		BS 8110 Pt. 2 Section 5
High strength	Each aggregate has ceiling strength for a given particle size. Crushed rock aggregates may be necessary for concrete grades above 60N/mm^2.		

6.1.4 Water

BS 3148 includes requirements for the testing of water for its suitability for use in concrete. However it does not give any limits with which the water should comply although some suggestions for the interpretation on the test results are given in an Appendix.

Water suitable for drinking is suitable for concrete. Where, however, untreated water is obtained from the ground surface after having passed through organic materials such as peat, it would be advisable to test it before using it in concrete. Water from deep boreholes is generally satisfactory in the UK.

6.1.5 Admixtures

6.1.5.1 *General*

The Code fully recognises the contribution which admixtures can make to improve certain properties of concrete by their chemical and/or physical effects. The British Standard for admixtures BS 5075 gives specific requirements for accelerating, retarding, water reducing, air-entraining admixtures and superplasticizers.

It is important to appreciate that the behaviour of one or more admixtures in a concrete mix depends upon their interaction with the particular cement and aggregate materials being used. If these materials are changed the behaviour of the admixtures may be very different.

The frost resistance of concrete depends to a large extent on its permeability, and the provision of adequate curing and the degree of saturation of the concrete when exposed to frost. Concretes with a high degree of saturation and subject to de-icing salts have increased risk of frost damage.

In such cases air entrainment should be specified in terms of the average air content of concrete in accordance with **6.2.3.2**.

The limitations on the total chloride content in concrete given in **6.2.5.2** are supported by limitations on the chloride ion content of admixtures which should not exceed 2% by mass of the admixture or 0.03% by mass of the cement when used in prestressed or reinforced concrete with any type of cement, or unreinforced concrete with cements complying with BS 4027 and BS 4248.

6.1.5.2 *Admixture specifications*

6.1.5.3 *Approval and performance of admixtures*

6.1.5.4 *Concrete durability*
Any chloride ion in the admixture should be included in the calculation of the total chloride contents in Table 6.4.

The Na_2O equivalent in any admixture should be included in the calculation of the total alkali content (**6.2.5.4**).

6.1.5.5 *Air-entraining agents*

6.2 Durability of structural concrete

This section treats all aspects of design to achieve durability and therefore gives a broader perspective than, for example, Sections **3.3** and **4.12** which are concerned specifically with the requirements for cover and concrete quality, particularly as they influence sizing of sections at the design stage. Design also means identifying the structural form and constituent materials appropriate to the life-time and environment.

In addition to the general environment (**6.2.3.1** and as defined in more detail in **3.3.4**), "freezing and thawing and de-icing salts" (**6.2.3.2**) and "exposure to aggressive chemicals" (**6.2.3.3**) are identified as other broad types of exposure condition.

6.2.1 General

6.2.2 Design for durability
As indicated in the Code in Clause **2.1.1**, durability is an aspect of the structure that has to be considered carefully and consciously taken account of in design. This implies a consideration of facets of design, materials and construction, and a convenient check list for these in the different stages is:

Design	–	assessment of environmental conditions during expected life
	–	geometry of structure and sections to improve weathering properties, i.e. control of flow of water
	–	cover to reinforcement and its adequacy
	–	depending on severity of environment, surface protection to concrete
Materials	–	constituents and their quality
	–	mix proportions
Construction	–	mixing, placing and compaction of concrete
	–	curing
	–	accuracy of formwork

- achieving the specified cover
- appropriate quality assurance procedures.

6.2.2.1 *Shape and bulk of concrete*
The emphasis should be on ensuring good drainage of water and the avoidance of standing pools and rundown water. Equally the cracks referred to are not those controlled by the clauses in Section **3** but those which may occur when the chosen geometry and bulk of the section make them virtually unavoidable – in other words, badly designed!

The particular aspects requiring attention as regards the cover have been taken into account in deriving Table 3.4 and no further adjustments are necessary.

6.2.2.2 *Depth of concrete cover and concrete quality*
The alkaline environment provided by fresh concrete protects reinforcement. From experience, appropriate combinations of cover and concrete quality ensure that in well defined environments the effects of carbonation of the concrete and of penetration of chlorides do not lead to unacceptable corrosion of the reinforcement during the expected life of the structure or component (**2.1.1**). Within limits, a trade-off is possible between free water/cement ratio, cement content and thickness of concrete cover to achieve the same nominal protection, except that for more severe exposure conditions the available combinations become more restricted.

The cover for a given strength, using the reduced concrete grades given in **3.3.5.2**, and exposure condition, e.g. Table 3.4, is broadly in line with that in Table 19 of CP110 except for increases of 5mm for mild and moderate exposure of lower concrete grades. These increases reflect concern that the durability of some buildings is proving less than had been anticipated. Variability of strength tends to be greater at lower grades and typical variations in cover have proportionately greater effect at lower covers. These influences are significant together only for mild and moderate exposure. In addition, however, restrictions are placed on minimum cement content and maximum free water/cement ratio to provide adequate impermeability for the particular thickness of cover. Although compliance with compressive strength can be demonstrated, compliance with limits for water/cement ratio and cement content is difficult to demonstrate, especially in hardened concrete. Based on analysis of a substantial number of records from ready mixed concrete plants (**6.5**) it is possible to specify a lowest grade of concrete which, if achieved, will ensure the limits on cement and water/cement ratio for 95% of materials in current use. The inclusion of these 'lowest grades' in Tables 3.4 and 4.8 represents a practical approach to achieving compliance with the necessary quality of concrete, although it should not be taken to imply that durability is a function only of compressive strength. It follows that the reduced values of grade in Clause **3.3.5.2** do not represent relaxations as such but are values that it will seldom be possible to use because of the difficulty of demonstrating compliance with the other limitations.

Clause **3.3.5.2** does not permit these values of grade to be used for mixes containing pfa or ggbfs even though **3.3.5.5** indicates that the protection to reinforcement should be equal to that of Portland cement concrete if the 28 day strengths are equal. The restriction arises because data for maximum water/cement ratio and minimum cement content in relation to durability are not available for concretes containing pfa or ggbfs in the same way that they are for Portland cement concrete. Although some pfa or ggbfs mixes may conform to the limiting values in Table 3.4 and **3.3.5.2** the wide range in percentage additions permissible means that this is not generally true. For all but the lowest percentage additions a proportionately greater mass of pfa or ggbfs will almost certainly be required. Put another way, the strength equivalence data are based on assumptions about minimum cement content in Table 3.4 for Portland cement concrete which are not necessarily true for pfa or ggbfs concrete.

Because the equivalence concept is based on broad comparisons with limited data it is reasonable to exercise some caution, given the concern to avoid premature deterioration in service. This concern extends to sulphate resisting Portland cement in **3.3.5.6** for very severe or extreme exposure conditions even though increased cover is recommended for achieving equivalent protection to reinforcement.

6.2.3 Exposure conditions

6.2.3.1 *General environment*

6.2.3.2 *Freezing and thawing and de-icing salts*

Air-entraining agents
The resistance of concrete to freezing and thawing depends to a large extent on its permeability, the provision of adequate curing and the degree of saturation of the concrete when exposed to freezing, concrete with a higher degree of saturation being the more liable to damage. The use of salt for de-icing roads greatly increases the risk of damage from freezing and thawing.

The use of de-icing chemicals can cause concrete deterioration through two different mechanisms. Firstly, the melting of ice and snow produces pools of water available to be absorbed by the concrete. This can raise the level of saturation in the concrete and the salt solution remains liquid at lower temperatures than pure water. Thus concrete may be subjected to many cycles of freezing and thawing at a much higher degree of saturation than if the de-icing salt had not been used. Secondly, de-icing salts increase the presence of chlorides which, in reinforced concrete, can pose a corrosion risk.

Air-entraining agents entrain controlled amounts of air in concrete, and greatly improve its durability and in particular its resistance to damage on freezing. Air-entrainment causes some loss in strength but, as a designed mix is required, this will be offset automatically. The engineer should specify air-entrainment where the concrete will be in contact with de-icing salt and should specify the average air content of the concrete in accordance with **6.2.3.2**. Site control of air content is covered by BS 1881: Part 106.

Care is required in the selection of air-entraining admixtures. It is recommended that products be obtained from reliable firms having a technical department capable of advising on the use of the product. The admixture must not only cause the entrainment of the air in the required amount, despite varying mixing and agitating times, but must also lead to the correct size and spacing of the air bubbles in the freshly mixed concrete. When those requirements are met, the air is reasonably stable in the fresh concrete, which can then be handled and compacted by vibration without serious loss of air. It should be noted that difficulties may be met in entraining air into mixes containing pfa.

6.2.3.3 *Exposure to aggressive chemicals*
This Clause is concerned with aggressive chemicals external to the concrete. The same chemicals may be introduced in the mix constituents (**6.2.5**) and have an aggressive internal effect. Concrete used in agricultural situations may be subject to acidic solutions, e.g. food processing, silage effluent[6.6, 6.7]. Engineers should be particularly wary of old industrial tips and the chemicals they may contain[6.8].

The omission of values for cement content and free water/cement ratio against class 1 in Table 6.1 is covered by the footnote to the Table and arises because different values may be appropriate and are stated elsewhere in the Code. For concrete in contact with non-aggressive soil (i.e. class 1 of Table 6.1), Table 3.2 defines the environment as 'moderate'; for a moderate environment Table 3.4 giving cover to reinforcement requires a minimum cement content of $300 kg/m^3$ and a maximum water/cement ratio of 0.60: these values then apply to class 1 of Table 6.1. However, unreinforced concrete is treated in **6.2.4.2**, and for a moderate environment, Table 6.2 requires a minimum cement content of $275 kg/m^3$ and a maximum free water/cement ratio of 0.65.

Based on longstanding practice and absence of durability problems in class 1 non-aggressive soil conditions, concrete made with normal-weight aggregate and used for foundations (strip and trench-fill) to low-rise structures (**6.2.4**) may have a lower cement content not less than $220 kg/m^3$ if the grade is not less than C20. Under these conditions the recommendations for increased cover to any reinforcement in **3.3.1.4**, for concrete cast against uneven surfaces, will usually apply.

The presence of water is necessary for sulphate attack to occur; attempts to dry one surface of concrete can exacerbate flow of moisture and the rate of attack.

6.2.4 Mix proportions

6.2.4.1 *General*
This Clause picks up the general principles for achieving durable reinforced concrete,

given in **6.2.1**, and focuses on mix proportions by reference to Tables 3.4, 4.8, 6.1 and 6.2. It emphasises the importance of achieving the lowest free water/cement ratio compatible with producing placed concrete of uniform consistency and of ensuring the specified minimum cement contents.

If it is necessary to use admixtures it should be ensured that the limiting values are still met because the values in Tables 3.4, 4.8, 6.1 and 6.2 are based on data on concretes made without admixtures.

It is equally important to be aware of the behaviour during curing of concretes containing high cement contents, particularly in excess of 550kg/m^3, when high drying shrinkage or thermal stresses may be induced.

6.2.4.2 *Unreinforced concrete*
Table 6.2 is analogous to Table 3.4 except of course there are no requirements for cover.

6.2.4.3 *Mix adjustments in Tables 6.1 and 6.2*
The changes or adjustments which may be made to values in Table 6.2 are again analogous to those relating to Table 3.2. However, recognizing that in some cases it may be appropriate to specify prescribed mixes, recommendations are given for mixes described in BS 5328 which will provide the necessary cement contents and meet the free water/cement ratio limits.

6.2.5 Mix constituents

6.2.5.1 *General*
The importance of proper selection and control of materials is emphasised.

6.2.5.2 *Chlorides in concrete*
Control of the risk of corrosion of embedded metal by chlorides is dealt with by the limits in Table 6.4, which represent a small modification to the stricter limit of 0.06% introduced in 1977 which excluded some inland aggregates previously regarded as completely satisfactory. Although a very low limit for chloride is required in this category it is considered that the risk of corrosion would not be increased by raising the limit from 0.06% to 0.1%. To achieve the revised limits, washing of sea-dredged aggregates is essential.

It is considered that there is sufficient information and experience of the use of cements complying with BS 4027 or BS 4248, for the chloride limit to be set at 0.2%, subject to continuing review. The 0.2% limit applies to both plain and reinforced concrete. It is needed in plain concrete for sulphate resistance purposes and in reinforced concrete for both sulphate and corrosion resistance. Where the type or use of concrete lies in more than one category, e.g. steam cured concrete using a sulphate resisting cement, the more onerous limit should be applied. The value of 0.4% for most reinforced concrete represents a simplification for the previous method of expression.

6.2.5.3 *Sulphates in concrete*

6.2.5.4 *Alkali-silica reaction*
A revised edition of the *Guidance notes on minimising the risk of alkali-silica reaction*, together with a set of Model Specification Clauses was published for public comment in October 1985[6.4].

It must be emphasised that the recommendations relate to conditions found in mainland Britain, and before using them Engineers working outside that area should satisfy themselves that local conditions are comparable.

The recommendations in the Code are in line with those given in the September 1983 Guidance Notes. The revised edition includes some important changes with the current advice being as follows:

As the three elements of moisture, high alkali levels and reactive silica aggregates all have to be present for damage to occur, it is only necessary to eliminate one of them to minimise the risk of ASR. The Guidance Notes recommend various ways in which this may be achieved, but stress the importance of giving as wide a choice of methods as possible to the contractor to minimise costs.

Taking the four sub-paragraphs in Clause **6.2.5.4** in turn:

(1) Controlling moisture will only be successful if the equilibrium relative humidity in the concrete is less than 75%. This can be the case in dry, well-ventilated parts of buildings. It will not apply to foundations even if waterproofed, to external members, or to those subjected to condensation.

(2) Guaranteed low alkali cement to BS 4027 has less than 0.6% alkali content. This requirement has to be specified at the time of ordering. Provided that their water-soluble alkali content is taken into account, either ggbfs or pfa can be used as a partial replacement for BS 12 Portland cement to reduce the alkali content of the cementitious materials below 0.6%.

(3) When avoidance of ASR is based on limiting the alkali content of the concrete to a maximum of $3kg/m^3$, all sources of alkali have to be taken into account. In particular the contribution of sodium chloride whether from aggregates or from mixing water must be included.

(4) If ggbfs or pfa are included in the concrete mix as a partial replacement for Portland cement, the revised Guidance Notes require the inclusion of the water-soluble alkali content of whichever diluent is used.

In the case of ggbfs, the control of alkalis can be achieved in one of two ways:

(a) replacement of cement by ggbfs at a minimum level of 50% so that the combination has an acid-soluble alkali content of less than 1.1%,

(b) replacement of cement by ggbfs at a level greater than 30% such that the acid-soluble alkali in the ggbfs when combined give a total alkali content of not more than 0.6%.

Suitable pfa can be used as a replacement of 30% or more of the Portland cement, provided that the total alkali level in the concrete does not exceed $3kg/m^3$ when the acid-soluble and water-soluble alkalis of the Portland cement and pfa respectively are taken into account.

There are other matters covered in the Guidance Notes which the Code refers to but does not cover in detail. In the absence of a recognised test a list is given of those aggregates which are considered to be non-reactive. In addition, the reactive rock types chert and flint are considered to be safe provided that they are present at a level greater than 60% of the combined coarse and fine aggregates.

Structures which are considered to be particularly vulnerable to attack by ASR include those subjected to high humidity and those buried in waterlogged ground. Highway structures come into this category and are in addition subjected to frequent saturation with de-icing salts. In such cases, more rigorous precautions may be necessary.

For further information, see also references 6.2, 6.3, 6.4.

6.2.6 Placing, compacting, finishing and curing

6.3 Concrete mix specification

6.3.1 General

Following the publication of CP110 in 1972, the British Standard *Methods for specifying concrete* (BS 5328) was published in 1976, and revised in 1981. It was intended that BS 5328 should provide a single standard for concrete to be referred to in all codes and specifications for concrete. Unfortunately the publication and revisions of these documents have not kept in step and different terminology has been used for the types of concrete mixes as shown in Table H6.3.

Irrespective of the detailed terminology, the fundamental difference between a 'designed' mix and a 'standard' or (special) 'prescribed' mix lies in the responsibility for selecting the mix proportions, the form of specification, the materials which can be used and the parameters for judging compliance. These differences are shown in Table H6.4.

It is the Engineer's responsibility to select the concrete grade together with any limits required on the mix proportions, the requirements for fresh concrete and the types of materials which may or may not be used to meet his strength, durability and any other

Table H6.3 Types of concrete mixes in British Standards

CP110 1972	BS 5328 1976, 1981	BS 8110 BS 5328 (revision in preparation)
Designed special ordinary	Designed	Designed
Prescribed special ordinary Table 50	Special prescribed Ordinary prescribed Table 1	Prescribed Standard*

*In the Code this is incorrectly termed 'Ordinary Standard'.

Table H6.4 Characteristics of different types of mix

Type of mix	Designed mix	Prescribed mix	Standard mix
Permitted grades	All grades	All grades	C7.5 – C30
Mix specified in terms of	Performance (strength grade)	Mix proportions	Mix from Table
Responsibility for mix design	Producer	Engineer	Engineer selects
Permitted materials	Generally complying with a wide range of British Standards	Free to specify, or restrict, any material	Complying with a restricted range of British Standards
Main parameter used for judgement of compliance	Strength	Mix proportions	Mix proportions

special requirements. Wherever possible, limitations on materials and mix proportions should be kept to the minimum needed in order that the concrete producer can make the best use of his knowledge and experience of local materials.

6.3.2 Selection of compressive strength grade

The grades of concrete required should be selected from those given in BS 5328 (Table H6.5).

Table H6.5 Compressive strength

Concrete grade	Characteristic compressive strength at 28 days
	N/mm^2 (= MPa)
C2.5	2.5
C5	5.0
C7.5	7.5
C10	10.0
C12.5	12.5
C15	15.0
C20	20.0
C25	25.0
C30	30.0
C40	40.0
C45	45.0
C50	50.0
C55	55.0
C60	60.0

The minimum grades and/or other specified requirements for reinforced, prestressed and unreinforced concrete and different conditions of exposure are given in

Table 3.4 for reinforced concrete
Table 4.8 for prestressed concrete
Table 6.2 for unreinforced concrete
Table 6.1 for concrete exposed to sulphate attack.

BS 8110 deals primarily with concrete for structural purposes. However, if concrete is required for non-structural uses, such as blinding or backfill, then the mixes given in Table H6.5 may be appropriate.

6.3.3 Limitations on mix parameters for durability

The free water/cement ratio is an important factor governing the durability of concrete and should always be the lowest value compatible with producing fully compacted concrete without segregation or bleeding. A minimum cement content is a primary requirement for durability. The cement content required for a particular water/cement ratio can vary significantly for different mix constituents. Where adequate workability is difficult to obtain at the maximum free water/cement ratio allowed, an increased cement content, the use of ggbfs or pfa and/or the use of plasticizing or water-reducing admixtures should be considered.

Mixes are frequently specified in terms of prescribed mixes. In such cases, the importance of minimum cement content and free water/cement ratio in determining durability suggests that concrete mixes should preferably be specified in terms of (special) prescribed or standard mixes.

With prescribed mixes, the Engineer has the responsibility for specifying the mix proportions and ensuring that these will provide the required performance. Moreover, with a prescribed mix, strength testing is not a means of judging compliance.

There are some occasions when a prescribed mix may be suitable such as:

(a) where the Engineer has had successful experience in the past of a prescribed mix made with particular constituent materials from known sources
(b) where the concrete is to be provided by a contractor and there is insufficient time for the collection of data, or the scale of work or economy does not justify the application of mix design procedures
(c) where special architectural finishes such as exposed aggregate are required.

In Table 1 of BS 5328, ordinary prescribed (or standard) mixes are given in nominal terms by mass of dry aggregate to be used with 100kg of cement, for the lower grades of concrete from C7.5 to C30.

As far as BS 8110 is concerned, the ordinary prescribed (or standard) mixes will only cover the grades C25 and C30. Since they have to take account of such a wide range of materials, limitations are applied to the types and gradings of aggregates which can be used and the cement contents are conservatively high.

As strength is not a criterion with prescribed mixes, compliance with the specified mix proportions has to be assessed by either:

(a) observation of the batching,
(b) examination of the autographic records of the batch weights used, or
(c) results of analysis tests on the fresh concrete with the requirement that proportions shall be within ±10% of the value specified.

Compliance with the specified maximum free water/cement ratio may be assessed using workability test results provided satisfactory evidence is available on the relationship between free water/cement ratio and workability for the materials used.

The cement content will affect the appearance of the hardened concrete, the handling and placing characteristics of the fresh concrete and performance during setting, hardening and curing when, for example, bleeding and 'settlement' after initial compaction may occur. If a mix is specified only by reference to the size of aggregate, slump and strength, then some qualities of the fresh or hardened concrete may be inadequate. Variability and deficiencies in grading of aggregate may necessitate a minimum cement content to reduce the sensitivity of the mix to bleeding, grout loss, colour variation, poor local compaction etc.

Therefore, when checking the cement content of a proposed mix for any concrete, assessment should be made of:

(a) the likely variability in mix materials

(b) the workability requirements
(c) the surface finish
(d) other special placing requirements, e.g. pumping
(e) the permeability of the hardened concrete.

When concrete mixes are specified either in terms of a minimum cement content or a maximum water/cement ratio, some difficulties may occur in establishing compliance with these requirements. Analysis of fresh concrete is not a generally accepted test at present and continuous observation of the materials batched is not always practicable. As an alternative, assurance of compliance with mix proportions can be obtained by adopting a compressive strength grade as suggested below[6.5].

From a comprehensive survey of concrete mixes manufactured throughout the UK, basic relationships were obtained between the average compressive strength at 28 days and cement content, and free water/cement ratio and cement content as shown in Figures H6.1 and H6.2. These data apply to ordinary Portland cements, 75mm slump and coarse aggregate of nominal maximum size 20mm. From such data applied to local materials, it is possible to establish the average compressive strength level which will satisfy any combination of maximum free water/cement ratio and minimum cement content.

For any given requirement, the equivalent strength grade may therefore be obtained from one or other of the following methods.

Method A
Use of data from records or from trial mixes relating to cement content, water/cement ratio and mean strength (M), representative of the particular materials and workability proposed for use. The equivalent grade is taken as $(M-10)$ N/mm^2.

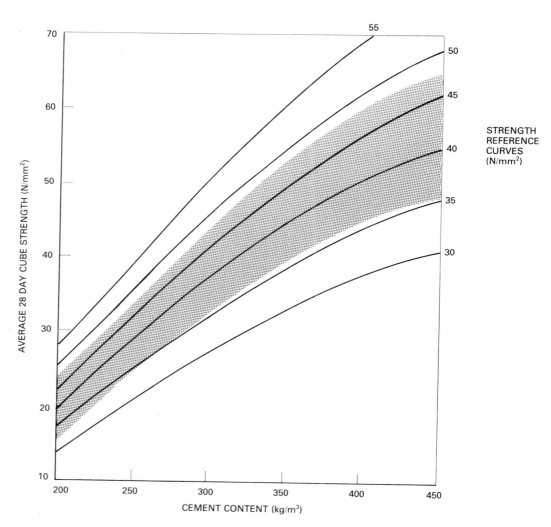

Figure H6.1: Relationship between strength and cement content of concrete made with OPC, 75mm slump and coarse aggregate with maximum size 20mm.

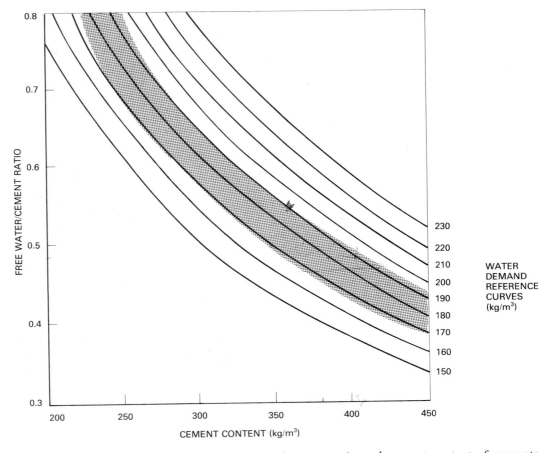

Figure H6.2: Relationship between free water/cement ratio and cement content of concrete (OPC, 75mm slump, 20mm coarse aggregate).

Method B

For any given cement content and water/cement ratio, Tables H6.6 and H6.7 may be used to determine the controlling grade. These values provide a probability of about 95% that the cement content and water/cement ratio requirements will be met using United Kingdom materials (British ordinary Portland cement, aggregate of 20mm nominal maximum size in a concrete having a slump of 75mm). Modifications to the equivalent grades given in Tables H6.6 and H6.7 to allow for other specified requirements are given in Table H6.8.

Table H6.6 Equivalent grades for cement content

Minimum cement content (kg/m^3)	Equivalent grade
220 – 230	C20
240 – 260	C25
270 – 280	C30
290 – 310	C35
320 – 330	C40
340 – 360	C45
370 – 390	C50
400 and above	Use method (A)

Table H6.7 Equivalent grades for free water/cement ratio

Maximum free water/cement ratio	Equivalent grade
0.70	C25
0.65	C30
0.60	C35
0.55	C40
0.50	C45
0.45	C50
less than 0.45	Use method (A)

Table H6.8 Modifications to Tables H6.6 and H6.7 to allow for other specified requirements

Specified requirement		Adjustment to the equivalent grade in Tables H6.6 and H6.7
Workability (slump)	25mm	+5*
	100mm	0
Nominal maximum aggregate size	10mm	0
	14mm	0
	40mm	0
Aggregate type	Lightweight	Use method (A)
Cement complying with	BS 4027	0
	BS 12 (rapid hardening)	+5
	BS 146	0
	BS 6588	0
	BS 1370	Use method (A)
Admixtures	Water reducing agents	+5*

*Only when cement content is the critical parameter determining grade.

6.3.4 Specification of constituent materials

6.3.4.1 *General*
A list of the clauses giving information on the effects of materials on the properties of concrete is given in Table H6.9.

6.3.4.2 *Cements, ggbfs and pfa*

6.3.4.3 *Aggregates*

6.3.4.4 *Admixtures*

6.3.5 Fresh concrete
Workability and cohesion of the fresh concrete should be suitable for the conditions of handling and placing so that after compaction concrete surrounds all reinforcement, tendons and ducts and completely fills the formwork. Excess bleeding should be avoided as this can lead to plastic settlement cracking and/or poor quality surfaces.

The characteristics which have the major effect on the properties of fresh concrete are

workability (**6.3.5.2**)
air content (**6.1.5.5** and **6.2.3.2**)
temperature (**6.2.2.1**, **6.7** and **6.8**)
minimum and maximum density (**6.3.5.3**)
aggregate grading (**6.1.3.4**).

Table H6.9 Clauses relating to the effects of materials on the characteristics of concrete

Property of material or concrete	Cement, ggbfs or pfa	Aggregates	Admixtures
Strength			
Early development	6.1.2.1		6.1.5
Very high		6.1.3.9	
Low heat evolution	6.1.2.2		
	6.1.2.5		
Materials			
Limits on:			
grading		6.1.3.4	
sulphates	6.2.5.3	6.2.5.3	6.2.5.3
chlorides			6.1.5.4
			6.2.5.2
shell content		6.1.3.5	
flakiness		6.1.3.6	
density		6.1.3.11	
Avoidance of:			
high moisture movements		6.1.3.7	
other effects		6.1.3.8	
Improved resistance to:			
sulphate attack	6.1.2.4		
	6.2.3.3		
ASR	6.2.5.4	6.2.5.4	
freezing and thawing			6.1.5.5
			6.2.3.2
wear		6.1.3.12	
fire		6.1.3.10	
chemical attack	6.1.2.2		
	6.2.3.3		

Of these characteristics, the Engineer would not normally be concerned with workability, since this would be decided by the Contractor.

6.3.5.1 *General*

6.3.5.2 *Workability*

6.3.5.3 *Density*

6.3.6 Concrete to meet special requirements

Concrete mixes made with most British cement and aggregate can be designed to meet the requirements of strength, durability and workability under normal conditions of exposure. Where special requirements are needed, guidance is given in the Code and this is summarised in Table H6.9.

6.4 Methods of specification, production, control and tests

6.4.1 Specification and acceptance of mix

Specification can best be done by the use of forms, as in Appendixes A, B and C:

Appendix A   Form for specifying a designed mix or a prescribed mix, in accordance with BS 5328
               Section 1: Essential items
               Section 2: Optional items

Appendix B   Form for specifying a standard mix in accordance with BS 5328

Appendix C   Materials for use in standard mixes

The exchange of information should include:

(a) nature and source of constituent materials and any alternatives which may be used;
(b) manufacturers' certificates for cement, ggbfs and pfa;
(c) proposed quantity of each material for prescribed mixes;
(d) details of admixtures;
(e) any changes in mix composition;
(f) for designed mixes, information on suitability of proposed mix proportions to meet a specified strength based either on previous production data or on trial mixes;
(g) suitability of proposed mix proportions to meet a specified maximum free water/cement ratio or minimum cement content;
(h) any other information.

6.4.2 Production, supervision and tests

Compliance with characteristic compressive strength

Compliance with the characteristic strength is based on individual test results and on groups of test results.

Where compressive strength is specified, the first result alone cannot be used to judge compliance with the specified characteristic strength. Compliance with the specified characteristic strength shall be assumed if:

(a) the average strength determined from the first 2, or the first 3 consecutive test results, or from consecutive, but non-overlapping, groups of 4 test results complies with the appropriate limits in column A of Table H6.10, and
(b) any individual test result complies with the appropriate limits in column B of Table H6.10.

Table H6.10 Compressive strength compliance requirements

Specified grade	Test results	A Average of first 2, or first 3, or of 4 consecutive, non-overlapping test results exceeds the specified characteristic strength by at least:	B Any individual test result is not less than the specified characteristic strength minus:
C20 and above	first 2	$1N/mm^2$	$3N/mm^2$
	first 3	$2N/mm^2$	$3N/mm^2$
	consecutive 4	$3N/mm^2$	$3N/mm^2$
C7.5 to C15	first 2	$0N/mm^2$	$2N/mm^2$
	first 3	$1N/mm^2$	$2N/mm^2$
	consecutive 4	$2N/mm^2$	$2N/mm^2$

Compliance with specified mix proportions (prescribed and standard mixes only)

BS 5328 details the compliance requirements for mixes specified in terms of mix proportions and these are summarised in Table H6.11.

6.4.3 Additional tests on concrete for special purposes

Other requirements may be specified that are not described in detail in this Code, such as modulus of elasticity of concrete. Compliance with those requirements should be determined only in association with the detailed description of the method of test and with tolerances which take appropriate account of variability due to manufacture, sampling and testing. A British Standard method of test should be used whenever it is appropriate.

Other information on the strength of concrete in structures is given in BS 6089.

H6.11 Compliance with specified mix proportions

Specified properties	Compliance requirements
Minimum or maximum cement content (i) By observtion of batching or from autographic records	Cement content not less than 95% of specified minimum or more than 105% of specified maximum
(ii) Fresh analysis tests in accordance with DD 83 *Assessment of the composition of fresh concrete*	Limits agreed with concrete producer, based on DD 83
Maximum free water cement ratio	Workability results, based on relationship between free water/cement ratio and workability
Equivalent grades	Compliance based on equivalent grade agreed as satisfying minimum cement content or maximum free water/cement ratio
Workability (designed and prescribed mixes) Slump	±25mm or $\pm\frac{1}{3}$ of the specified value, whichever is the greater
Slump (sample taken in accordance with 12.2 of BS 5328)	Specified value Tolerance 25mm +35mm −25mm 50mm ±35mm 75mm and over $\pm\frac{1}{3}$ of specified slump plus 10mm)
Vebe	±3s or $\pm\frac{1}{5}$ of the specified value, whichever is the greater
Compacting factor	±0.03 where specified value is 0.90 or greater ±0.04 where specified value is less than 0.90 but more than 0.80 ±0.05 where specified value is 0.80 or less
Flow table	Specified value ±50mm
Air content of concrete	Individual samples $\pm1.5\%$ of the required value Average of 4 consecutive determinations $\pm1.0\%$ of the required value
Temperature of fresh concrete	Not less than specified minimum value less 2°C Not more than specified maximum value plus 2°C
Density of fully compacted concrete	Not less than 95% of specified minimum value or more than 105% of specified maximum value.

6.5 Transporting, placing and compacting concrete

6.5.1 Transport of concrete

6.5.1.1 *General*
Concrete should be transported as rapidly as possible because any undue delay may cause the workability to decrease to the extent that it cannot be properly compacted as required by Section **6.5.2**. The rate of loss of workability with time depends on a number of factors including cement type, admixtures, concrete temperature and the rate of evaporation of water from the concrete. Guidance on acceptable intervals between mixing and placing concrete is given in BS 5328.

6.5.1.2 *Transport and delivery of ready-mixed concrete*
Before ready-mixed concrete is delivered, the site should ensure that the truck can gain access to the intended point of discharge and that, when discharged, the concrete can be transported to the point of placing in accordance with the requirements of Clause **6.5.1.1**. Further information on the handling of ready-mixed concrete is given in BS 5328.

6.5.2 Placing and compacting concrete

Prior to placing the concrete, checks should be made on the rigidity and tightness of the formwork and on the fixing of reinforcement and prestressing ducts. Particular attention should be given to ensure that sufficient spacers in number, location and quality have been used and that they are securely fixed and do not become dislodged during the placing of the concrete.

Particular care should be taken when placing concrete under box outs, top sloping forms or other complex shapes where air pockets might form. Extra care is required when casting against permanent formwork if, like woodwool, it can absorb energy from the concrete whilst it is being compacted.

Thorough compaction is essential if the hardened concrete is to have the intended strength and durability. For general guidance see reference 6.9. Further information on placing concrete in deep lifts is given in reference 6.10 and on concreting underwater in reference 6.11.

When concrete is placed in deep lifts with reinforcement near the upper surface, consideration should be given to re-vibrating the top surface of the concrete to prevent plastic settlement cracking. This is a particular problem with concretes containing ggbfs or retarders.

Finishing times are increased with concretes containing mixtures of OPC with ggbfs or pfa. This can be an advantage in hot weather, but in mild or cold conditions it may require overtime working to ensure a properly floated surface and adequate abrasion resistance.

6.6 Curing

6.6.1 General

Appropriate curing is essential for achieving the strength and durability of concrete in structures. The areas most affected by poor curing are the surface zones and these are the critical zones with respect to durability. Abrasion resistance depends on the quality of the concrete in the top few millimetres and the protection of reinforcement depends on the quality of the concrete in the cover. If the curing is inadequate the concrete may not be durable nor provide adequate protection to the reinforcement despite full compliance with the specification in all other aspects.

Several references provide information on curing when members are of considerable bulk or length[6.12, 6.13], the cement content of the concrete is high[6.13], the surface finish is critical[6.14, 6.15] or special or accelerated methods are to be applied[6.16].

6.6.2 Minimum periods of curing and protection

Curing should ideally be carried out until the capillary voids are discontinuous, but at present it is not possible to establish the precise times when this occurs. The figures in Table 6.5 provide a useful guide but are *minima* and may need to be exceeded. The times quoted relate to both the ambient conditions and the average surface temperature of the concrete. The ambient conditions can vary during the period of curing. Conditions which started as 'good' can deteriorate to 'average' or 'poor' and the curing periods should be increased. For example, if the 'good' conditions do not last for the 'average' time, curing needs to be applied for the remainder of the 'average' period or the outstanding proportion of the 'poor' period. Proportions of the curing times can be used to calculate the curing period but it may be simpler to cure for the longer period. CEB Bulletin 166 gives additional information on curing[6.17].

Concrete and ambient temperatures will vary throughout the curing period and the daily average values can usually be taken as the mid value between the maximum and the minimum readings. At 0°C the water in concrete freezes, expands and disrupts the concrete. Temperatures between 1 and 5°C are not harmful to concrete, but the rate of strength gain is very slow and therefore for practical reasons Clause **6.6.2** requires a minimum concrete temperature of 5°C. BS 5328 states that the temperature of the concrete at the time of delivery shall not be less than the specified value less 2°C which in practice means the acceptance of any concrete over 3°C. When one considers that an unheated form is likely to cause the concrete in the surface zone to cool, a delivery temperature of 3°C is too low. It would be prudent to specify a minimum concrete temperature of 7°C which in practice will mean that any concrete not at 5°C or greater can be rejected.

It should be noted that the necessary curing times are increased when the OPC in a mix is partially replaced by ggbfs or pfa. This is to compensate for the lower rate of strength development.

Ideally, curing should start as soon as the concrete has been placed and should not be interrupted during the whole of the period given in Table 6.5.

6.6.3 Methods
Further information on methods of curing are given in references 6.10 and 6.15. Thermal curing of large pours is described in references 6.12 and 6.13.

6.7 Concreting in cold weather

6.7.1 General
Experience from Northern Europe and Canada shows that it is possible to concrete throughout the winter, but in some parts of the UK it may be worth considering whether it would be acceptable and economic to suspend concreting for a short period. It has to be appreciated that in very severe conditions it may not be possible to transport concrete to or around a site.

6.7.2 Concrete temperature
Guidance on this may be obtained from references 6.18 and 6.19.

6.8 Concreting in hot weather

Further information on concreting in hot weather is given in references 6.20 and 6.21.

6.9 Formwork

6.9.1 Design and construction
The design and construction of formwork and falsework has a significant effect on the appearance and durability of concrete structures. Some of the references given in BS 8110 for loading or pressures have been superceded. The current recommendations are given in references 6.22 and 6.23.

6.9.2 Cleaning and treatment of forms
The type of release agent used can influence the appearance of the concrete surface and the life of the formface[6.23]. The release agent may also affect the bond of paint or other surface treatments subsequently applied to the concrete surface.

6.9.3 Striking of formwork

6.9.3.1 *General*
Early removal of formwork can reduce cycle time for both in situ and precast work. This can be achieved safely by the use of accelerated curing techniques[6.16, 6.24].

6.9.3.2 *Striking period for cast in situ concrete*
Table 6.6 is based on a grade 20 concrete and as the lowest grade PPFAC reinforced concrete is C30, this may be used to determine the striking times of PPFAC concretes. Table 6.6 should not be used for slag-based blended hydraulic cement concretes unless evidence is produced to show its applicability for the particular materials being used on the site.

The heading in Table 6.6 "16°C and above" does not rule out shorter periods before striking if the calculation using the equation in the last column is carried out.

The effects of temperature on the rate of gain of strength (maturity) are different for blended hydraulic cement concretes. The maturity rules used for OPC concretes are unlikely to be applicable and a maturity calculation based on activation energies is recommended.

The strength of concrete in a structural element can be assessed for striking purposes by using temperature-matched curing[6.25], pull-out tests[6.26], break-off tests[6.27] or penetration tests[6.28]. Care is needed to ensure that a safe (conservative) relationship is used to convert instrument reading to equivalent cube strength.

An unintentional change in the wording in the section on striking formwork supporting concrete in flexure from CP110's '10N/mm^2 in cubes of equal maturity to the structure' to BS 8110's '10N/mm^2 strength in the structure' may lead to an incorrect interpretation of this clause. What is intended is 10N/mm^2 in cubes of equal maturity to the structure and an amendment is being issued to change the text to clarify this point. The ideal method of curing cubes under the same conditions as the concrete in the element is by using temperature-matched curing[6.25].

In partially completed structures, local bond stresses on partially embedded reinforcement may be the controlling criterion. Unfortunately, the table of local bond stresses has not been included in BS 8110 and therefore reference should be made to CP110 or reference 6.24.

6.10 Surface finish of concrete

6.10.1 Type of finish
Guidance on the wide range of finishes which may be obtained is given in references 6.14 and 6.29-6.32.

6.10.2 Quality of finish
Guidance on the specification and production of high quality finishes is given in reference 6.33. Where the quality of the surface is important, it is essential that specifier and contractor liaise closely before and after the tender stage to develop a mutual understanding of the quality required. Demonstration or trial panels can be of immense help in developing this understanding.

6.10.3 Type of surface finish
Smooth off-the-form and board-marked finishes can form the basis of a wide range of internal finishes produced by the application of paint or other coatings.

6.10.4 Production
Guidance on the production of surface finishes is given in references 6.14 and 6.29-6.32.

6.10.5 Inspection and making good
Obtaining a high-quality durable finish when making good is a skilled operation which should be undertaken by a specialist.

6.10.6 Protection
Vulnerable areas of surface may merit permanent protection to avoid discoloration or physical damage.

6.11 Dimensional deviations

Formwork is made and erected within some tolerances – whether or not they are specified and checked – and at some cost which will depend considerably on the level of the tolerance adopted. Even when no special attention is given to tolerances, experience determines some upper limit to the deviation from the specified nominal dimensions because excessive inaccuracy would cause construction difficulties, resulting in increased cost, or would produce work of unacceptable quality. Within the range of tolerances used in practice, however, an increase in precision will generally be accompanied by an increase in formwork costs.

The engineer is usually concerned with tolerances on the finished concrete, whether cast in situ or precast. For precast concrete, the deviations of the relevant dimension of the mould from the nominal dimension specified should normally be smaller than the specified tolerances for the concrete, to account for such factors as:

(a) the inaccuracy of the measurement system used when making and assembling the mould
(b) the change in size of the mould with repeated uses
(c) the changes in size of the mould with changes of temperature when the concrete is cast
(d) the deformation of the mould during casting
(e) the change in size of the finished concrete due to changes in the conditions to which it is exposed between casting and checking.

These factors are also valid for in situ concrete but, in addition, the following should also be taken into account:

(f) the accuracy of setting out
(g) the uncertainty of fixing the formwork correctly in relation to the setting out positions
(h) the deflection of any supporting falsework during casting.

When tolerances are specified, therefore, it is essential that they be related to a clearly defined and stated checking procedure with a precision of measurement appreciably greater than the tolerance allowed. The level of tolerance selected should not be out of proportion to the other uncertainties inherent in the construction.

6.11.1 General

6.11.2 In situ concrete

6.11.3 Precast concrete members

6.11.4 Prestressed units

6.11.5 Position of reinforcement and tendons

6.11.6 Position of connecting bolts and other devices in precast concrete components

6.11.7 Control of dimensional accuracy

6.11.8 Checking of dimensional accuracy

6.12 Construction joints

Further information on the forming of construction joints is available in reference 6.10. Particular care should be taken with construction joints in liquid retaining structures (BS 5337). If reinforcement levels are low, restrained thermal contraction or restrained drying shrinkage are likely to manifest themselves at construction joints.

The Code is understandably brief when describing good practice in relation to construction joints because of the very wide range of circumstances in which construction joints have to be made.

Instead of the weak porous concretes sometimes seen, the quality of concrete in kickers should be at least equal to that of the main structure. Since, to obtain a fully compacted concrete in a kicker, the proportion of fine to total aggregate is likely to have to be increased, the maximum size of the aggregate reduced and the workability of the concrete increased compared with the concrete in the structure, it is evident that the proportion of cement in the concrete for kickers should generally be greater than that in the main part of the structure. This is liable to result in a concrete of darker colour than the rest of the structure; hence, where the appearance of the work is of high importance, kickers are best avoided.

Ineffective clamping of the forms to hardened concrete all too often leads to leakage of mortar from the subsequent pour and therefore to an unsightly appearance.

The need for full compaction of concrete in the vicinity of construction joints is emphasized, particularly as the effectiveness of compactive effort is often reduced close to a mass of hardened concrete. Although the possibility of using a rather higher workability concrete at the joint is often discussed, this is not practicable when ready-mixed concrete is used. The best way of attaining full compaction is therefore to use vibrators and to reckon that they will have to be used for considerably longer, perhaps twice as long, near joints as compared with the bulk of the structure.

No recommendations are made about the moisture condition of the hardened concrete against which a new concrete is to be placed; the concrete should not, however, be so dry as to draw excessive quantities of water from the concrete being placed; conversely the concrete should not have puddles of free water laying on it as this might inhibit good bond between the old and new concretes. The Code also makes no recommendations about the use of a layer of fresh mortar or grout on the hardened concrete just before the new concrete is to be placed. Although good joints have been produced by using mortar or grout, the technique appears to present more problems than it solves; it is therefore best avoided in most situations and emphasis placed instead on a high compactive effort.

Note that the surface treatment selected for joints may be defined by considerations of interface shear (**5.4.7**).

6.13 Movement joints

Poor performance of movement joints can affect the serviceability and durability of a structure. If joints cannot move, this may cause the structure to crack excessively or for other joints to open excessively allowing ingress of deleterious materials. Special attention needs to be paid to joints which include a waterbar as some types are particularly vulnerable to the consequences of poor workmanship. For further information, see Part 2, Section **8**.

6.14 Handling and erection of pre-cast concrete units

REFERENCES

6.1 HARRISON, T.A. and SPOONER, D.C. The properties and use of concretes made with composite cements. Wexham Springs, Cement and Concrete Association. Interim Technical Note 10. 1986.

6.2 SOMERVILLE, G. Engineering aspects of alkali-silica reaction. Wexham Springs, Cement and Concrete Association. Interim Technical Note No.8, October 1985.

6.3 HOBBS, D.W. Expansion of concrete due to alkali-silica reaction. The Structural Engineer, January 1984. Vol.62A, No.1, pp 26-34.

6.4 THE CONCRETE SOCIETY. Minimising the risk of alkali-silica reaction. Guidance Notes and Model Specification Clauses. Draft for Public Comment. London, The Society, 1985.

6.5 DEACON, C. and DEWAR, J.D. Concrete durability – specifying more simply and surely by strength. Concrete. February 1982. Vol.16, No.2, pp 19-21.

6.6 KLEINLOGEL, A. Influences on concrete, New York. Frederick Ungar Publishing Co. 1950. 281pp.

6.7 EGLINTON, M.S. Review of concrete behaviour in acidic soils and ground waters. London, Construction Industry Research and Information Association. Technical Note 69. 1975. 52 pp.

6.8 BARRY, D.L. Material durability in aggressive ground. London, Construction Industry Research and Information Association. Report 98. 1983. 60 pp.

6.9 BLACKLEDGE, G.F. Man on the job: Placing and compacting concrete. Wexham Springs, Cement and Concrete Association. 1980. 45.108. 28 pp.

6.10 CEMENT AND CONCRETE ASSOCIATION. Concrete practice. Wexham Springs, Cement and Concrete Association. 1984. 48.037. 63 pp.

6.11 THE CONCRETE SOCIETY. Underwater concreting. London, 1971. 52.018. 13 pp. Technical Report No. 3.

6.12 BAMFORTH, P.B. Mass concrete. London, Concrete Society Digest No. 2. 1985. 53.046. 8 pp.

6.13 HARRISON, T.A. Early-age thermal crack control in concrete. London, Construction Industry Research and Information Association, Report 91, 1981. 48 pp.

6.14 MONKS, W. Appearance matters – 1: Visual concrete: Design and production. Wexham Springs, Cement and Concrete Association. 1980. 47.101. 28 pp.

6.15 DEACON, R.C. Concrete ground floors: their design, construction and finish. Wexham Springs, Cement and Concrete Association. 1986. 48.034. 28 pp.

6.16 FIP Guide to good practice – Acceleration of concrete hardening by thermal curing. London, Federation Internationale de la Precontrainte. 1982. 15.907.

6.17 CEB Guide to durable concrete structures. Lausanne, Comite Euro-International du Beton. Bulletin 166. 1985.

6.18 PINK, A. Winter concreting. Wexham Springs, Cement and Concrete Association. 1978. 45.007. 19 pp.

6.19 HARRISON, T.A. Tables of minimum striking times for soffit and vertical formwork. London, Construction Industry Research and Information Association. Report 67. 1977. 23 pp.

6.20 SHIRLEY, D.E. Concreting in hot weather. Wexham Springs, Cement and Concrete Association Construction Guide. 1980. 45.013. 7 pp.

6.21 ACI/305R-77. Hot weather concreting. Detroit, American Concrete Institute Manual of Concrete Practice. 1985: Part 2. pp 305R-1 to 305R-17.

6.22 CLEAR, C.A. and HARRISON, T.A. Concrete pressure on formwork. London, Construction Industry Research and Information Association. Report 108. 1985. 31 pp.

6.23 THE CONCRETE SOCIETY/INSTITUTION OF STRUCTURAL ENGINEERS. Formwork. A guide to good practice. London, 1986.

6.24 HARRISON, T.A. The application of accelerated curing to apartment formwork systems. Wexham Springs, Cement and Concrete Association. 1977. 45.032. 8 pp.

6.25 BRITISH STANDARDS INSTITUTION. Method for temperature-matched curing of concrete specimens. London, BSI DD92:1984. 4 pp.

6.26 BICKLEY, J.A. North American experience with pull-out testing. Paper presented at Nordisk Betonkongress. 22 may 1980. 12 pp.

6.27 JOHANSEN, R. In situ strength evaluation of concrete – the 'Break-off' method. Concrete International. Vol. 1, No. 9, September 1979. pp 44-51.

6.28 BUNGEY, J.H. Testing by penetration resistance. Concrete. Vol. 15, No. 1, January 1981. pp 30-32.

6.29 MONKS, W. Structural concrete finishes: a guide to selection and production. Wexham Springs, Cement and Concrete Association Reprint 1/80. 16pp.

6.30 MONKS, W. Appearance matters – 7: Textured and profiled concrete finishes. Wexham Springs, Cement and Concrete Association. 1986. 47.107. pp 12.

6.31 MONKS, W. Appearance matters – 8: Exposed aggregate concrete finishes. Wexham Springs, Cement and Concrete Association 1985. 47.108. pp 16.

6.32 MONKS, W. Appearance matters – 9: Tooled concrete finishes. Wexham Springs, Cement and Concrete Association. 1985. 47.109. pp 8.

6.33 WILSON, J.G. Specification clauses covering the production of high quality finishes to in situ concrete. Wexham Springs, Cement and Concrete Association. 47.010. pp 12. 1970.

Appendix A: Form for specifying a designed mix or a prescribed mix in accordance with BS 5328

Section 1: Essential items

Type of mix (ring one)	Designed or Prescribed			
Permitted type(s) of cement (ring those permitted)	BS 12(OP)	BS 12(RH)	BS 146	BS 1370
	BS 4027	BS 4246	BS 4248	BS 6588
	BS 4027 (low alkali)			

Combinations with ggbfs or pfa (Permitted or not permitted)	ggbfs to BS 6669	Permitted	Not permitted	Required (see Section 2)
	pfa to BS 3892: Part 1	Permitted	Not permitted	Required (see Section 2)

Permitted type(s) of aggregate (ring those permitted)	Coarse	BS 882	BS 877	BS 1047	BS 1165
		BS 3797			
	Fine	BS 882	BS 877	BS 1165	BS 3797

Nominal maximum size of aggregate (ring one)	40mm	20mm	14mm	10mm

Designed mixes only

Grade (ring one in Group A, B or C)

Group A			Group B	Group C
Compressive			Flexural	Indirect-tensile
C2.5	C15	C40	F3	IT2
C5	C20	C45		
C7.5	C25	C50	F4	IT2.5
C10	C30	C55		
C12.5	C35	C60	F5	IT3

Minimum cement content . . . . kg/m^3

Rate of sampling for strength testing

Number of cubic metres per sample *or*
Number of batches per sample

Prescribed mixes only

Mix proportions

cement	. . . . . . kg
fine aggregate	. . . . . . kg
coarse aggregate	. . . . . . kg

. . . .
. . . .

Section 2: Optional items

Workability (enter value for one only)

Slump	. . . . . mm
Vebe	. . . . . s
Compacting factor	. . . .
Flow table	. . . . . mm

Maximum free-water/cement ratio . . . .

Maximum cement content . . . . kg/m^3

Special cement(s) and
combinations of ggbfs or pfa

Special requirements
for aggregates

Coarse:
Fine:

Admixtures
Pigments
ggbfs
pfa

Specified:

Prohibited

Quantity required . . . .

Air content
. . . . . % by
volume

Temperature of
fresh concrete

. . . . °C maximum
. . . . °C minimum

Density of . . . . kg/m^3 maximum
fresh concrete . . . . kg/m^3 minimum

Maximum chloride content . . . . % by weight of cement

Specification of
trial mixes

Details of test
procedures

Method of assessment
of concrete

As BS 5328
Or (details of method). . . . .

Other requirements

Appendix B: Form for specifying a standard mix in accordance with BS 5328

Standard mix number (ring one)		SM1 SM2 SM3	SM4 SM5 SM6
Permitted type(s) of cement (ring those permitted)		BS 12 (OP) BS 12 (RH) BS 146 BS 6588	BS 12 (OP) BS 12 (RH) BS 146 BS 6588 BS 4027
Combinations with ggbfs or pfa (ring those permitted)		ggbfs to BS 6699 pfa to BS 3892 Part 1	ggbfs to BS 6699 pfa to BS 3892 Part 1
Permitted type(s) of aggregate (ring those permitted)	Coarse Fine All-in	BS 882 BS 1047 BS 882 BS 882	BS 882 BS 1047 BS 882 N/A
Nominal maximum size of aggregate (mm) (ring one)		40 20	40 20 10
Workability (ring one)		Medium High	Medium High
Any additional information			

152

Appendix C: Materials for use in standard mixes

Standard Mixes	SM1, SM2, SM3	SM4, SM5, SM6
Cement	BS 12 (OP or RH) BS 146 BS 6588	BS 12 (OP or RH) BS 146 BS 6588 BS 4027
Ground granulated blastfurnace slag	Where cement to BS 146 is permitted, ggbfs complying with BS 6699 may be combined with cement to BS 12 at the mixer as specified in **6.1.2.**	
Pulverized-fuel ash	Where cement to BS 6588 is permitted, pfa complying with BS 3892: Part 1 may be combined with cement to BS 12 at the mixer as specified in **6.1.2.**	
Coarse aggregate (see Note 1)	BS 882 BS 1047	BS 882 BS 1047
Fine aggregate	BS 882	BS 882 (see Note 2)
All-in aggregate (see Note 3)	BS 882	Not allowed
Admixtures	Not allowed	Not allowed

Note 1. Single-sized coarse aggregates. Where several sizes of single-sized coarse aggregates are used, they shall be combined in such proportions that the combined grading falls within the limits given in BS 882 or BS 1047 for graded aggregate of the appropriate nominal size except that a tolerance of up to 5% may be applied. This tolerance may be divided between the sieves within the total of 5.5%.

Note 2. The purchaser should satisfy himself that concrete made with crushed gravel or rock fines, blended fine aggregate or fine aggregate grading type F will provide the performance he requires.

Note 3. With all-in aggregates, it is preferable that the fine content is at the higher end of the range.

SECTION SEVEN. SPECIFICATION AND WORKMANSHIP: REINFORCEMENT

7.1 General

Hot-rolled steel bars in grades 250 and 460 are required to conform to BS 4449. Grade 250 bars are of circular cross-section with a plain surface, and are available in sizes from 6mm to 50mm. Grade 460 bars, which have a higher carbon content, are usually rolled with a ribbed surface to meet the requirements for Type 2 bars and are available in the same nominal sizes as grade 250 bars.

BS 4461 specifies requirements for rolled steel bars, other than plain round bars, that have been cold-worked to increase their yield stress. The method of cold-working is not specified in the Standard, but it normally consists of twisting the bar while it is held longitudinally; extension in tension alone is not satisfactory since this treatment raises the yield stress in tension but lowers it correspondingly in compression. The bars may be either of plain square (or chamfered square) cross-section (Type 1) or of circular cross-section with ribs (Type 2). The latter form is normal nowadays.

Cold reduced steel wire to BS 4482 is supplied mainly for the manufacture of reinforcing fabric and for the mass production of reinforcement for precast concrete products. The wire may be plain, indented (Type 1) or deformed in sizes from 5mm to 12mm. For the indented wire, the size, spacing and depth of indentations are given. It should be noted that this wire is not of high enough strength to be used for prestressing concrete.

BS 4483 deals with reinforcing fabric manufactured from plain or deformed wires or bars complying with BS 4449, BS 4461 or BS 4482. Its main uses in building are in floor slabs and walls, as secondary reinforcement for developing fire resistance, and in precast products.

Each of the specifications sets a number of requirements for mechanical properties, which are summarized in Table H7.1 with some of the other detailed requirements.

The Standard also set limits for the deviations from the nominal mass of the material as supplied. As the test results are calculated on the cross-sectional area of the bars and the design calculations are based on the nominal cross-sectional area or mass, any under-sized bars will be over-stressed in design and this over-stress must be accommodated within the partial safety factor, γ_m, for the steel. For hot-rolled bars of 12mm size and above, the cross-sectional area is allowed to be as much as 2.5% under-size for the batch and 4% under-size for individual bars; the corresponding figures for cold-worked bars are 3% and 4.5% respectively.

In exceptional circumstances, when enhanced durability is required (see **2.2.4** in general terms), reinforcement that offers some integral protection against corrosion may need to be considered. Three main types are available commercially, namely; galvanized, epoxy-coated and stainless steel reinforcement. Galvanized and epoxy-coated reinforcement is obtained by coating normal reinforcement to BS 4449 or BS 4461 and stainless steel reinforcement is available which complies with the requirements of BS 4449 other than weldability.

Evidence about the performance of galvanized steel in concrete is confusing, even though it has been used for some years. While in some marine conditions its corrosion protection has considerably improved the durability of reinforced concrete, many exposure studies have shown that corrosion protection in chloride-bearing concrete is increased only marginally over the performance of uncoated steel. However, it offers an undoubted increase in corrosion resistance in carbonated, but chloride-free, concrete. The durability of galvanized reinforcement is enhanced by chromate treatment which also depresses initial alkali-induced corrosion (See BRE Digest 109). Epoxy-coated bars have not been used extensively in the UK but have in the US.

The protection provided by an epoxy coating depends on the continuity of the film and its freedom from gaps, even of pinhole size, occurring during manufacture. The protection is also affected by the coating's ability to withstand damage from abrasion and impact during bending and handling on site. There is a wide range of epoxy coatings but those applied as powder coatings and thermally cured provide the lowest risk of pinholing of the epoxy layer. Cut ends of bars should be protected, e.g. by painting with a compatible epoxy. The quality achievable is improving but it should be appreciated that a defective coating which permits oxygen and moisture to penetrate beneath the coating may allow sub-film corrosion of the reinforcement to occur. Coated and uncoated bars should not be mixed. The great advantage of epoxy-coated bars is that they limit corrosion-induced damage and so facilitate repair.

Stainless steel, so far, has had limited use as reinforcement for economic reasons; the only technical reason is the need to provide sufficient oxygen to maintain the oxide film on the steel. Thus, stainless steel is of least value in anaerobic conditions in the presence of chlorides. Under low covers where the environment is aerobic the advantages over plain carbon steel are significant. In the absence of a product standard it is important to select an appropriate grade of stainless steel. An austenitic non-free machining grade, such as 304 or 316, should be used. Type 316 is not essential for low cover applications; the cheaper type 304 gives adequate performance in carbonated concrete. Tests may be necessary to establish suitable conditions under which bars of this material may be bent satisfactorily, because residual stresses may be above the threshold to initiate stress corrosion cracking in certain environments.

Further information on galvanized, epoxy-coated and stainless steel reinforcement may be obtained from reference 7.1.

Table H7.1 British Standard requirements for reinforcing bars for concrete

BS	Type of reinforcement	Preferred sizes (mm)	Specified characteristic strength (N/mm²)	Composition of steel	Other requirements
4449	Hot-rolled plain round bars Grade 250	(6)* 8 10 12 16 20 25 32 40 (50)†	250 (Yield stress or stress for 0·33% total strain; the tensile strength should be at least 15% greater than actual yield stress, the yield stress should not exceed 425)	$C \not> 0.25\%$ $S \not> 0.06\%$ $P \not> 0.06\%$ (Carbon equivalent $\not> 0.42\%$)	Minimum elongation on $5.65\sqrt{area} = 22\%$. Bend test through 180° around a former with a diameter double the nominal size of bar. Rebend test (if specified) through 45° around a former with a diameter double the nominal size of bar, then heated to 100°C for 30 min, cooled and bent back through at least 23°.
4449	Hot-rolled high-yield deformed steel bars Grade 460	As for grade 250 bars	460 (Yield stress or stress for 0·43% total strain; the tensile strength should be at least 15% greater than actual yield stress)	$C \not> 0.30\%$ $S \not> 0.05\%$ $P \not> 0.05\%$ (Carbon equivalent $\not> 0.51\%$)	Minimum elongation on $5.65\sqrt{area} = 12\%$. Bend test and rebend tests as for grade 250 bars but with a former of diameter three times the nominal size of bar for the bend test and five times the nominal size of the bar for the rebend test.
4461	Cold-worked steel bars Grade 460	As for hot-rolled bars	460 (Yield stress or stress for 0·43% total strain; the tensile strength should be at least 10% greater than actual yield stress)	$C \not> 0.25\%$ $S \not> 0.06\%$ $P \not> 0.06\%$ (Carbon equivalent $\not> 0.42\%$)	Minimum elongation on $5.65\sqrt{area} = 12\%$. Bend and rebend tests as for hot-rolled high-yield deformed bars to BS 4449.
4482	Cold-reduced plain and deformed steel wire	5 6 7 8 9 10 12	460 (Yield stress or stress for 0·43% total strain; the tensile strength should be at least 5% greater than the actual yield stress and not less than 510)	$C \not> 0.25\%$ $S \not> 0.06\%$ $P \not> 0.06\%$ (Carbon equivalent $\not> 0.42\%$)	Rebend test as for cold worked steel bars.

*If a bar smaller than 8mm is required, 6mm is recommended.
†If a bar larger than 40mm is required, 50mm is recommended.

7.2 Cutting and bending

Attention needs to be given to the correct dimensions in bending and cutting of reinforcement if the required tolerances on the position of reinforcement and thickness of concrete cover in **7.3** are to be achieved in construction. Bending dimensions are given in BS 4466 which specifies the cutting and bending tolerances in Table H7.2.

Table H7.2 Cutting and bending tolerances

Dimensions of bent bars (mm)		Tolerances (mm)	
over	up to and including	plus	minus
–	1000	5	5
1000	2000	5	10
2000	–	5	25
Dimensions of straight bars – all lengths		25	25

The minimum permissible diameters for bends in bars are set out in Table H7.3.

It is not always practicable to bend binders, links and stirrups to diameters that correspond to the diameters of the main bars to which they are fixed. Allowance for the effect of any lack of fit on the position of the main bars should therefore be made in design.

Table H7.3 Minimum diameter of former

Type of material		Minimum diameter of former
Grade 250 steel to BS 4449		$4\phi^*$
Grade 460 steel to BS 4449 and BS 4461	$\phi \leqslant 20$	6ϕ
	$\phi \geqslant 25$	8ϕ

$^*\phi$ is the size of the bar, i.e. the diameter of a circle of equivalent area.

7.3 Fixing

See commentary on **3.12.1.3**, **3.12.1.4** and **7.2**.

7.4 Surface condition

The surface of the reinforcement should be free from any material which is likely to reduce the bond with the concrete or lead to corrosion of the steel. When loose rust and scale have been removed, the remaining rust is known to benefit bond with the concrete, particularly for plain bars. If steel must remain in position in the formwork for more than a few days before casting, it may be coated with cement grout to prevent rusting.

In particularly aggressive environments the desirability of grit blasting the reinforcement should be considered.

7.5 Laps and joints

See **3.12.8.9**.

7.6 Welding

The ease with which reinforcing bars may be welded depends upon the carbon equivalent value of the steel. Bars to BS 4461 and grade 250 bars to BS 4449 are considered to be readily weldable, provided that the requirements of BS 5135 and the manufacturer's recommendations are observed. Grade 460 bars to BS 4449 are considered to be weldable. Welding should be avoided where reinforced concrete members are to be subjected to large numbers of repetitions of substantial loads. The fatigue strength of beams in which the links have been welded to the main bars can be reduced by as much as 50%.

7.6.1 General

7.6.2 Use of welding

7.6.3 Types of welding

7.6.3.1 *Metal-arc welding*

7.6.3.2 *Flash butt welding*

7.6.3.3 *Electric resistance welding*

7.6.3.4 *Other methods*

7.6.4 Location of welded joints

7.6.5 Strength of structural welded joints

7.6.6 Welded lapped joints

REFERENCE

7.1   MARSDEN, A.F.. Special reinforcing steels. Concrete Society Current Practice Sheet No. 103. Concrete. Vol.19, No.9, September 1985. pp 19-20.

SECTION EIGHT. SPECIFICATION AND WORKMANSHIP: PRESTRESSING TENDONS

8.1 General

Although specific reference is made to BS 4486 and BS 5896, it is reasonable to use other types of steel tendon that have been shown to have properties not inferior to the materials described in the British Standards. There are no explicit requirements regarding steel making or chemical composition, except that the air and air/oxygen bottom-blown processes should not be used and the cast analysis should not show more than 0.04% sulphur or more than 0.04% phosphorus.

The main types of steel used in the UK for prestressing are all covered by the British Standards noted, i.e. tendons processed from hot steel bar or fabricated from cold-drawn steel wire, often in the form of seven-wire strand. A summary of the preferred sizes and strengths of tendons is given in Table H8.1 together with the main requirements of the British Standards.

Table H8.1 British Standard requirements for prestressing tendons for concrete

BS	Type of tendon	Nominal diameter or size (mm)	Nominal tensile strength (N/mm²)	Nominal steel area (mm²)	Specified characteristic load — breaking load (kN)	Specified characteristic load — 0.1% proof load (kN)	Minimum elongation at max. load or fracture (%)	Modulus of elasticity (kN/mm²)	Relaxation — Initial load as % of breaking load	Relaxation — Max. relaxation after 1000 hours
4486	Hot-rolled bar (smooth or ribbed)	20	1030	314	325	260	6·0 at fracture	165±12 for bars as rolled and stretched	60	1·5
		25		491	505	410			70	3·5
		32		804	830	670			80	6·0
		40		1257	1300	1050				for all bars
	Hot-rolled and processed	20	1230	314	385	340	4·0 at fracture	206±10 in other cases		Relax. class 1 / Relax. class 2
		25		491	600	530				
		32		804	990	870				
5896	Cold-drawn wire (stress-relieved)	4	1670	12·6	21·0	17·5	3·5 at max. load	205±10 for all wires	60	4·5 / 1·0
		4	1770	12·6	22·3	18·5			70	8·0 / 2·5
		4·5	1620	15·9	25·8	21·4			80	12·0 / 4·5
		5	1670	19·6	32·7	27·2				for all wires / for all wires
		5	1770	19·6	34·7	28·8				
		6	1670	28·3	47·3	39·3				
		6	1770	28·3	50·1	41·6				
		7	1570	38·5	60·4	50·1				
		7	1670	38·5	64·3	53·4				
	7-wire standard strand	9·3	1770	52	92	78	3·5 at max. load	195±10 for all strands	60	4·5 / 1·0
		11·0	1770	71	125	106			70	8·0 / 2·5
		12·5	1770	93	164	139			80	12·0 / 4·5
		15·2	1670	139	232	197				for all strands / for all strands
	7-wire super strand	8·0	1860	38	70	59				
		9·6	1860	55	102	87				
		11·3	1860	75	139	118				
		12·9	1860	100	186	158				
		15·7	1770	150	265	225				
	7-wire drawn strand	12·7	1860	112	209	178				
		15·2	1820	165	300	255				
		18·0	1700	223	380	323				

Note. See BS 4486 and BS 5896 for further information, including tolerances and ductility tests, and requirements for cold drawn wire in mill coil.

BS 4486 gives the requirements for bars which are produced by hot rolling low alloy steels under controlled conditions, so that, as the bar leaves the last rolls, the temperature is at the right stage in the cooling cycle to give a fine pearlitic structure. The bars are next cold worked by stretching under about 90% of the characteristic strength, permanent stretch being carefully controlled. The bars have a maximum length of 18m, the ends being machined and threads formed by cold rolling in the machined length. Longer tendon lengths are obtained by coupling bars together. Bars are normally smooth but may also be rolled with a ribbed surface.

BS 5896 gives the requirements for round cold-drawn wire, which may either have a plain surface or be indented or crimped to improve bond with the concrete. The Standard differentiates between three categories of material: pre-straightened wire with normal relaxation properties; pre-straightened wire with low relaxation properties; and 'as drawn' wire in mill coils. The last-mentioned type of wire was used when prestressing was introduced into this country some fifty years ago. Since then, substantial improvements in properties have been obtained by the development of new techniques in production.

The wire is drawn from hot-rolled rod, which has been patented by heating in a continuous furnace to about 1000°C followed by cooling in a lead bath at about 500°C to impart to the steel a suitable microstructure for drawing. After removal of scale in a pickling treatment, the rod is passed continuously through a series of water-cooled dies which reduce its cross-sectional area by between 60% and 80% and increase the tensile strength by between two and three times. After passing through the final die, the wire is wound on to the drawing capstan and then has a coil diameter of 0.6 to 0.7m. To maintain continuity of the processes, one length of rod is welded to the next. These welds are cut out before the steel is supplied as wire, unless special lengths of wire are required; in that case, welds made before the patenting process may be accepted.

In this form, the wire is used for pre-tensioning in the manufacture of some precast products such as pipes and railway sleepers. Under stress, it exhibits substantial permanent deformation even at low levels of stress with a considerable relaxation of stress at levels corresponding to those at transfer. Since wire in mill coils does not pay out straight, it is unsuitable for post-tensioned tendons. For post-tensioning, wire should be purchased from the manufacturer in a pre-straightened form: straightening wire from mill coils by the purchaser is not recommended.

Pre-straightened wire is obtained by straightening the mill coils; it is then either subjected to heat treatment at a fairly low temperature to relieve the effects of straightening or to special treatment (sometimes termed stabilizing) to further reduce relaxation losses. The former material is described in BS 5896 as wire with class 1 relaxation and the latter as wire with class 2 relaxation. Each is wound into coils of large diameter to pay out straight, 2.0m for 6 and 7mm wire, 1.5m for 5mm wire and 1.25m for 4 and 4.5mm wire.

Most cold-drawn wire used in prestressing has a plain smooth surface. It has been shown, however, that greater reliability of bonding with the concrete can be obtained by indenting the surface, and bond may be substantially improved by crimping. Wires of 3mm size or larger may be supplied with an indented surface, the form of indent being agreed between the manufacturer and the purchaser. Relevant information for design is given in **4.10**, but for the purpose of specification the only effect on the required mechanical properties is to reduce the specified bend test from four reverse bends to three reverse bends.

BS 5896 also gives the requirements for seven-wire strand, which is produced by spinning six cold-drawn wires in helical form around a straight core wire of slightly larger size. Welds are permitted in the individual wires provided that they were made before patenting. After the stranding process, standard and super strands are subjected to heat treatment to produce class 1 normal relaxation strand and to an additional treatment to produce class 2 low relaxation strand. Drawn strand is produced by drawing a seven-wire strand through a die under controlled tension and temperature. As a result, the product has low relaxation and the wires exhibit a characteristic non-circular shape. Strand, which is produced in sizes ranging from 8 to 18mm, is either coiled or put on to reels with a minimum diameter of 800mm.

The Standards for tendons require the manufacturer to keep records of test results for inspection by the purchaser or his representative. This is necessary to determine compliance with the requirement for the specified characteristic strength of the tendons, which requires that not more than 5% of the test results should fall below the specified characteristic strength f_{pu}, and that none should be less than $0.95 \, f_{pu}$. Both Standards also require the manufacturer to provide load-extension curves for the estimation of the extension of tendons in stressing operations.

Since the characteristic strength of a tendon is specified in terms of breaking load, dimensional accuracy does not directly affect the ultimate strength of prestressed concrete members.

Further information on the manufacture and properties of steel for prestressing tendons may be obtained from reference 8.1.

8.2 Handling and storage

Since nearly all the types of tendon in general use have a high tensile strength imparted by cold-working, it is important that they should not be subjected to temperatures which would impair their properties. In handling and storage, therefore, the tendons should not be near cutting or welding operations without proper safeguards.

Experience does not suggest that corrosion causes serious problems when reasonable care is taken to provide good conditions of storage for tendons. It must be recognized, however, that the steel used in tendons is susceptible to severe corrosion in circumstances where ordinary reinforcement would suffer little damage. Protection from ground damp is essential, because severe corrosion has resulted when sulphates or other salts in the soil have come into contact with the steel. Corrosion may also be caused by stray welding currents or even the presence of bacteria near the steel. In coastal construction, protection from airborne spray and salt is needed.

Where storage is prolonged, provision should be made for regular inspection of tendons for pitting. Visual examination for surface pitting is required and metallurgical inspection should be made in cases of doubt. Reductions in tensile strength resulting from severe and unacceptable levels of corrosion may be quite small and changes in mechanical properties may be assessed better from the changes in ductility revealed by bend tests or the extension at fracture.

8.3 Surface condition

To avoid superficial rusting, the manufacturer usually gives the steel a protective coating which needs to be removed by the method suggested to obtain good bond; if light surface rusting has developed, however, removal of the coating is not necessary.

It has been established experimentally that light surface rusting of hard-drawn wire has little or no effect on the static or fatigue strength of members in which it is incorporated.

8.4 Straightness

Except for cold-drawn wire supplied in mill coils, wire and strand complying with British Standards should pay out reasonably straight. As straightening modifies the properties of steel substantially and in some respects adversely, it should be done only under the manufacturer's control.

8.4.1 Wire

8.4.2 Strand

8.4.3 Bars

8.5 Cutting

Pre-tensioned tendons of wire or strand may be cut flush with the ends of units. No special measures for protecting the ends of the tendons against corrosion are then required.

The method of cutting should not impart shock to the tendon, as this might impair bond or cause slip in the anchorage if the tendons have not been grouted.

8.6 Positioning of tendons and sheaths

The recommendations on accuracy of placing apply to both pre-tensioned and post-tensioned tendons. Provided that the tolerance of ±5mm is maintained, there should be no difficulty in satisfying the requirement that the actual cover should be not less than the nominal cover less 5mm.

These tolerances are so small that they are unlikely to affect compliance with requirements for serviceability and ultimate limit states except for very shallow members. In practice, it will often be necessary to agree larger tolerances on positioning.

In short members with pre-tensioned steel, it is usually sufficient to position the tendons at their ends only, but for long members some intermediate supports, which may be withdrawn before the completion of casting, may be required to prevent the tendons being displaced by vibration or other cause during the filling of the moulds. For post-tensioning, the positioning of the tendons is usually governed by the positioning of the sheaths or duct-formers which should therefore be fixed firmly during concreting. If sheaths are used, it may be desirable to place the tendon in the sheath before concreting, thereby stiffening the sheath, and to support the sheaths either temporarily or permanently at centres of at least 0.75m. Maintenance of the true cross-sectional form of sheaths and ducts and avoidance of leakage is needed to minimize frictional effects during the stressing operations.

8.7 Tensioning the tendons

8.7.1 General

If prestressed concrete construction is to resist cracking and comply with the requirements for construction, the prestressing forces imposed must be as required in the design; success therefore depends on the skill and accuracy with which the prestressing operations are carried out in the field and in the factory. All tensioning should be done under the direct control of a supervisor with thorough experience of the various stressing operations involved.

The choice of system of prestressing to be used in particular circumstances does not usually present difficulty. Pre-tensioning is normally used for the mass production of similar units, such as floor beams. If they can be readily transported, they are precast in the concrete products factory, but if they are too large to be handled easily then they may be made on a prestressing bed at the site. Post-tensioning is most frequently employed in large structures and carried out in situ as construction proceeds. However, where sites are very constricted, it may be more convenient to precast the members in short sections in the factory and to assemble them on site; one advantage of this is that it gives better control of the concrete production.

Each of the methods of post-tensioning available has particular advantages which may make it more suitable in certain circumstances. For short members, bars with threaded ends are most suitable because losses of prestress due to draw-in, which could be excessive with wire or strand, are completely avoided. Bars can carry the largest prestressing forces in individual tendons but strand has the advantage if they have to be curved. Large tendons can be built up from groups of strands which may be anchored together or in individual anchorages, or from individual wires anchored in groups by wedge-anchorages or by button-heading in a special anchorage assembly. For particularly long tendons, both wire and strand have the merit of being available in long lengths and so do not need connectors. The longer the tendon, the less the significance of the loss of prestress due to draw-in of the grips.

8.7.2 Safety precautions

During the life of a prestressed concrete structure, the concrete and the steel are usually most severely stressed during the operations associated with tensioning and transfer, at a time when the strength of the concrete is not fully developed and the anchoring of the steel may be only temporary. It is then, therefore, that the risk of failure and of accident is greatest. Although it is not possible to safeguard personnel completely from the risks of such an accident, reasonable precautions should always be taken when working with or near tendons which have been tensioned or are in the process of being tensioned. Personnel should not stand in line with the tendons, anchorage or jacking equipment. Simple protective measures such as stout timber shields should be placed in line with the tendons and behind the jacks to protect those passing in the course of their duties.

Each factory or site will call for separate consideration of the most reasonable form of protection. It must be emphasized, however, that the most effective safety precaution is the proper supervision and training of personnel in prestressing techniques. Manufacturers' instructions for the use of stressing equipment should always be followed closely.

Notes for guidance with regard to safety precautions for prestressing operations are provided in references 8.2 and 8.3.

8.7.3 Tensioning apparatus

Item (c) requires that the elongation of the tendon be measured. This measurement should be checked against the elongation calculated from the load–elongation % relationship supplied by the manufacturers of the tendons for the batch of material being used.

8.7.4 Pre-tensioning

8.7.4.1 *General*

8.7.4.2 *Straight tendons*

8.7.4.3 *Deflected tendons*

8.7.5 Post-tensioning

8.7.5.1 *Arrangement of tendons*

8.7.5.2 *Anchorages*

8.7.5.3 *Deflected tendons*

The requirement refers to deflectors for external tendons, as the curvature of internal tendons will be determined by that of the ducts which will be usually less onerous than the limit given here.

The use of deflectors of smaller radius of curvature or with a larger angle of deflection is permitted as long as test data on the loss of strength are obtained. Some experimental results (see reference 8.4) for strand of 12mm diameter show that the loss of strength is less than 10% for a ratio of deflector radius to tendon diameter of 2. There is therefore considerable scope for testing, but it should be noted that the secondary stresses that develop at sharp changes in curvature would have an adverse effect on fatigue strength under cyclic loading and could aggravate an otherwise passive situation should mildly corrosive conditions develop in the region of the deflector.

8.7.5.4 *Tensioning procedure*

8.8 Protection and bond of prestressing tendons

The recommendations apply only to post-tensioned steel; pre-tensioned steel is adequately protected by the concrete cover, provided that the requirements for thickness of nominal cover and for quality of concrete in **4.12.3.1.2** are satisfied. The primary reason for grouting internal tendons and for encasing external tendons in concrete is to protect the steel against corrosion and fire.

A secondary but important consideration is the effect of grouting and encasement on stiffness and strength. If other materials based on bitumen, epoxy resins or rubber are used, there may be a reduction in stiffness and strength which will need to be allowed for and the fire resistance may be affected. Great care is needed in selecting materials which are not bound by cement, to ensure not only that they are not harmful to the steel but that they cannot become so under conditions that could develop in the ducts over a prolonged period.

8.8.1 General

8.8.2 Protection and bond of internal tendons

8.8.3 Protection and bond of external tendons

8.9 Grouting of prestressing tendons

8.9.1 General
Further guidance on preparing and grouting ducts is given in reference 8.5.

8.9.2 Ducts

8.9.2.1 *Duct design*

8.9.2.2 *Construction*

8.9.3 Properties of grout

8.9.3.1 *General*

8.9.3.2 *Fluidity*

8.9.3.3 *Cohesion*

8.9.3.4 *Compressive strength*

8.9.4 Composition of grout

8.9.4.1 *General*

8.9.4.2 *Cement*

8.9.4.3 *Water*

8.9.4.4 *Sand and fillers*

8.9.4.5 *Admixtures*

8.9.4.6 *Chloride content*

8.9.5 Batching and mixing of grout

8.9.6 Grouting procedure

8.9.6.1 *Trials*

8.9.6.2 *Injection*

8.9.6.3 *Injection procedure*

8.9.7 Blockages and breakdown

8.9.8 Maintenance and safety

8.9.9 Grouting during cold weather

8.9.10 Precautions after grouting

8.9.11 Checking the effectiveness of grouting

REFERENCES

8.1 LONGBOTTOM, K.W. Steel for prestressed concrete. Concrete Society Digest No. 4. 1984. 8 pp. Publication 53.048.

8.2 THE CONCRETE SOCIETY. Safety precautions for prestressing operations (post-tensioning). Notes for guidance. Concrete Society Data Sheet. 1980. 2 pp. Publication 53.031.

8.3 THE CONCRETE SOCIETY. Safety precautions for prestressing operations (pre-tensioning). Notes for guidance. Concrete Society Data Sheet. 1982. 4 pp. Publication 53.036.

8.4 VANDEPITTE, D. RATHE, J. and KERCHAERT, P. Loss of strength of prestressing strand due to severe curvature. Revue C Tijdschrift. Vol 4, No 9. 1966. pp 275-283.

8.5 BUDGE, C.J. Preparing and grouting ducts in prestressed concrete members. Wexham Springs, Cement and Concrete Association Construction Guide. 1981. 8 pp. Publication 47.012.

PART 2. CODE OF PRACTICE FOR SPECIAL CIRCUMSTANCES

PART 2
SECTION ONE. GENERAL

1.1 Scope

1.2 Definitions

1.3 Symbols

PART 2
SECTION TWO. NON-LINEAR METHODS OF ANALYSIS FOR THE ULTIMATE LIMIT STATE

2.1 General

2.2 Design loads and strengths

2.2.1 General

2.2.1.1 *Choice of values*

2.2.1.2 *Analysis phase*

2.2.1.3 *Element design phase*

2.2.2 Selection of alternative partial factors

2.2.2.1 *General*

2.2.2.2 *Statistical methods*
The situations where adequate statistical data are likely to be available for this approach to be contemplated are currently rare. Nevertheless, there are possibilities such as where acceptance tests are carried out on mass produced units. In this case, a statistical evaluation of γ_m might be feasible.

2.2.2.3 *Assessment of worst credible values*
Some explanatory remarks on Table 2.1 may be helpful as it should be interpreted with some care.

(a) Adverse loads.

The greater the number of different, independent, types of loading considered to be acting together on a member, the lower is the probability of them all being at their worst credible value together, hence the lower partial factor suggested for (c). Case (c) assumes dead load, and at least two other types of loading acting together (e.g. dead+live+wind).

(b) Beneficial loads.

It must be noted that the worst credible beneficial load is its *minimum* credible value. The factor of 1.0 is therefore not directly comparable with the partial factors applied to characteristic loads in Part 1 of the Code: it is being applied not to a characteristic value but to an estimate of the lowest value of the load that is considered credible.

2.2.2.4 *Worst credible values for earth and water pressures*
The 'worst credible' approach to assessing design loads was first developed in the ground engineering field[2.1] and this is an area where it is particularly applicable and where other methods of assessing partial factors are particularly suspect.

2.2.3 Implications for serviceability
If significantly lower partial factors are used than those given in Part 1 of the Code, then the stress under service loads will be significantly higher. This, in turn, will mean that deformations under service loads (cracking and deflections) will be greater: hence the necessity for this warning.

2.3 Restrictions on use

This is the wrong title – it should read 'Non-linear methods'.

2.3.1 General

2.3.2 Basic assumptions

2.3.2.1 *Design strengths*

2.3.2.2 *Material properties*
Figure 2.1 has been taken from the CEB Model Code:1978[2.2] with minor modifications to convert from cylinder to cube strength.

2.3.2.3 *Loading*

2.3.3 Analysis methods

2.4 Torsional resistance of beams

2.4.1 General

2.4.2 Symbols

2.4.3 Calculation of torsional rigidity ($G \times C$)

2.4.4 Torsional shear stress
The nominal torsional shear stress is calculated by assuming a plastic shear stress distribution. Torque levels giving a nominal shear stress less than $v_{t\,min}$ in Table 2.3 do not cause a significant reduction in flexural and shear strengths[2.3] and may be ignored. The upper limit v_{tu} for the sum of the flexural and torsional shear stresses is the same as for shear alone and is to prevent a premature compressive failure of the concrete. The background to this requirement and the special limitation to prevent corner spalling in small sections is described in reference 2.4.

2.4.4.1 *Rectangular sections*

2.4.4.2 *T-, L- or I-sections*
In the treatment of T-, L- or I-sections, it has been assumed that a whole section can be divided into rectangles each of which attracts a torque approximately proportional to its theoretical torsional stiffness.

2.4.4.3 *Hollow sections*
The treatment of thin-walled box sections has been omitted because the provision of diaphragms or transverse reinforcement to resist cross-sectional distortion is outside the scope of this clause. Where distortion has been properly provided for, the St Venant torsion may be designed for by calculating the maximum nominal stress from the Bredt formula.

2.4.5 Limit to shear stress

2.4.6 Reinforcement for torsion

2.4.7 Area of torsional reinforcement

The reinforcement formulae are based on the equations for an orthogonal truss with 45° compressive struts[2.5]. The reasons for the efficiency factor of 0.8 are described in reference 2.4. All of the torsion should be resisted by reinforcement although the capacity of the concrete in flexural shear is unaffected.

2.4.8 Spacing and type of links

The detailing requirements have been chosen to give reasonable control of cracking. They are more stringent than those for shear because of the different overall stress configuration. It is particularly important to resist the tendency for the corners to spall[2.4] owing to the resultant of the diagonal compressive forces in adjacent faces of the member. For this reason, the pitch and cover to the closed links should be as small as practicable.

2.4.9 Arrangement of longitudinal torsion reinforcement

2.4.10 Arrangement of links in T-, L- or I-sections

2.5 Effective column height

2.5.1 General

Reference 2.6 gives further information on the rigorous definition of effective heights of columns.

2.5.2 Symbols

2.5.3 Stiffness of members

2.5.4 Relative stiffness

The assumption of $\alpha_c = 1.0$ for bases designed to resist moment is appropriate to pad footings. Where a mass concrete base is provided with depth and width greater than, say, four times the depth of the column cross-section, it will be reasonable to assume a rigid fixing, i.e. $\alpha_c = 0$.

2.5.5 Braced columns: effective height for framed structures

Equations 3 to 6 are simplifications of the buckling equations derived for regular frames. Figure H(2)2.1 shows the buckling modes considered, from which it will be seen that the effective length must always be less than the actual length for a braced frame and always greater than the actual length for an unbraced frame.

2.5.6 Unbraced columns: effective height for framed structures

See above.

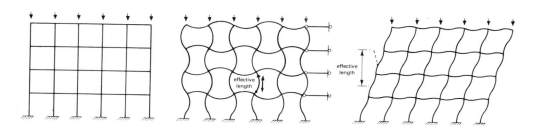

Figure H(2)2.1: Buckling modes for rectangular frames.

2.6 Robustness

2.6.1 General

2.6.2 Key elements
Where key elements have to be designed, the γ_m factors should be those given for exceptional loads or localised damage. The values of γ_f on the dead load and on any live load that it may be considered appropriate to include, should be 1.0 and 1.05 respectively. No factor need be applied to the 34kN/m².

Special considerations apply when it is desired to check whether a length of plain wall will withstand 34kN/m²; the following method is suggested.

Step 1: Assess axial preload on the wall, due to dead load only.

Step 2: Consider mode of collapse to be by formation of yield lines at top, bottom and centre of wall (Figure H(2)2.2).

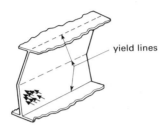

Figure H(2)2.2. Formation of yield lines in a wall subjected to lateral loading.

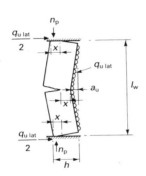

Figure H(2)2.3 Configuration of wall at ultimate conditions.

Step 3: Sketch deflected shape under ultimate conditions, taking ultimate deflection a_u at central yield line equal to $e_a = l_e^2/2500\,h$ as given in **3.9.4.16** of Part 1 (Figure H(2)2.3).

Step 4: Determine neutral axis depth x at yield lines from

$$x = (n_p/0.3f_{cu})(1.3/1.5)\text{mm}$$

where n_p is the preload in kN/m run.

The equation for x is derived from the simple rectangular stress-block as explained in the commentary to **3.9.4.15** of Part 1. The 1.3/1.5 ratio adjusts for the different γ_m factor.

Step 5: Determine ultimate lateral load $q_{u\,lat}$ by taking moments about centre of stress-block at central yield line. This gives

$$q_{u\,lat} = 8n_p(h-a_u-x)/l_w^2$$

Step 6: Check for shear. Shear force at upper and lower yield lines should be less than or equal to one-quarter of the axial load n_p.

Example. Wall, 5m long, 150mm thick, $f_{cu} = 30$N/mm², clear height between floor slabs 2.3m, preload 180kN/m run. Check resistance to 34kN/m².

$l_e = 0.75 \times 2300 = 1725\text{mm}$

$e_a = 1725^2/(2500 \times 150) = 8\text{mm} = a_u$

$x = (180/0.3 \times 30)(1.3/1.5) = 17\text{mm}$

Therefore $q_{u\,lat} = 8 \times 180(0.150 - 0.025)/2.3^2$

$= 34\text{kN/m}^2$, which checks.

Shear at base $= 34 \times 1.15 = 39\text{kN/m run}$

Permitted $= 180/4 = 45\text{kN/m run}$, which checks.

It should be noted that 180kN/m run is a substantial preload which would be unlikely to be realized in the topmost storeys of a structure. In such cases, it will be necessary either to provide reinforcement tying (see **3.12.3.7** of Part 1) over the whole wall area or to provide local strengthening.

2.6.2.1 *Design of key elements (where required in buildings of five or more storeys)*

2.6.2.2 *Loads on key elements*

2.6.2.3 *Key elements supporting attached building components*

2.6.3 Design of bridging elements (where required in buildings of five or more storeys)

Any building component that is normally not load-bearing may be taken into account. There are limitless possibilities here over the range of types of structure (and their usage) covered by this Code and the value of the loading is left to the discretion of the engineer; in general, all permanent loads would be considered and some fraction of imposed loading – this will depend on usage and special consideration may have to be given to warehouses, plant rooms, etc. Only rarely will it be necessary to consider debris loading, because of the relative magnitudes of the safety factors for normal and exceptional loads and also because of the force requirements.

The bridging method outlined above will be the most appropriate for precast concrete structures made of load-bearing elements. This involves the further necessity to define a 'lateral support': this may be either a substantial partition at right-angles to the wall being considered and tied in to it or, alternatively, a narrow width of the wall itself which has been locally stiffened and is capable of resisting a specified horizontal force.

2.6.3.1 *General*

2.6.3.2 *Walls*

2.6.3.2.1 *Length considered lost*

2.6.3.2.2 *Lateral support*

REFERENCES

2.1 SIMPSON, B. PAPPIN, J.W. and CROFT, D.D. An approach to limit state calculations in geotechnics. Ground Engineering. Volume 4, No.6. September 1981.

2.2 CEB-FIP. Model Code for Concrete Structures. Paris, Comite Euro-International du Beton. Bulletin d'Information N 124/125-E. April 1978.

2.3 HSU, T.T.C and KEMP, E.L. Background and practical application of tentative design criteria for torsion. Journal of the American Concrete Institute. Vol.66, No.1. January 1969. pp12-23.

2.4 SWANN, R.A. The effect of size on the torsional strength of rectangular reinforced concrete beams. London, Cement and Concrete Association. March 1971. 8pp. Publication 42.453.

2.5 LAMPERT, P. Torsion and bending in reinforced and prestressed concrete members. Proceedings of the Institution of Civil Engineers. Vol. 50. December 1971. pp 487-505.

2.6 CRANSTON, W.B. Analysis and design of reinforced concrete columns. London, Cement and Concrete Association. 1972. 28pp. Publication 41.020.

PART 2
SECTION THREE. SERVICEABILITY CALCULATIONS

3.1 General

This Section contains a substantial amount of explanatory material – far more than is commonly provided in Part 1 of the Code. Additional information is therefore only required for relatively few clauses.

There is, however, one general point about serviceability calculations which, even though it is touched on in the Code, needs reiterating. By their nature, serviceability calculations cannot be accurate. This arises from our inability to predict the properties of concrete which influence the deformations of the structure. Some of the problems with prediction of these properties will be considered below.

(1) *Tensile strength*

The deformation under load, particularly of lightly reinforced members, is critically affected by the tensile strength of the concrete. This is illustrated schematically in Figure H(2)3.1. Normally, the information about the concrete available to the person doing the calculation is just its compressive strength. There is no reliable, unique relationship between the compressive and tensile strength of concrete. Unless a great deal more is known about the concrete than just its cube strength, it is doubtful if the tensile strength can be estimated to a better accuracy than ±30%.

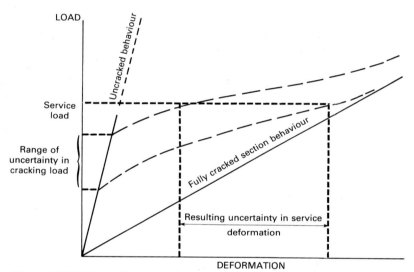

Figure H(2)3.1: Influence of uncertainty about tensile strength of concrete on deformation.

(2) *Behaviour of concrete in the tension zone after cracking*

After cracking, the concrete between the cracks continues to carry some tension and therefore this concrete adds significantly to the overall stiffness. The amount of this contribution is very variable and cannot be predicted with precision.

(3) *Creep and shrinkage*

These characteristics are not known with any precision in normal circumstances and yet contribute 50% or more to the total deformation. They will depend on the exact details of the mix used, the loading history and the environmental history. There can be significant differences in behaviour between members cast in early summer compared with those cast in late autumn. Differences in formwork striking times and propping procedures could also have a substantial effect. The person attempting calculations is unlikely to be able to define any of these factors, but needs to put bounds on their effects.

The calculation methods used in this Section are based on simplified assumptions about section behaviour; however, in view of the major uncertainties discussed above, it is doubtful if a more rigorous approach could be justified.

Another feature of serviceability calculations is that they can be checked against the actual behaviour of the structure. Since calculation and reality are most unlikely to agree, this tends to undermine the confidence of the designer. Calculations cannot be expected to predict what the deflection or crack width will actually be; they can be used to set bounds on the likely values, and it is important that they are used in this way, so that positive practical action is taken by the designer to ensure serviceable and durable structures (see Section **7**, regarding the required accuracy of calculations).

3.1.1 Introduction

3.1.2 Assumptions

3.2 Serviceability limit states

3.2.1 Excessive deflections due to vertical loads

3.2.1.1 *Appearance*
The limit on sagging of span/250 follows the recommendations of a committee of the Institution of Structural Engineers on the testing of structures[3.1]. A survey of beams and slabs in Germany conducted by Mayer, where sag had given rise to complaints[3.2] produced about 50 examples. The measured sag was less than span/250 in only two of these examples, and span/300 was the smallest sag which gave offence. The selected limit thus has some practical justification. When the designer can show that greater sag is unlikely to give rise to trouble, this limit might be increased to span/200. A limit to precamber is not given; however, a reasonable limit would seem to be about $L/250$. If greater precambers are needed, then the structure must be a very flexible one and could give rise to problems due to general 'liveliness'.

3.2.1.2 *Damage to non-structural elements*
The basic problem is that partitions, since they tend to be vertical, are very stiff and generally cannot follow the deflection of the floor or beam which supports them. If the partition possesses a reasonable degree of tensile strength, the floor can deflect away from the partition, leaving a gap between the partition and the floor of much the same magnitude as the deflection. This, of course, can be hidden by skirtings or similar details. Unfortunately, with permanent partitions (e.g. blockwork), the bottoms of the partitions

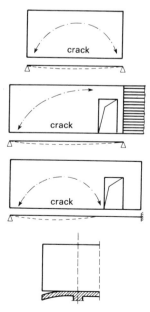

Figure H(2)3.2: Partition wall damage – cracks between wall and floor due to a self-supporting wall.

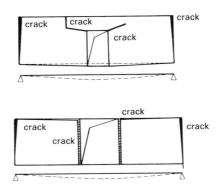

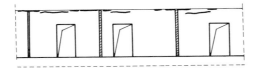

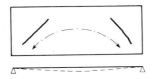

Figure H(2)3.3: Partition wall damage – cracks at joints between wall and ceiling and towards exterior wall due to rotation or movement of individual wall panels.

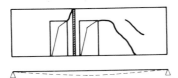

Figure H(2)3.4: Partition wall damage – inclined cracks due to shear.

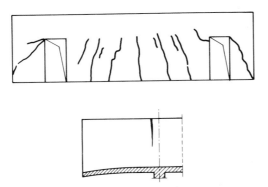

Figure H(2)3.5: Partition wall damage – vertical cracking due to flexure.

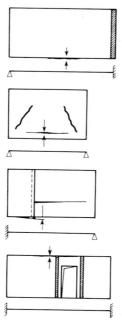

Figure H(2)3.6: Partition wall damage – types of damage related to different structural configurations.

are frequently held down by the floor screeds. In this case, the bottom of the partition is pulled down and cracks appear in the body of the wall. These can be large and unsightly. The presence of openings (e.g. doors, windows) in partitions tend to produce weaknesses and will often act as crack initiators. A paper by Clarke, Neville and Houghton-Evans[3.3] gives illustrations of the type of damage that can occur in particular cases and the relevant Figures are reproduced here (H(2)3.2 – H(2)3.6).

Masonry is generally fairly brittle and it seems clear that, if a floor or beam below a masonry partition deflects, then that deflection will be accommodated very largely by cracks (i.e. 10mm of deflection over the length of a wall is going to produce a total crack width of the order of 10mm somewhere). While the accommodation of vertical deflection by horizontal cracking can produce large cracks, the cantilever example shown in Figure H(2)3.5 is capable of producing quite startlingly large cracks even where the deflection is relatively small.

Figure H(2)3.7, taken from reference 3.4, shows the damage produced in model walls where various forms of deformation are imposed on the lower edges of the walls. It can

Figure H(2)3.7: Cracking of model walls due to sagging or hogging (from Ref. 2.3.4).

be seen that hogging deformations cause much greater disruption than sagging deformations.

This concludes the discussion of the types of damage that can commonly occur. It is far from complete but gives a general idea of the general forms of damage which can be met. The next question to consider is the limitations to deflections required to keep damage within acceptable limits.

Much of the work done on damage to partitions has been concerned with allowable settlement of foundations rather than the deflection of members supporting walls; nevertheless, the data should have some relevance.

One of the earliest investigations of this problem was that by Skempton[3.5]. He related damage to angular distortion (Figure H(2)3.8).

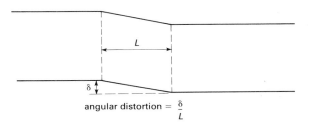

Figure H(2)3.8 Skempton's definition of angular distortion

He concluded that δ/L should be limited to $L/300$. This would appear to be more equivalent to a limit to mid-span deflection of a beam of $L/600$.

Mayer, who collected information from buildings in which deflections had caused complaint, reported the results shown in Figure H(2)3.9. The deflections occurring after construction of the partitions could not, of course, be measured and are therefore estimated values. It will be seen that these results, obtained from studies of deflection problems in buildings, are not inconsistent with the results obtained from considerations of damage due to foundation settlement. Both sources suggest that deflections would have to be limited to around $L/1000$ if damage is to be avoided with any certainty.

It must be concluded that it is impossible to give universally applicable limits for allowable deflections and the designer should really establish limits appropriate to the particular structure and type of partition. The values given in this clause are those given in the ISO standard ISO 4356-1977 which has been approved by the UK, but the point is made that the values are only indicative.

3.2.1.3 *Construction lack of fit*

3.2.1.4 *Loss of performance*

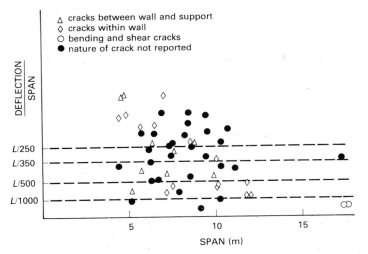

Figure H(2)3.9: Damage to partitions as a function of calculated deflection of supporting structure (Ref. 3.2).

177

3.2.2 Excessive response to wind loads

3.2.2.1 *Discomfort or alarm to occupants*

3.2.2.2 *Damage to non-structural elements*

3.2.3 Excessive vibration

Research has been carried out on the response of humans to vibration. For further information on this, for example, see reference 3.6.

3.2.4 Excessive cracking

3.2.4.1 *Appearance*

Clearly the width of crack which will be acceptable is very dependent on the particular circumstances and a code could not possibly give more than a guide. Factors likely to influence acceptable crack widths are:

(a) surface texture of concrete
(b) distance of observers from surface
(c) exposure conditions (in surfaces exposed to weather, cracks can become accentuated by dirt and by exudations of calcium carbonate)
(d) aesthetic importance of element (a crack in, say, the entrance lobby of a prestige office block is likely to lead to more complaints than the same crack in, say, a pigsty).

3.2.4.2 *Corrosion*

In recent years a considerable effort has been put into establishing what relationship, if any, exists between crack width and corrosion[3.7]. The general conclusion from such studies is that small cracks (say less than 0.5mm) very rarely pose any particular corrosion risk, whatever the nature of the environment. However, very few studies have been carried out in circumstances where the cracks follow the line of a reinforcing bar rather than crossing it. In the absence of reliable information on this question, it therefore seems prudent to limit widths to about 0.3mm.

3.2.4.3 *Loss of performance*

Leakage is probably the commonest manifestation of loss of performance caused by cracking. Investigations of leakage through cracks have been carried out[3.8] but have not been entirely conclusive. It seems probable that cracks passing right through a section with widths less than 0.2mm will fairly rapidly seal themselves and would therefore not cause significant loss of water in a water-retaining structure.

3.3 Loads

3.3.1 General

3.3.2 Dead loads

3.3.3 Live loads

3.4 Analysis of structure for serviceability limit states

3.5 Material properties for the calculation of curvature and stresses

3.6 Calculation of curvatures

The approach used for calculating shrinkage curvatures is given in reference 3.9.

3.7 Calculation of deflection

3.7.1 General

3.7.2 Calculation of deflection from curvatures

3.8 Calculation of crack width

3.8.1 General

3.8.2 Symbols

3.8.3 Assessment of crack widths

The basis of equation 12 is given in reference 3.10. Equation 13 can be derived approximately from the assumptions given in **3.6** as follows:

If the tensile stress at the tension face is f, then the force carried by the concrete in tension (Figure 3.1) will be given by:

$$f_t = [b_t(h-x)f]/2$$

This can be converted to an effective strain reduction in the steel of:

$$f_t/A_s E_s = [b_t(h-x)f]/2A_s E_s$$

Clause **3.6** gives values of 1 and 0.55N/mm^2 for the stress in the concrete at the steel level under instantaneous and long-term loads respectively. The corresponding values of f will be slightly larger than the values but x, calculated on the basis of a cracked section, will be underestimated. What has been done is to assume a value of $\frac{2}{3}\text{N/mm}^2$ for f and assume that this will cope adequately with the various uncertainties. This gives an approximate value for the steel strain as:

$$\varepsilon_{sm} = \varepsilon_s - [b_t(h-x)]/3A_s E_s$$

Equation 13 assumes a linear distribution of strain over the tension zone.

Figures H(2)3.10 and H(2)3.11 may be used for calculating the properties of cracked sections. In the Figures, α_c is the modular ratio and I_c is the second moment of area of the cracked section.

For cracking in pure tension, equation 12 is somewhat approximate. Recent work by Williams[3.11] provides more information.

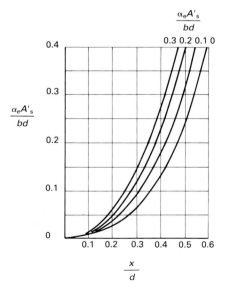

Figure H(2)3.10: Neutral axis depths for rectangular section.

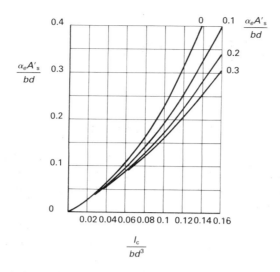

Figure H(2)3.11. Second moments of area of rectangular sections.

3.8.4 Early thermal cracking

3.8.4.1 *General*

The information used in the drafting of this section has been taken from references 3.12 – 3.14 which give considerably more detailed information.

3.8.4.2 *Estimating early thermal crack widths*

REFERENCES

3.1 INSTITUTION OF STRUCTURAL ENGINEERS. The testing of structures. 1964. 24pp.

3.2 MAYER, H. Bauschaden als folge der durchbiegung von stahlbeton – bauteilen. Report No.68. Materialprufungsamt fur das bauwesen der technischen hochschule Munchen. 1966.

3.3 CLARKE, C.V. NEVILLE, A.G. and HOUGHTON-EVANS, W. Deflection – problems and treatment in various countries. American Concrete Institute. Deflections of concrete structures. Special Publication SP43.

3.4 INSTITUTION OF STRUCTURAL ENGINEERS. Structure – soil interaction – A state of the art report. The Institution. 1978.

3.5 SKEMPTON, A.W. and McDONALD, D.H. The allowable settlement of buildings. Proceedings of the Institution of Civil Engineers. Vol.5. December 1956.

3.6 AMERICAN CONCRETE INSTITUTE. Vibrations of concrete structures. American Concrete Institute, Publication SP60. Detroit. 1979.

3.7 BEEBY, A.W. Cracking and corrosion. Concrete In the Oceans Report. No.1. CIRIA/UEG. London, Cement and Concrete Association. Dept of Energy. 1978.

3.8 CLEAR, C.A. The effects of autogenous healing upon the leakage of water through cracks in concrete. Wexham Springs, Cement and Concrete Association. Technical Report, May 1985. 42.559.

3.9 HOBBS, D.W. Shrinkage-induced curvature of reinforced concrete members. Wexham Springs, Cement and Concrete Association. Development Report 4. November 1979.

3.10 BEEBY, A.W. The prediction of crack widths in hardened concrete. The Structural Engineer. Vol.57A, No.1. January 1979.

3.11 WILLIAMS, A. Tests on large reinforced concrete elements subjected to direct tension. Wexham Springs, Cement and Concrete Association. Technical Report, April 1986. 42.562.

3.12 HARRISON, T.A. Early age thermal crack control in concrete. CIRIA Report No.R91. 1981.

3.13 THE CONCRETE SOCIETY. Non-structural cracks in concrete. Technical Report No.22. 1982. Publication 53.038.

3.14 BAMFORTH, P. Mass concrete. Concrete Society Digest No.2. London 1985. 8pp. Publication 53.046.

PART 2
SECTION FOUR. FIRE RESISTANCE

A SUMMARY OF THE APPROACH TO FIRE RESISTANCE

In the thirteen years between the introduction of CP110 and this Code there have been a number of important reports issued on the fire resistance of concrete elements.

From the viewpoint of the design of structures in the United Kingdom these are (in chronological order):

1975 (The Orange Book)	*Fire resistance of concrete structures* – Report of a Joint Committee of the Institution of Structural Engineers and the Concrete Society.
1978 (The Red Book)	*Design and detailing of concrete structures for fire resistance* – Interim Guidance by a Joint Committee of the Institution of Structural Engineers and the Concrete Society.
1980 (The BRE Guidelines)	*Guidelines for the construction of fire resisting structural elements* by R E H Read, F C Adams and G M E Cooke – A Building Research Establishment Report published by the Department of the Environment.

The content of these three reports (where relevant) has been incorporated into this Code. The four principle changes from CP110:1972 are:

1. The concept of continuity

CP110:1972 distinguished between simply-supported concrete elements and those where conditions of restraint could be incorporated into the structure, such that the fire resistance of a concrete element could be increased. In the use of the old Code from 1972 onwards very few constructions have been able to demonstrate the advantages of higher fire resistance from such restraint. The 1978 report put forward the concept of achieving better fire resistance through continuity in structural elements, which was adopted as the principle on which the concrete elements section of the 1980 BRE Report was prepared (Tables 4.3, 4.4 and 4.5).

2. Variation of width of section and cover

The present tabular data in the 1980 BRE Guidelines state for any concrete element the required minimum width and appropriate concrete cover. In the majority of cases at the lower ends of fire resistance (i.e. up to two hours) the requirements for minimum widths are below those which most designers would wish to use in practice. Consequently, some increase in the minimum width requirement could be justified on practical grounds.

Table H(2)4.1. Variation of minimum width of member and cover to reinforcement

Minimum increase in width (mm)	Decrease in cover	
	Dense concrete (mm)	Lightweight concrete (mm)
25	5	5
50	10	10
100	15	15
150	15	20
200	15	25
250	20	25
350	20	30
450	20	35

(Refer to clause **4.3.5** in Part 2)

It was also evident that the results of fire testing both in this country and abroad have shown that flexural elements, (i.e. beams and ribs) have higher periods of fire resistance when the width of the beam or rib is increased. Consequently, there emerged a viewpoint that some small reductions in concrete cover for beams and ribs could be established if the minimum values for widths of these flexural elements were increased. A table of adjustments to concrete cover for increase in minimum width was therefore produced, Table H(2)4.1. By adopting the more realistic practical minimum widths for beams and ribs, it was found possible to reduce the concrete covers required, particularly in the continuous support situation.

3. Provision of supplementary reinforcement

The requirements of BS 8110 centre around the concept of nominal cover to reinforcement or prestressing steel for durability, as well as fire resistance. An area of conflict that had to be resolved within CP110 was the requirement to position a layer of D49 mesh at 20mm from the face of beams, ribs and columns wherever cover to the main steel exceeded 40mm for dense concrete or 50mm for lightweight concrete. This requirement was negated by the new requirements for durability, whereby a cover of 20mm to a steel mesh was unacceptable. A working party examined the requirement for supplementary reinforcement and decided to relegate its importance in favour of three other methods:

- an applied finish to enhance fire resistance
- provision of sacrificial steel in the main tensile zone
- provision of a fire resistant false ceiling to the underside of floors

Supplementary reinforcement in the form of a D49 mesh implanted in concrete cover was not, however, rejected outright for the BRE have proved in fire tests on beams that such a construction improves fire resistance of flexural elements. However, this mesh cannot now be used where durability requirements set a nominal cover above 20mm. (Refer to Table 3.4 in Part 1).

4. Design for fire resistance by calculation

In thirteen years of Code development and the issue of major reports it has been possible to promulgate design for fire resistance based on first principles. Consequently this Code is the first to include such design principles as opposed to compliance with tabular data on minimum width of section and required concrete cover to steel.

Apart from the changes introduced by the four principal items stated above this Code also makes further minor changes from those to be found in CP110:1972 viz:

- rationalisation of tabular data for columns
- additional tabular data for reinforced concrete walls
- simplification of construction types for ribbed floors
- removal of data on additional protection from tables.

PARTS 1 AND 2 OF THE CODE
Fire resistance is treated at two levels in the code.

Part 1 gives simplified recommendations for use in the majority of dense concrete structures either reinforced (**3.3.6**) or prestressed (**4.12.3.1.3**).

Part 2, Section **4** gives detailed recommendations for fire resistance in any concrete structure.

Part 2, Section **5** gives simplified recommendations for use in the majority of reinforced lightweight concrete structures. No simplified recommendations are given for prestressed lightweight concrete structures.

This treatment of fire resistance between two parts of the Code is unfortunate as the designer has no single point of reference as existed in Section 10 of CP110:1972. The reason for the split in treatment was the Code Committee's insistence that reference to cover to steel whether for fire, durability or other should be available in one section. This was achieved in Section **3.3** of Part 1.

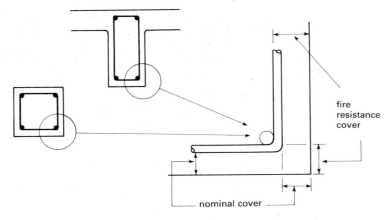

Figure H(2)4.1: Nominal cover and fire resistance cover in beams or columns.

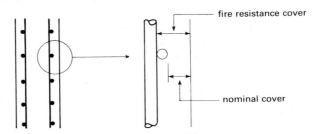

Figure H(2)4.2: Nominal cover and fire resistance cover in walls or slabs.

Before embarking on a clause by clause explanation of Section **4** of Part 2 it is necessary for the designer to appreciate the significance of the word 'cover' used in this Code.

CONCRETE COVER TO STEEL

Section 10 of CP110:1972 made reference to concrete covers to reinforcement or prestressing steels which were the distances from the exposed face of the concrete to the edge of the main tensile steel – bar, strand, wire.

It is very important for the designer using *this Code* to appreciate that the use of the term "nominal cover" will give differing values to the term "cover" used in fire resistance depending on the use of secondary steel such as stirrups, lacers, links etc. For example:

Beams – links must be used (**3.4.5** of Part 1)
Columns – links must be used (**3.12.7** of Part 1)
Ribs – links not usually required, therefore the nominal cover is usually equal to the fire resistance cover
Walls – vertically reinforced with lacers horizontally

Therefore great care is needed in reference to the word cover to distinguish between the two meanings. For ease of reference to fire resistance the designer should note:

Part 1	generally refers throughout to *nominal* covers
Part 2, Section **4**	refers throughout to *fire resistance* covers
Part 2, Section **5**	refers to *nominal* covers.

4.1 General

The handbook on the Unified Code (i.e. Section 10 of CP110) gave a description of the behaviour of concrete elements in fire with figures showing the effect of temperature on material properties. This description is still valid thirteen years later but is not reproduced here in the interests of brevity.

In the intervening thirteen years a much better understanding of the roles of the structure in fire resistance has emerged. Apart from the three reports mentioned in the opening summary to this section there have been other reports, technical papers and conferences which have advanced knowledge considerably. The designer is therefore referred to these which, among others, can be listed as:

Date	Title and author(s)	Publisher
1975	FIP/CEB *Recommendations for the design of reinforced and prestressed concrete structural members for fire resistance*	Cement and Concrete Association
1978	FIP/CEB Report on *Methods of assessment of the fire resistance of concrete structural members*	Cement and Concrete Association
1978	*Assessment of fire-damaged concrete structures and repair by gunite.* (Technical Report No 15)	The Concrete Society
1979	*Concrete for fire resistant construction,* Cembureau	Cement and Concrete Association
1979	*Spalling of normal weight and lightweight concrete on exposure to fire,* Ir W J Copier	Heron (Netherlands) Vol 24, No 2, 1979
1980	*An international review of the fire resistance of lightweight concrete,* J C M Forrest	The Concrete Society & The International Journal of Lightweight Concrete Vol 2, No 2, June 1980
1982	*Design of concrete structures for fire resistance.* Preliminary Draft of an Appendix to the CEB-FIP Model Code	CEB (Lausanne)
1982	*The effects of elevated temperatures on the strength properties of reinforcing and prestressing steels,* R Holmes, R D Anchor, D J Cook and R N Crook	The Structural Engineer, Vol 60B, No 1, March 1982
1983	*A basis for the design of fire protection of building structures,* Margaret Law	The Structural Engineer, Vol 61A, No 1, January 1983
1983	International Seminar, *Three decades of structural fire safety,* 22-23 February 1983	Building Research Establishment
1984	*Guidance for the application of tabular data for fire resistance of concrete elements,* J C M Forrest and Margaret Law	Institution of Structural Engineers
1984	*Spalling of concrete in fires,* H L Malhotra (Technical Note 118)	CIRIA (London)
1985	*Fire resistance of ribbed concrete floors,* R M Lawson (Report No 107)	CIRIA (London)

4.1.1 Methods
Three methods are available for use by the designer to determine the fire resistance of a concrete element.

4.1.2 Elements

4.1.3 Whole structures

4.1.4 Surfaces exposed to fire
The present state of knowledge denies determination of the fire resistance of an assembly of concrete elements. Some research centres in Europe and the USA are currently working on the fire resistance of complete frames by mathematical modelling but no practical applications capable of being used in codes, are yet available.

4.1.5 Factors affecting fire resistance
Consequently the designer is required to ensure that the details of concrete member sizes, cover, disposition of steel reinforcement or prestressing strand, and choice of materials achieves the desired response of the structure under fire attack.

4.1.6 Spalling of concrete at elevated temperatures

During preparation of the Code further research in the UK was commissioned by CIRIA. The report was written by H L Malhotra and published in 1984 as Technical Note 118 under the title *Spalling of concrete in fires*. A summary of this report from CIRIA News, January/February 1985 is given below.

"Spalling is the breaking off of layers or pieces of concrete from the surface of a structural element, and can occur when reinforced concrete is exposed to the high and rapidly rising tmperatures experienced in fires. Spalling may be insignificant in amount and consequence, such as surface pitting or the fall of a small piece from an arris, or it can seriously affect the stability of the construction because of the extensive removal of concrete from reinforcement or because it causes holes to appear in slabs or panels. It can occur soon after exposure to heat, accompanied by violent explosions or it may happen when the concrete has become so weak after heating that, when cracks develop, pieces fall off the surface. All these phenomena are covered by the expression 'spalling'.

Over the last twenty years or so, various national and international codes have suggested that measures are needed to prevent spalling when dealing with certain types of concrete or when the cover to the reinforcement is large. These requirements created difficulties on site, leading to increased cost and problems of control. The resulting criticisms necessitated a re-examination of the basis of the earlier requirements and further knowledge which has become available over the last decade by experiments as well as by study of actual fires.

Technical Note 118 *Spalling of concrete in fires* presents the results of the first part of a CIRIA research project intended to provide a basis for future code recommendations. It describes, collates and assesses existing information in the literature, from laboratory tests and reports of the effects of actual fires on buildings. This leads to a review of the causes of spalling as recently understood, the ways in which it may be controlled and, particularly, the areas in which more research is needed, including recommendations for further experimental study."

4.1.7 Protection against spalling

In concrete structures the concrete cover protects the steel reinforcement or tendon from becoming overheated and and losing strength. This concrete cover can spall away under fire attack exposing the steel.

Subject to the method of detailing employed by the designer such spalling can be ignored if alternative paths for load transference or capacity are available. Where they are not then the designer has to ensure that the concrete cover remains sufficiently unimpaired for the period of fire resistance required.

CP110:1972 recommended the use of a secondary reinforcement system as follows:

"Supplementary reinforcement will be required in those cases indicated in the table when the cover to all the bars and tendons under consideration is more than 40mm. When used, supplementary reinforcement should consist of expanded metal lath or a wire fabric not lighter than $0.5kg/m^2$ (2mm diameter wires at not more than 100mm centres) or a continuous arrangement of links at not more than 200mm centres incorporated in the concrete cover at a distance not exceeding 20mm from the face."

This requirement arose from the test programme, by the Fire Research Station in 1968, on concrete beams when the use of such a mesh as secondary reinforcement was found to be advantageous in increased fire resistance for simply-supported beams. The test specimens were manufactured under laboratory conditions whereby the mesh could be accurately located at 20mm from the faces of the beam and without regard to cost or time implications in manufacture.

Regrettably via CP110 this requirement was imposed on the construction industry at large with the result that the use of such a mesh led to many cases, well documented, of poorly compacted concrete, displaced mesh positioning and increased costs of concrete site production. The use of such mesh became abhorrent to those concerned with the production of good quality homogeneous concrete. During preparation of this Code the important aspects of durable concrete were incorporated as the concrete cover requirements for durability (refer to **3.3** in Part 1). It was realised that the requirements for supplementary reinforcement mesh would be in conflict with those for durability and alternative measures for protection against spalling would be necessary. A working party of the Code Committee (including representativs from the Building Research Establishment) advised alternative measures as given in this clause so as to resolve the matter.

However the use of a mesh as supplementary reinforcement was not removed from the Code as otherwise the test experience by the BRE would be negated. Instead the use of a mesh was down-graded in favour of the four alternatives and suitable cautionary notes included in the clause.

4.1.8 Detailing

An understanding of the requirements for good detailing is given in the 1978 Report – Design and Detailing of Concrete Structures for Fire Resistance – Interim Guidance by a Joint Committee of the Institution of Structural Engineers and the Concrete Society. Two principal aspects from reports of existing fires are:

Bottom reinforcement in slabs – The designer should check that at least 50% of the main steel is anchored at both ends (i.e. avoid the staggered straight bar arrangement whereby only one end is anchored in a beam zone).

Top reinforcement in beams and slabs – Does the length of steel from the support enable the beam or slab to adopt a 'near cantilever' structural action at the limit state in fire?

4.2 Factors to be considered in determining fire resistance

4.2.1 General

4.2.2 Aggregates

For the purposes of the Code, concrete materials are divided into two classes (i.e. dense and lightweight). The aggregates used in these classes are given.

Unlike CP110:1972 no separate subdivision of dense concretes made from calcareous as opposed to siliceous aggregates is made. This is a retrograde step after thirteen years but reflects the evidence obtained by the BRE that there is no superior fire resistance from limestones (calcareous) over gravels (siliceous) in a flexural mode in fire. Concrete section sizes for beams and slabs are therefore identical for either type of dense aggregate. For the compression mode however there is no just cause to penalise columns and it would be reasonable to use CP110:1972 values for concrete sections made from calcareous aggregates. The values for fully exposed columns are as follows:

Period of fire resistance (hours)	0.5	1	1.5	2	3	4
Minimum dimension of column (mm)	150	190	200	225	275	300
(Compare with Table 4.2	150	200	250	300	400	450)

4.2.3 Cover to main reinforcement

The designer is referred to the summary introduction to this Section for a clear understanding of the use of the word 'cover'. As stated throughout this Section, reference is made to the fire resistance cover unless specifically called nominal cover.

(a) Floor slabs
During the preparation of the Code significant strides in new knowledge of the behaviour of one-way spanning and two-way spanning ribbed floors was made. The information gained suggests that the concept of average cover should now only apply to solid slabs with multi-layer reinforcement or to one-way spanning ribbed floors. Two-way spanning ribbed floors have been examined by CIRIA in a programme of testing during 1984/85 leading to CIRIA Report No 107 in 1985 *Fire resistance of ribbed concrete floors*. The designer is referred to a full description of the tests, summary and conclusions. In relation to cover the report states:

"To clarify the use of the tabular data in BS 8110, the definition of minimum cover to the bars in the ribs of two-way spanning floors (such as waffle slabs) is taken to be to the lower bars. The increased cover to the bars in the transverse ribs is not important, because of the ability of the slab to redistribute moment from any heat-affected area."

The last sentence is invariably valid because waffle floors are usually cast as in situ construction where adequate continuity of structural action is available from each of the two spans concerned.

(b) Rectangular beams
Note 2 given in this clause refers to the relative heating effect on corner bars compared with the others. Corner bars are heated from two directions with equal intensity. All other bars have the main heat applied from one direction only. It is good detailing practice to arrange for the majority of the fully stressed tensile bars/tendons to be grouped away from the corner.

(c) I-section beams
On a practical note these beam types are rarely found in in-situ construction as they are usually the product of precast works. Where volume production is required for such applications as floor beams in system construction it is usual to undertake a fire test (method 2). The requirements of this clause are therefore usually checked against the behaviour of the test model after initial sizing of the concrete section.

Of great importance in these beam types is the retention of the web of the beam in fire, and the use of web reinforcement as shown in Figure 4.2 is essential. There have been some notable fire test failures where early collapse of the web has resulted in the premature failure of the beam.

4.2.4 Additional protection
The values given in this clause represent a more conservative approach to the use of applied materials to enhance fire resistance than the values obtainable from CP110:1972. In putting forward these values the BRE considered that insufficient test evidence was available from the use of modern applied finishes to be specific for each period of fire resistance for each material. The intention of this clause is therefore to aid the designer with initial sizing of concrete section and applied finish and then to seek more direct information on the fire resistant qualities of the applied finish from selected manufacturers at the detailed design stage.

4.2.5 Floor thickness

4.2.6 Width of beams
The designer is referred to Section **4.3.5** for the influence of width of beams on cover requirements for given periods of fire resistance.

4.2.7 Distinction between ribs and beams
The requirement to distinguish between ribs and beams in this clause was inserted to ensure that rib spacing did not move too far apart and consequently negate the role of a ribbed floor as a floor rather than a topping over a series of beams. The original maximum spacing proposed was 1.2m but representations from the precast industry enabled the Code Committee to raise the spacing to 1.5m so that double 'T' units of width 3.0m could be made if required, to match construction widths in the USA for example.

4.2.8 Beams and floors

4.2.9 Columns
Figures 4.2 and 4.3 have been prepared to illustrate the general intention of construction on which the tabular data in Tables 4.2, 4.3, 4.4 and 4.5 are based. The sketches are idealised and the designer should ensure the relevance of the important factors of minimum dimensions, thicknesses and covers in the design of the concrete element concerned.

4.3 Tabulated data (method 1)

4.3.1 Method by design from BRE Guidelines

The summary introduction to this Section of the Handbook explained that the BRE Guidelines, published in 1980, were used as the basis for the tabular data in this Code. In turn the BRE Guidelines were based on the tabular data contained in the 1978 Report – *Design and detailing of concrete structures for fire resistance* (the Red Book). Consequently the tabular data given represent the combined input of the three organisations over seven years' deliberations. It is anticipated that any alterations to BRE Guidelines in the future will be in conjunction with BSI revisions to the text of this Code.

4.3.2 Support conditions: simply-supported and continuous

4.3.3 Use of tabular data

Examples of continuous constructions are given in the 1978 Report, *Design and detailing of concrete structures for fire resistance* (the Red Book). The 1978 report also indicates how the fire resistance of concrete elements varies with applied load, viz increases in fire resistance for lightly loaded elements and vice versa.

4.3.4 Spalling of nominal cover

The designer should note that the onset of the required protection against spalling now starts when the *nominal* cover, i.e. the cover to the outermost steel, exceeds 40mm/50mm respectively for dense and lightweight concretes and not the *fire resistance* cover as in CP110:1972. (Refer to this Handbook covering clause **3.3.6** of Part 1.)

4.3.5 Variation of cover to main reinforcement with member width

Table 4.1 was produced following modern evidence from fire tests that as beam widths were increased there were small permissible reductions in concrete cover to maintain the same period of fire resistance. No such facility was available in Section 10 of CP110:1972 and in many cases designers were using concrete beam and rib sections well above the minimum required but having no benefit in decrease of required concrete cover.

Table 4.1 was therefore used to prepare revised concrete covers to those given in BRE Guidelines to suit practical everyday widths of beams at 200mm wide and ribs at 125mm wide. These concrete covers are given in Tables 3.5 (reinforced concrete) and 4.9 (prestressed concrete) of Part 1 of the Code.

Table 4.1 can also be used to vary the covers of beams and ribs from those given in the BRE Guidelines viz Tables 4.3, 4.4 and 4.5 of the Code.

The proviso that the cover to beam steel should not be reduced to a value lower than that for a solid concrete floor is necessary to ensure retention of fire engineering principles.

4.3.6 Reinforcement

BRE Guidelines and hence the tabulated data in the Code are based on fire tests held in the UK where the variation of material properties of UK reinforcing steels and prestressing tendons (to British Standards) under heating are well known and documented. This clause alerts the designer to consider the heating effects on other steels the strength properties of which do not conform to the pattern given in Figure 4.5 or to British Standards.

Tables applicable to method 1

Table 4.2 Reinforced concrete columns

The exposure gradings are illustrated in Figure 4.3. The designer should note that for practical purposes the covers given in this table should be reduced by the dimension of the link to arrive at the nominal cover given in Part 1.

Table 4.3 Concrete beams

The designer should note the requirement for the onset of protection against spalling, i.e. when the nominal cover exceeds 40mm for dense concrete and 50mm for lightweight concrete.

Table 4.4 Plain soffit concrete floors

Table 4.5 Ribbed open soffit concrete floors
The footnote on cover is incorrect as floor reinforcement does not normally have any links. Consequently the cover to the main reinforcement is also the nominal cover.

Table 4.6 Concrete walls with vertical reinforcement
Walls are grouped into three categories depending on the percentage of vertical reinforcement viz:

– less than 0.4% (note 0.9% is a printing error)
– 0.4% to 1%
– over 1%

The values in the table extend the range available from CP110:1972.

4.4 Fire test (method 2)

This brief clause covers the requirements for constructions not conforming to the general arrangements outlined in this section. Also where precast units in volume production would benefit economically by a suitably designed fire test programme to verify the fire resistance of a manufactured unit.

4.5 Fire engineering calculations (method 3)

4.5.1 General

4.5.2 Principles of design

4.5.3 Application to structural elements
This method of determining fire resistance by calculation is confined to the flexural mode of behaviour of beams and slabs in fire. For an understanding of the principles to adopt the designer is referred to Chapter 8 of the 1978 Report, *Design and detailing of concrete structures for fire resistance* (the Red Book).

4.5.4 Material properties for design

4.5.5 Design curve for concrete

4.5.6 Design curve for steel
The designer should note that the curves given in Figures 4.4 and 4.5 are design curves derived from experimental data over many test regimes.

4.5.7 Design
The basis of the calculation approach to the design for fire resistance of an element in flexural mode, i.e. beam, rib or slab, follows fire engineering principles. These principles dictate that the element should, over the required period of fire resistance, support the moving pattern of loading provided by the detailing of the reinforcement/tendons within the section. At the end of the fire resistance period the reduced moment of resistance of the element under attack should still be greater than or at least equal to the applied moment. This principle is illustrated in Figure H(2)4.3. For simplicity of approach the ultimate moment of resistance (M_u for the simply-supported condition and M_s for the continuous case) is reduced to 50% by the heating effect at the end of the fire resistance period. This approach is based on the strength of the steel being reduced to 50% of its ultimate strength as indicated in Figure 4.5.

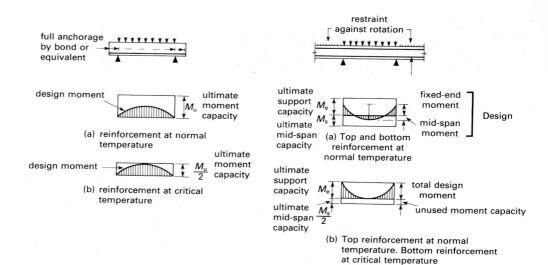

Figure H(2)4.3: Structural effects of temperature.

PART 2
SECTION FIVE. ADDITIONAL CONSIDERATIONS IN THE USE OF LIGHTWEIGHT AGGREGATE CONCRETE

5.1 General

5.1.1 Introduction

The clauses in this Section are additional to those elsewhere in the Code, and deal with situations where change is necessary in the general design provisions to cover cases where lightweight aggregate concrete is used.

The Code stresses that the properties of any particular type of lightweight aggregate can be established far more accurately than for most naturally occurring materials, and recommends obtaining specific data from the aggregate producer, in preference to using generalised tabulated information. Indeed, with any one source of aggregate, a wide range of properties can be obtained, by varying the manufacturing and production processes in a controlled manner. This permits considerable flexibility to the designer, but makes the derivation of general Code clauses difficult; for that reason, most Code clauses on lightweight aggregate concrete tend to be on the conservative side.

For reinforced or prestressed concrete, the Code suggests grade 20 as a minimum. This means that the density of lightweight aggregate concrete will normally be in the range 1,500-1,900kg/m^3 (or 60–80% of that for normal-weight concrete). However, the material can have advantages other than that of reduced weight, notably in terms of strain capacity, stability at high temperatures (fire resistance) and good insulation characteristics; equally, there are some disadvantages, compared with normal-weight concrete, and these must be accounted for in design. In very general terms, some design properties are listed in Table H(2)5.1 below: but, for the design of a particular structure, using a particular aggregate, recourse should be made to the data from the aggregate producer – as the Code suggests.

Table H(2)5.1 Some design properties of lightweight aggregate concrete, compared with the same grade of normal-weight concrete

Property	Relation to same grade of normal-weight concrete	Notes
Strength	the same	
Density	60-80%	}the upper end of the range
Stiffness	50-70%	}obtains for higher grades
Expansion	65-80%	
Creep	higher	}usually because the paste
Drying shrinkage	higher	}content is higher
Shear strength	75-85%	
Anchorage bond	80-85%	
Bearing capacity	60-75%	
Permeability	higher	

The Code makes no specific reference to prestressed lightweight aggregate concrete. In general, the provisions of Section **4**, Part 1 may be taken as applicable – modified by the requirements of this Section. Additionally, attention may have to be given to:

Loss of prestress — Loss of prestress may be higher with lightweight aggregate concrete. This will be due mainly to greater deformation of the concrete, either by elastic shortening or caused by greater creep and shrinkage. This requires careful checking, since overall loss of prestress can increase by as much as 50%.

Transmission length — The values calculated by equation 60 in **4.10.3** of Part 1 of the Code should be increased by 50%, in the absence of appropriate test data.

Shear in prestressed As for reinforced concrete (see **5.4** below), the design concrete
lightweight concrete shear stress should be taken as 0.8 times that for dense concrete.

5.1.2 Symbols

5.2 Cover for durability and fire resistance

Table 5.2 sets out the nominal covers to all steel to meet specified periods of fire
resistance. This table is prepared in similar format to Tables 3.5 and 4.9 in Part 1 for
reinforced concrete and prestressed concrete respectively.

The table should contain the same footnotes as Tables 3.5 and 4.9 referring to:

(a) the 10mm stirrup allowance to beams and columns
(b) covers related to minimum dimensions given in Figure 3.2
(c) anti-spalling measures.

It is to be hoped that these footnotes will be added in later amendments to the Code.

The designer should note that to cover the full range of fire resistance up to four hours
there is no need to incorporate any additional measures to reduce the risk of spalling
for any continuous construction. This reflects the generally much better spalling behaviour
in fire of flexural elements made from lightweight concrete.

For exposure conditions other than Mild, Table 5.1 requires 10mm additional cover
when compared with Table 3.4 in Part 1 of the Code. This is because lightweight concrete
is usually more permeable since it has a greater paste water content than a normal-weight
concrete of the same strength. Lightweight aggregate has a porous structure, and with
lower grade concretes in particular, careful attention should be given to curing, to ensure
that the porous particles do not provide an easy path for carbon dioxide, thus accelerating
carbonation.

Table 5.2, on the other hand, requires less cover for fire resistance than that required
by Table 3.5 in Part 1; the differences range from 5 to 15mm. This reflects the generally
better performance of lightweight aggregate concrete in fires. Exactly why this is so is
not completely proven, but it is generally attributed to a greater strain capacity, in fires
of limited duration, due to some combination of reduced stiffness, a lower coefficient
of thermal expansion (8×10^{-6} per °C, compared with 11×10^{-6} per °C) and thermal
diffusivity.

In practice, this means that for lightweight aggregate concrete, cover will almost always
be dictated by durability requirements, except possibly for deep beams in buildings.
With corrosion protection being the main issue, there are perhaps greater incentives
with lightweight aggregate concrete to consider special measures for lowering
permeability, such as additives or even protective coatings.

5.3 Characteristic strength of concrete

5.4 Shear resistance

This clause in effect permits the use of conventional shear design methods, but sets
limiting design concrete shear stresses at 80% of those for equivalent normal-weight
concrete. Normal design shear stresses are calculated at critical sections and subsequent
design is based on how these stresses relate to limiting design concrete shear stresses.
The basic method has not changed for decades, but some of the limiting values have,
as more data have become available.

Although the method is convenient for design use, it does not directly reflect how a
beam carries shear forces in practice – this is generally assumed to be a combination of
dowel action of the main reinforcement, aggregate interlock across shear cracks and a
contribution from the flexural compression zone. The argument for reducing the shear
capacity of lightweight aggregate concrete is based on a reduced contribution to shear
from aggregate-interlock – this is because the aggregate itself can crack, leading to
smoother faces on each side of the crack, and hence less interlock. With some types of
lightweight aggregate, this might not happen, and higher stresses could be justified. In

the light of present knowledge, however, this could only be on the basis of comparative data between similar beams of dense and lightweight concrete.

5.5 Torsional resistance of beams

See **5.4**.

5.6 Deflections

In general, direct calculation will be the most realistic and economic method of checking on deflections since the method given in **3.4.6.3** of Part 1 of the Code will be conservative. The approach used will depend on the accuracy required from the calculation but, in general, the input to the calculation should be based on properties determined from the aggregate to be used: in particular, there is a need for precise data on elastic moduli, and on creep and shrinkage characteristics.

5.7 Columns

The significant change here, compared with **3.8** in Part 1 of the Code, is that the slenderness limit for a short column is set at 10, irrespective of whether the column is braced or unbraced. In part, this is to further limit the risk of deflection-induced moments. In addition, it is suggested that the clear distance between end restraints should not exceed fifty times the minimum thickness of the column.

5.7.1 General

5.7.2 Short and slender columns

5.7.3 Slender columns

5.8 Walls

Similar restrictions are introduced here as for columns – for similar reasons. For slender walls (**5.8.3**), the changes in the values for the divisors represent conservative assessments of the relative moduli of dense and lightweight concrete, in the context of equations 34 and 44 of Part 1.

5.8.1 General

5.8.2 Stocky and slender walls

5.8.3 Slender walls

5.9 Anchorage bond and laps

Test data indicate reduced values for anchorage bond, when lightweight aggregate concrete is used (and even greater reductions for local bond, which is very rarely critical in practice). The Code sets this reduction at 20%, leading to increased lap and anchorage lengths, which can be something of a problem for shallow short-span members. Good detailing is essential in any case, not just for these structural reasons but also to ensure proper cover for durability.

5.10 Bearing stress inside bends

The limiting bearing stress given in this clause is one-third less than that obtained by equation 50 in **3.12.8.25.2** in Part 1 of the Code, for dense concrete. In reality, bearing stresses depend very much on the lateral restraint provided, and this reduction is an attempt to allow for the fact that lightweight aggregate may crush more easily due to its porous nature.

REFERENCE

5.1 FEDERATION INTERNATIONAL DE LA PRECONTRAINTE (FIP). Manual of lightweight aggregate concrete. Second edition. Surrey University Press/Blackie & Son, Glasgow. 1983.

PART 2
SECTION SIX. AUTOCLAVED AERATED CONCRETE

6.1 General

Autoclaved aerated concrete is a lightweight cellular material and does not normally contain coarse aggregate. It is made by introducing air or other gas into a slurry of cement and sand, pulverized-fuel ash or other suitable material. For structural purposes, the material is autoclaved, i.e. cured in high pressure steam chambers. The material is thus made in a factory to produce various precast structural units, which, in addition to their low density ($400-1,000 kg/m^3$, oven dry), have good thermal properties and fire resistance.

This Section stresses that the manufacturer is responsible for the design of the units, which should meet the general requirements of Section **2**, Part 1 of this Code; certainly, the manufacturer's recommendations regarding the use of these units should always be carefully followed.

The properties of the material, the design considerations, and the production of structural units are fully described by Short and Kinniburgh[6.1]. Additional information may be obtained from the CEB Manual[6.2], particularly on design and detailing. More recently, a volume edited by Wittman[6.3] contains numerous papers on moisture movement, and on creep and shrinkage characteristics.

6.2 Materials

6.2.1 Cement

6.2.2 Water

6.2.3 Fine materials

6.3 Reinforcement

Owing to its porosity and low alkalinity, aerated concrete does not afford the same protection against corrosion of the steel as does normal concrete, and so the reinforcement must be specially treated by protective coatings. These should resist moist heat, be chemically inert towards the steel and adhere to it, have sufficient mechanical strength to resist impact and abrasion in handling, and should not be brittle nor deteriorate with age. Coating methods now in use have been well proven, even for long exposures under corrosive conditions; in general, they are based either on a mixture of rubber latex and cement, or on special bituminous compounds.

Reliance cannot be placed on the bond between the aerated concrete and the reinforcement, and hence all bars must be provided with suitable anchorages. One of the most common ways of achieving this is by cross-bars, welded to the main reinforcement; hence the reference in this clause to the use of mats or cages. This means that it is important that units should not be cut on site, except in accordance with the manufacturers' instructions.

Due to the nature of the manufacturing process, it is difficult to incorporate shear reinforcement. In slabs, shear reinforcement need not be provided, as long as the manufacturer has allowed for the shear in his design by, for example, increasing the depth of the units. However, in lintels and single beams, shear reinforcement should be provided, broadly in accordance with the principles in Section **3**, Part 1 of this Code.

6.4 Production of units

The compressive strength of autoclaved aerated concrete is directly related to its density, ranging from $2-3N/mm^2$ at $400 kg/m^3$ to $5-8N/mm^2$ at $800 kg/m^3$. Strength is also dependent on moisture content, and can increase by 20% or more if the moisture content falls significantly below 10%. The Code requires that the average strength of 12 specimens minus 1.64 times their standard deviation is not less than $2N/mm^2$; normally these measurements will be taken at relatively high moisture contents, and hence a further gain in strength can be expected as the units dry out in service to 3–4% moisture content by volume.

6.4.1 General

6.4.2 Quality control

6.4.3 Marking of units

6.4.4 Dimensions and tolerances

6.4.5 Rebating and grooving

6.5 Methods of assessing compliance with limit state requirements

Here the responsibility for the design is placed firmly with the manufacturer, and an indication given that prototype testing will be required. In practice, manufacturers have undertaken development testing over many years, and therefore have an extensive data bank to draw on, in formulating design procedures. Deformation generally is influenced not just by stress level in service, but also by moisture content, ambient temperature and relative humidity.

6.6 Erection of units

6.7 Inspection and testing

REFERENCES

6.1 SHORT A and KINNIBURGH W. Lightweight concrete. London. Applied Science Publishers Ltd. Third Edition, 1978. 464pp.

6.2 COMITE EUROPEEN DU BETON. CEB Manual of autoclaved aerated concrete – design and technology. The Construction Press. London. 1978. p90.

6.3 WITTMAN F.H. (Editor). Autoclaved aerated concrete, moisture and properties. Developments in Civil Engineering, 6. Elsevier Scientific Publishing Co., Oxford. 1983. p380.

PART 2
SECTION SEVEN. ELASTIC DEFORMATION, CREEP, DRYING SHRINKAGE AND THERMAL STRAINS OF CONCRETE

7.1 General

This Section is not concerned with providing minimum requirements to satisfy any particular limit state. It is concerned with different aspects of deformation, and attempts to provide helpful information on deformation and movements, for use at the detailed design stage perhaps at a time when the concrete specification has not been finalized, and hence the precise properties of the mix are not known.

The point is strongly made in this Section that the designer should first decide how accurate his assessment need be, since this will affect the way he approaches the design. In effect, there are three levels of accuracy implicit in this Section as a whole; these are:

(a) information required to assess the general overall response of the structure to the design loads, and hence to calculate the resulting forces and moments. This reduces to the selection of a suitable value for the modulus of elasticity, which can be used to define the stiffness of the structure as a whole. Here, the mean values given in Table 7.2 are usually sufficient, but care may be necessary if limestone or lightweight aggregates are to be used.

(b) information required, as part of routine design, to assess deformation and movements – of concrete the material, of individual elements, and of the structure as a whole – with a view to determining how to cope with these in the design. This will involve identifying the source of the movement, quantifying the likely effect (perhaps bracketing the potential range of movement in doing so), prior to taking decisions on whether to deal directly with the stresses so induced, or to make provision for the strains involved (by providing movement joints for example). It is this level of accuracy that Section **7** is intended to cover.

(c) the assessment made in (b) above may reveal a level of deformation such that more precise data are required, before final design and detailing decisions are possible. The Code then suggests that the only way to obtain these data is by tests carried out on concrete made with the materials to be used in the actual structure.

The information contained in Section **7** is intended as guidance in predicting in-service movement. This is clearly shown by the various sub-headings, which are concerned with:

– Elastic deformation
– Creep
– Drying shrinkage
– Thermal strains.

However, to obtain a proper overall perspective, it is important to remember that other forms of movement can occur, particularly at an early age when the concrete is still plastic (plastic shrinkage, plastic settlement) or when it has just hardened (early age thermal contraction, crazing). These deformations are essentially intrinsic, being dependent on the constituent materials, concrete technology, workmanship, etc. Dealing with this type of movement is primarily a concrete technology issue, and guidance is available in the literature[7.1, 7.2]. However, in coping subsequently with in-service movement, it is important to remember that this early age movement (and how it is dealt with) will all too often provide the basis or datum line for all subsequent movement.

Movement and deformation are mainly a serviceability issue; however, excessive deformation or a failure to deal properly with movement in design can cause cracking, or the opening of joints or other defects, all of which can accelerate deterioration and affect durability.

7.2 Elastic deformation

The provisions in this Section are based substantially on reference 7.3. Elastic modulus depends predominantly on the type of aggregate used, but is also influenced by the grade of concrete. The relative importance of these factors is clearly shown in equation 17 and Table 7.2. Table 7.2 also shows the wide range of values that can occur in practice for any particular grade, and the Code suggests that it would be prudent to consider a range of values in a particular case, in order to bracket the movement that could occur. Although no allowance for an increase in strength with age beyond 28 days is permitted in Part 1 of the Code when dealing with limit state requirements, Table 7.1 has nevertheless been included here, since, in dealing with movements, the assessment should be as accurate and realistic as possible.

7.3 Creep

The recommendations in this Section are based mainly on reference 7.4. A great deal of research has been done on creep over the years, but mainly under controlled laboratory conditions and some care is necessary in applying laboratory data to actual structures in service. Figure 7.1 is an attempt to present the best available information in a simplified way for design purposes. Creep depends on the stress in the element and on its stiffness. As Figure 7.1 indicates, the creep coefficient also depends on the environmental conditions, on the maturity of the concrete, on the aspect ratio of the cross-section, and also on the composition of the concrete itself. Additionally, creep and shrinkage effects are inter-related, although it is normal practice, as indicated here, to deal with them separately.

7.4 Drying shrinkage

This clause is also based on reference 7.4. Figure 7.2 shows the strong influence of relative humidity and of the aspect ratio of the cross-section. Mix proportions are also important, and attention is also drawn to the influence of highly shrinkable aggregates[7.5]. Figure 7.2 relates to plain concrete, and the influence of any reinforcement should also be taken into account. The Code gives a simple method for symmetrical reinforcement, but the influence of non-symmetrical reinforcement on curvature is more complex. In this context, a cross-reference is made to Section 3, Part 2 of the Code – and to equation 9 in clause **3.6** in particular. A more detailed treatment of the subject is given in reference 7.6.

7.5 Thermal strains

Figure 7.3 is taken direct from reference 7.4, which also contains a much more detailed version of Table 7.3.

REFERENCES

7.1 HARRISON, T.A. Early age thermal crack control in concrete. Report 91. London, Construction Industry Research and Information Association. 1981. 48p.

7.2 THE CONCRETE SOCIETY. Non-structural cracks in concrete. Technical Report No.22. The Concrete Society. London. 1982. 38p.

7.3 TEYCHENNE, D.C. PARROTT, L.J. and POMEROY, C.D. The estimation of the elastic modulus of concrete for the design of structures. Building Research Establishment, Garston. Current Paper CP 23/78. 1978. 12p.

7.4 PARROTT, L.J. Simplified methods of predicting the deformation of structural concrete. Wexham Springs, Cement and Concrete Association. Development Report No.3. October 1979. 11p.

7.5 BUILDING RESEARCH ESTABLISHMENT. Shrinkage of natural aggregates in concrete. BRS Digest 35 (second series). 1968.

7.6 HOBBS, D.W. Shrinkage-induced curvature of reinforced concrete members. Wexham Springs, Cement and Concrete Association. Development Report No. 4. November 1979. 19p.

PART 2
SECTION EIGHT. MOVEMENT JOINTS

8.1 General

Since the first national Code of Practice for reinforced concrete was published in 1934, structures have tended to become lighter and more flexible and hence more vulnerable to the effects of dimensional change. At the same time, materials have become stronger, with the result that structures are produced which are less tolerant in their intrinsic ability to accommodate movement, without special provisions being made. This means that more attention has to be given consciously to the treatment of movement in design; the mere existence of this Section of the Code highlights that fact.

Section 7, Part 2 of the Code gives guidance on calculating deformations due to factors such as creep, shrinkage and thermal movement; the commentary on that Section briefly mentions other factors, and gives references which permit these to be assessed. It will be obvious from Section 7 that the prediction of deformation is not an exact science, and engineering judgement is required in identifying and quantifying those factors which are of importance, in individual cases.

Even more judgement is required in deciding how to allow for these deformations in design – each with its associated variability. In broad terms, sources of movement can be considered in one of three classes:

(a) Intrinsic i.e. those due to change in the inherent properties of the materials and components. For concrete, this category would include early age thermal movement, plastic shrinkage and settlement, and, to some extent, drying shrinkage and creep.
(b) External i.e. those due to dead and imposed loading, to temperature and humidity change, etc.
(c) Time-dependent i.e. seasonal, diurnal.

This classification is significant in design, since the solution to each can be different; for example, some intrinsic sources of movement can be dealt with by reducing them to acceptable levels via concrete technology, whereas time-dependent sources cannot be avoided in this way and require accommodation as part of the design.

In any particular case, having identified, classified and quantified all relevant sources of potential movement and deformation, the designer is faced with making a choice between alternative strategies. Again, he has three basic approaches to choose from:

(a) Reduction of the deformation. This might be appropriate for many of the intrinsic sources of movement. By the use of protective or insulation systems, it might also be relevant for seasonal variations.
(b) Suppression of the deformation. In effect, this implies accepting built-in restraints, and coping with the resulting stresses by appropriate design of the individual elements and the structure as a whole.
(c) Accommodation of the deformation. This means allowing movement to physically take place.

In practice, some combination of these approaches will generally be most appropriate; however, if this is done, the required detailing associated with each should be compatible; the analyses of feedback on in-service performance indicates that this has not always been so, and that the general approach in designing for movement is often confused.

This Section of the Code effectively deals only with approach (c) as outlined above. The treatment can be no more than general in nature, and reference should be made to the literature for more detailed information[8.1, 8.2]

8.2 Need for movement joints

8.3 Types of movement joint

8.4 Provision of joints

8.5 Design of joints

REFERENCES

8.1 ALEXANDER, S.J. and LAWSON, R.M. Design for movement in buildings. Technical Note 107. Construction Industry Research and Information Association, London. 1981. 54pp.

8.2 RAINGER, P. Movement control in the fabric of buildings. Batsford Academic and Educational Ltd. 1983. 216pp.

PART 2
SECTION NINE. APPRAISAL AND TESTING OF STRUCTURES AND COMPONENTS DURING CONSTRUCTION

9.1 General

This Section is intended to cover cases where testing may be deemed necessary *during construction*. That point is stressed in **9.1**; model or prototype testing is specifically excluded, nor do the clauses relate to the appraisal of structures that have been in service for some time (where reference should be made elsewhere to the literature e.g. reference 9.1).

Testing, particularly load testing, is expensive, and the implication behind the whole of Section **9** is that it should only be used as a last resort; and should not be regarded as an easy option in a dispute situation. The approach is essentially a structured one. Firstly, there is the need to clearly establish that testing is necessary (**9.2**). **9.3** then defines the basic objective, namely to assess the structure as built and to determine if it meets the requirements of the original design. There then follows – in **9.4** and **9.5** – a progressive series of steps to be followed. Above all, any testing must be meaningful.

In general, the design and construction of structures which satisfactorily fulfil their intended function is made up of an overall 'package' which can be broken down into a series of discrete elements as follows:

(a) a proper assessment of loads and load effects
(b) the choice of performance criteria (e.g. deflection or crack width values)
(c) a choice of appropriate factors of safety, or design margins
(d) the use of representative 'models' for structural behaviour
(e) complying with material specifications
(f) achieving relevant standards of workmanship.

Doubts generally arise because of deficiencies in (e) and (f). Here, the importance of inspection and supervision cannot be over-emphasised in getting the construction right in the first place, and particular attention is drawn to reference 9.2. However, where something has gone wrong (**9.2**), then the implication of any test results obtained on the whole 'package' (a–f above) must be considered.

9.2 Purpose of testing

9.3 Basis of approach

9.4 Check tests on structural concrete

9.4.1 General
This clause emphasises that testing need not relate solely to strength. In general, a measure of in situ strength is a good guide to concrete quality, but BS8110 as a whole, and Sections **3** and **6** of Part 1 in particular, places great stress on the provision of adequate durability. Consideration may then be given to the use of covermeters, NDT techniques, gamma radiography, chemical analysis, surface absorption measurements (or other techniques to quantify permeability), etc.

9.4.2 Concrete strength in structures

9.5 Load tests on structures or parts of structures

9.5.1 General
Detailed recommendations on test procedures are given in reference 9.1.

9.5.2 Test loads

Since the basic objective is to 'calibrate' the structure as built against the original design, the magnitude of the test load must be sufficient to give reliable measurements of strains, deflections, etc. Various caveats are given in **9.5.2**, which are important in interpreting the results obtained and in matching the assessed performance against that expected in the original design. The levels of loading specified should be regarded as minimum values, since it is also important to remember that most designs are based on an 'envelope' approach using patterned loading. If the primary concern is about strength or stability of the structure, then there is a good case for increasing the test load up to 1.5 times the design live load, provided that this does not cause permanent damage, should the test prove satisfactory. Engineering judgement is absolutely essential in individual cases.

9.5.3 Assessment of results

Comparisons between measured and predicted results are essential. Where there are significant differences (say greater than 15–20%), then the first step should be to check that the structure is not carrying the load in a way different from that assumed in the design (due, say, to arching action, or the influence of 'non-load-bearing' elements). Material properties should then be re-checked. If there are still serious discrepancies in the results – using the criteria in **9.5.4** as guidelines – then additional special tests may have to be devised (**9.5.5**) to eliminate all extraneous factors or, alternatively, remedial action taken.

9.5.4 Test criteria

The values given are for general guidance only. The most important factor is that the test loads should be applied at least twice; repeatability, and the recovery of the structure after the load is removed, are perhaps the most important issues.

9.5.5 Special tests

This clause is intended primarily for precast units which, in the final structure, will act compositely with in situ concrete. However, the approach should also be considered for load testing of the type described in **9.5.2**, if discrepancies appear in the results (see commentary on **9.5.3** above).

9.6 Load tests on individual precast units

The two paragraphs in this clause cover quite different situations. The first simply says that if there are doubts about an element – for the reasons given in **9.2** – then that element should be treated like any other concrete element i.e. clauses **9.3 – 9.5** obtain. The second paragraph relates to Quality Assurance. A number of accredited QA schemes now exist for various precast components; here it is important to remember that QA generally relates to the entire production process, and gives a measure of assessed capability – testing is only one part of that assessment, and sampling would not be expected to exceed that laid down in the relevant technical schedule.

REFERENCES

9.1 INSTITUTION OF STRUCTURAL ENGINEERS. Appraisal of existing structures. July 1980. 60p.
9.2 INSTITUTION OF STRUCTURAL ENGINEERS. Inspection of building structures during construction. April 1983. 20p.

LIST OF TABLES

PART 1

LIST OF FIGURES

PART 1

PART 2